Classic Southwest Cooking

Classic
Southwest
Cooking

Over 200 Succulent Recipes
Celebrating America's
Great Regional Cuisine

Carolyn Dille & Susan Belsinger

Illustrations by Kathleen Gray Farthing

Biscuit Books, Inc.
Newton, Massachusetts

This book is fondly dedicated to Tomaso and Dick.

Interior design by Liney Li
Cover design by The Dunlavey Studio, Sacramento

Some of these recipes previously appeared in
Gourmet magazine.

Reprinted by arrangement with Prima Publishing,
A Division of Prima Communications, Inc.
First Biscuit Books Edition, 1996

Biscuit Books, Inc.
P.O. Box 610159
Newton, Massachusetts 02161

ISBN 0-9643600-3-9 (previously 1-55958-291-X, paper)

Printed and bound in the United States of America

00 99 98 97 96   5 4 3 2 1

Library of Congress Cataloging-in-Publication Data
Dille, Carolyn.
    Classic Southwest cooking: over 200 succulent recipes celebrating
America's great regional cuisine / Carolyn Dille & Susan Belsinger:
illustrations by Kathleen Gray Farthing. — 1st Biscuit Books ed.
      p.   cm.
    Originally published: Rocklin, CA: Prima Pub., c1994.
    Includes bibliographical references and index.
    ISBN 0-9643600-3-9 (cloth)
    1. Cookery, American — Southwestern style.   I. Belsinger, Susan.
  II. Title.
TX715.2.S69D56   1996
641.5979—DC20
                             96-42897
                                CIP

ACKNOWLEDGMENTS

With the reissue of this book, we are reminded of how many people helped us with it. Once again, the generosity and suggestions of our families and friends lightened the work and, looking back, fill it with the warmest memories. We greatly appreciate the help and expertise of Jeanne Croft at the University of New Mexico, Las Cruces, as well as June Rutherford of Hatch, New Mexico, unexcelled chile grower and storyteller. Tom and Joyce De Baggio contributed outstanding seed starts and recipe testing. Kathy Gray Farthing's fine illustrations highlight the world of Southwestern chiles. And special thanks to Martha Casselman, our agent, and Jennifer Basye, our editor, for their foresight and persistence in giving this work a new life.

Contents

Classic Southwest Cooking

Introduction

We should confess immediately that one of us, Carolyn, grew up in the Southwest and considers that food to be home food, soul food, the heart of childhood awakenings to flavor, the stuff of memories. Proust's reverie of the madeleine may not be bettered, but the recollection of chile pepper eating contests with her brother can still bring a ringing to Carolyn's ears and tears to her eyes. The rules were ten- and twelve-year-old strict: the chiles were pickled *güeritos* and there was no eating or drinking for thirty minutes after the last chile. She and her brother differ as to who holds the record.

Her mother's family had a ranch very close to the Arizona-Mexican border, and ate corn, beans, chiles, and meat like their Mexican neighbors, though they were Anglos from the Midwest. Grandmother kept making her favorite Midwestern recipes: biscuits and fruit pies. She was a plain cook, not a fine cook, but the family liked good food. The vegetable patch, the fresh eggs and hen-yard chickens, the pigs, and the range beef were important to their lives in a way that few Americans, even in the Southwest, can understand today. Food was livelihood and immediately life-sustaining in a very direct way. If cattle prices were down at least some of them could be butchered and air-dried. Growing spinach, tomatoes, and onions was an exercise in water-conservation (rinse water went to the vegetables, cooking water to the pigs), and a relearning of the seasons. The heat of an Arizona summer coupled with limited water shriveled rather than nourished garden plants, so late fall or early winter became the time to sow.

Though there are few small family ranches and farms in the Southwest today, home-style cooking is still a strong tradition, even in restaurants. A high percentage of them are owned and run by families. When Carolyn was growing up, virtually all restaurants were family-operated. Going out to dinner meant small Mexican restaurants, each of which had a specialty (green corn enchiladas, salsa, tacos), or small pit-barbecue places. The last had minimal amenities; the barbecue was often brought back home for Saturday night dinner. Now there are Northern Italian restaurants, haute and *nouvelle* French, Szechuan, Greek, Continental, and chain restaurants. These have and will influence the region's cooking in various ways, but a homey style and earthy ingredients continue to distinguish Southwestern food.

This past decade is not the first era in which change has been folded into the batter of Southwestern cooking. The Pueblo Indians, the Apaches, the Papagos, the Navajos, the Chiricahuas lived with corn, squash, wild greens, nuts, berries, game, and occasionally fish for a thousand years before the Spaniards moved into their homelands. The Spaniards brought foods from the Mexican Indians: chiles, tomatoes, tomatillos, chocolate; they also brought wheat, rice, grapes, orchard fruits, and the desire to recreate the dishes of Mexico and Spain in the Nuevo Méjico, which included much of Texas, all of New Mexico and part of southern Colorado, most of Arizona and southern California. The Spanish, and later the Mexicans, ruled the area for close to three centuries before Anglo-Americans began settling in earnest after the Mexican-American War of 1848. The Anglos brought with them beef cattle, a hunger for dairy products, more varieties of produce, and grand plans (largely realized) to make the desert earth productive.

This latest mix of foodstuffs and cultures had barely a century to proof before the last twenty years when new elements of change began to be stirred in. These included ideas and phenomena which affected cooking in every culture in the area: the nationwide interest in the role of food as a valuable part of civilization; technology in food production and preservation; agribusiness, its benefits and the search for solutions to its problems; nutrition and diet suitable to the twentieth century.

All the people who cook in the Southwest, in homes and restaurants, are taking part in this latest stage of the region's culinary evolution. The challenge they face daily is how to keep the well-loved traditional specialties, accommodate what is valuable and necessary in modern cooking, and still serve up richly-flavored and distinctive food. If the past is precedent, we think that they will blend new and old ingredients and ideas with sure and satisfying style.

Our aim has been to present the best of the region's specialties in recipes that are workable for the home cook, to lighten dishes by using less fat than is traditional, and to offer new recipes that show what cooks in the Southwest are doing today. This last group of dishes uses ingredients and seasonings that give Southwestern flavor to new combinations. Corn and Green Chile Lasagne; Dried Beef, Carrot, and Romaine Salad; and Duck Burritos are examples. Similarly, Tostadas with Egg Salad are a tasty variation of the traditional, very filling tostadas. They are less work than meat or bean tostadas, and more versatile, suited to impromptu summer brunches, lunches, or suppers. Serving classics like Crab and Scallop Ceviche with Guacamole together makes two dishes into a special party dish. With desserts we have worked with traditional ingredients to create lighter than traditional confections, such as Hazelnut Cake with Cajeta and Coconut, and Spiced Chocolate Soufflé that will satisfy the sweetest tooth, yet leave dessert lovers able to ask for more.

Deeper than the excitement and choices which accompany the new cooking is the love Southwesterners have for the basics. Corn, chiles, beans, and grilled meats have proved versatile and gratifying to many peoples for a very long time. Methods of preparation may be simplified or made easier today, people may eat more fish and vegetables, new dishes may be created and old ones lightened, but the taste of sun and earth will remain in the food.

CHAPTER ONE

Chiles & Other Ingredients

≡

Chile Peppers

Chiles are the *sine qua non* of Southwestern cooking. Their richness, pungency, and color liven the cook's palette, brightening humble and sophisticated dishes. Their vitamin A and C contents, greater than those of oranges, grapefruit, or lemons, gives them high nutritional value. Chiles remain an important part of the diet of the region; many people eat them every day, and more than once a day.

Originally brought from Mexico four centuries ago, chiles have become a Southwestern heritage, central to community and agricultural life. They still inspire passionate fans who hold festivals in the red and green harvest seasons, and form clubs, such as the International Connoisseurs of Green and Red Chile, to spread the good chile word.

The cuisines of the American Southwest use a relatively small number of chiles. Learning their names and characteristics is easy even for someone new to this food. There are several common names for some peppers. In our dictionary (page 13), we follow accepted usages and give as many names and spellings as we have heard and unearthed. As yet there is only broad agreement among chile experts (growers, botanists, and agronomists) on chile nomenclature. This is not surprising given the antiquity and worldwide cultivation of chiles. We refer to the plants and their fruits in general as *chile, chiles, pepper,* or *peppers. Chili* is a stew or a powder compounded of spices as well as ground chiles. These distinctions are noted in the recipes.

Choosing Chiles

Like other produce, chiles should present a good appearance. If fresh, they should be bright and glossy, smooth and unwrinkled, with no punctures, splits, or spots. Occasionally fresh jalapeños will have thin buff-colored vertical cracks. We have picked them from the garden with this condition; it does not affect their flavor as long as the skin is still unwrinkled. Fresh peppers in the market vary greatly in hotness according to their type, cultivation, and storage. There is really no way to tell exactly how hot they are except by tasting them, or asking the produce seller if he or she has eaten them. Fresh chiles can be stored for three or four days in a loosely closed plastic bag in the vegetable section of the refrigerator.

Dried chiles are often sold in cellophane packages. Whether you buy them this way or in bulk, they should have good color, flexibility, and shine. There should be no chile dust in the package or on the chiles; this indicates long storage or insects. *Chipotle* chiles are the only exception to these rules. Because they are smoke-dried, they are dull and brittle, with the tendency to break and accumulate some chile dust. It is best to buy dried whole peppers or choose a good supplier for ground red chiles and cayenne.

Handling Chiles

All chiles should be handled carefully, especially by those who are unfamiliar with them. Use small amounts if you are just beginning to eat chiles. A good way to check pungency is to slice off the stem and run your finger over the flesh attached to it. Then lick your finger; if the pepper is very hot you will know immediately and can adjust the amount you wish to use accordingly. If there is slight pungency or none, take a cautious little nibble of the flesh. Commercial growers are better able to standardize the hotness of the peppers, but there are variations even in canned or frozen roasted and peeled chiles. Pungency varies much more in garden-grown peppers. For this reason we do not use a hotness scale for chiles. These scales all rely on tasters, whose perceptions of pungency are naturally different.

Always wear rubber gloves to prepare chiles. Disposable surgical gloves, available at drugstores, are good for working with peppers. *Never* touch your eyes, nose, or lips while chiles are on the cutting board.

This advice, we must confess, is based on some long slow burns that resulted from dicing piles of peppers for large parties or canning. Some people can take the heat better than others, but it's best not to find out just how sensitive you are to capsaicin, the active pungent compound. Capsaicin is carried mainly in the white membrane of chiles; it flavors the seeds strongly, then the inner walls of the peppers.

Further real life confessions: we do not always wear gloves when working with just a few chiles. Still we feel the caveat is just. Only much practice will teach you how to hold a pepper so that you don't touch the inside flesh, how to let the knife do most of the work, how to scrape roasted chiles, and how to achieve a fine dice without capsaicin under your fingernails.

We always *do* wash our hands very well after preparing peppers. Usually soap and cold water will be sufficient. We've read some interesting suggestions for washing away capsaicin. Jean Andrews in *Peppers: The Domesticated Capsicums* found (and documents with a chemical formula) that household bleach diluted or full strength "completely eliminated the irritant effect." Huntley Dent in *The Feast of Santa Fe* suggests washing the hands well with salt and water. We hope you do not have to resort to these remedies. The outside skin of peppers contains no capsaicin so they may be handled as much as you like while choosing or harvesting them.

Roasting and Peeling Chiles

Many varieties of peppers have a tough skin which must be removed before the pepper is pleasant to eat. All the stuffing chiles, such as California, New Mexico, poblano, and mulato, need to be skinned. There are several methods for accomplishing this, of which we think roasting is the best for efficiency and flavor. Sweet bell peppers, red, green, or yellow, can be roasted using the same procedures. Roasting is the term always used with chiles, but blistering is a truer description of the operation. The chiles are placed over or under a flame, just long enough for the skin to blacken and loosen from the meat. A gas stove top, a charcoal grill, or an oven broiler can provide the flame. Each has its best case applications.

The stove top is good when there are just a few peppers to be roasted. The peppers can be placed directly on the stove grates, but they must be turned frequently to prevent over-roasting. Charcoal-grilled chiles have the best flavor, and if the grill is large many chiles can be roasted at the same time. If you grow your own chiles or can buy large amounts, you can use a grill to great advantage by roasting the chiles and freezing them. Oven broiling is a good technique when you have a dozen or so chiles to roast. Place the chiles on an aluminum foil-lined baking sheet as close to the broiler flame as possible. Whatever technique you use, the chiles should be completely blistered in 3 to 5 minutes. Every bit of skin must be loose, but not necessarily blackened. If the skin is not black, push it a bit with tongs to check for looseness. Over-roasting chiles will cause the flesh to dehydrate or to be so soft that stuffing them is difficult.

After the chiles are roasted, place them in a paper or plastic bag to steam for a few minutes. The skin may then be scraped with the blunt edge of a knife or slipped off under running water, though this rinses away some of the roasted flavor. Some black bits are attractive and tasty. If the peppers are to be used for chiles rellenos, care must be taken to slit them and remove the seeds without removing the stems.

Toasting and Grinding Chiles

Many recipes call for toasting dried chiles to bring out a deeper flavor. For this the chiles may be left whole, or seeded, stemmed, and broken or cut into large pieces. The chiles are put on an ungreased frying pan, griddle, or comal over medium heat and toasted for a brief time, 30 seconds to 1 minute, just until they start to release some fragrance. You must stand by and stir the chiles; if they are over-toasted they will be bitter.

To grind large dried chile pods, first stem and seed them. Cut or tear the pods into rather big pieces. Toast the pieces in one layer for no longer than 30 seconds. Grind about a half cup at a time in a blender or food processor. Finish the grinding in a spice grinder or clean coffee mill in small batches. The ground chile keeps well in a tightly-closed jar away from sunlight and heat. Small dried peppers, such as tepins or pequins, can be ground in a spice grinder without toasting or seeding.

Drying and Freezing Chiles

The large New Mexico/California cultivars can be dried in controlled circumstances. The flesh of jalapeño and red hot cherry peppers is too thick to be dried or frozen; they should be pickled. Small, thin-walled chiles, such as cayenne, Thai, tepin or pequin, and serrano, dry successfully in most conditions.

Home-drying chiles is most easily done in the Southwest, where the climate cooperates. There red, mature, whole chiles with no blemishes are tied by the stems with string and hung in the sun or spread on screens or baskets with air space below and left in the sun. The process takes three or four days of bright even sun and low moisture. If the peppers are spread, they will need to be turned a few times during the drying. *Comida Sabrosa*, by Irene Sanchez and Gloria Yund, gives good directions for making a *ristra*, a large string of clustered chiles to be hung and dried. Ristras are brilliantly festooned throughout New Mexico villages and cities in the fall.

To dry large chiles in areas with uneven sunshine, low temperatures, or high humidity, it is best to hang them inside where they will receive several hours of sunlight a day. The chiles should hang for a week to ten days, then finish drying in a 150-degree oven for 8 to 24 hours. The chiles should feel free of moisture, yet be leathery rather than brittle. We have successfully dried large chiles straight from the vine to the oven in 36 hours at 150 degrees. The quality is better and the expense is less if they are partially sun-dried.

The small peppers mentioned above are threaded through the stems with a needle and hung inside or out, depending on climate, where they receive plenty of sunshine, until they are completely dry and brittle. If the peppers are hung outside in a climate with humidity above thirty percent, they must be brought in at night to prevent mold. Small chiles can be oven-dried in 4 to 8 hours at 150 degrees. The time varies according to the size of the pepper, thickness of the flesh, and partial sun-drying. Home-dried chiles will keep until the next season in tightly-closed glass jars.

Some varieties of chiles can be frozen. The tough-skinned California and New Mexico chiles should be roasted as described above and frozen with the skins still on. Do not overcook the peppers, cool them to room temperature, lay them on baking sheets to flash freeze, then pack them in freezer bags. They will keep up to six months in the freezer, with the best flavor for the first two months. When they are thawed the skins slip off easily. Or they can be peeled, seeded, stemmed, and diced before freezing. Güero cultivars, jalapeños, and Hungarian hot peppers can be frozen raw. Pack them in freezer bags either whole or seeded and sliced. Freezing chiles in this manner retains their heat, but their texture is no longer crunchy. They are best used within three months. Thaw them in the refrigerator for salsas or add them frozen to soups or stews.

Growing Chiles

Growing your own peppers can give you the varieties still not available in markets outside the Southwest. If you can grow tomatoes, you should be able to grow peppers. They have similar requirements: heat and light (but not too much heat for the best fruit set) and plenty of water. Most chiles thrive in the climate of the Southwest, producing there the most flavorful and pungent fruits. In northern areas with less heat, peppers benefit by being grown on black plastic, with special attention to regular watering and fertilization. Popular seed catalogs carry common cultivar seeds, jalapeños, Anaheims, cayennes, and some others. Our source list gives the addresses of several suppliers who offer a wide variety of chile seeds.

Chiles make handsome container plants, especially the smaller varieties, such as Thai, red hot cherry, and cayenne. Even larger plants, such as New Mexico or Anaheim peppers or Hungarian Yellow Wax do well given large enough containers. For further information on growing capsicums refer to Jean Andrews' book or any good vegetable gardening book.

To ensure continuous fruit set and development on the plants, chiles should be harvested as soon as they are mature. Both green and red mature chiles have bone-white seeds. The first harvest of green chiles will have small- to average-sized peppers and will not be as abundant or pungent as later harvests. Toward the end of the season, chiles may be left on the vine to ripen red. These can be used fresh, or dried according to the drying methods previously discussed.

Chiles used in the foods of the Southwest and in this book are described in the *Dictionary of Chiles*. Throughout the dictionary *color* describes chiles in their ripe green stage, or red dried form. *Size* refers to average peppers. For a further fascinating look into the larger world of chiles, Diana Kennedy's *The Cuisines of Mexico*, and Jean Andrews's *Peppers: The Domesticated Capsicums* are remarkably informative and cannot be bettered.

Dictionary of Chiles

Anaheim

COLOR: medium light green turning to dark bright green and ripening to red
SIZE: 6 to 7 inches long and 1 to 1¾ inches wide
PUNGENCY: mild to slightly hot
SUBSTITUTES: New Mexico 6 or 6–4 and Numex Big Jim; hotter peppers are Mexico Improved and Sandia
OTHER NAMES: chile verde, relleno chile, stuffing pepper, mild green chile

This is one of the most popular relleno chiles. It is always used green for stuffing and sauces and must be roasted and peeled. The flavor is not particularly distinguished, although we have found good flavor and pungency from garden Anaheims. It has uniform growth and size; this and its mildness account for its appeal to canners and people who don't like the hotter chile varieties.

Ancho

COLOR: glossy mahogany red-brown
SIZE: 4 to 5 inches long and about 3 inches wide
PUNGENCY: mild to slightly hot
SUBSTITUTES: mulato, pasilla
OTHER NAMES: poblano, mulato, pasilla

The ancho chile is the dried poblano. No other chile, fresh or dried, has such confusing nomenclature. It is common to find the poblano called ancho, as well as mulato or pasilla, and vice versa, the ancho named poblano, mulato or pasilla. It is widely grown in Mexico and California, thriving there as it does nowhere else. Recent cultivars of the ancho/ poblano are smaller in size than older forms of the chile and do not have the clear heart shape. Anchos are sweet with something of an apple flavor and are much used in sauces, moles, and commercially in chili powders.

California

COLOR: glossy medium-dark red
SIZE: 6 to 8 inches long and 1 to 1½ inches wide
PUNGENCY: mild to fairly hot
SUBSTITUTES: New Mexico dried chiles, especially New Mexico 6 and Numex Big Jim
OTHER NAMES: red chile, chile colorado

California dried red chiles are cultivars of the Anaheim. They are smoother-skinned than most dried red chiles and are often strung in ristras like the New Mexico red chiles. Their flavor is rich with mild pungency, (though occasionally a hot one will appear in a ristra) making them good all-purpose chiles for sauces, soups, stews, and with most foods.

Cascabel

COLOR: dark reddish-brown with rather glossy skin
SIZE: ¾ to 1½ inches in diameter
PUNGENCY: fairly hot to hot
SUBSTITUTES: guajillo, New Mexico hot dried chiles
OTHER NAMES: chile bola

Almost entirely grown in Mexico, the cascabel is a round, smooth, shiny chile used in the dried form in the United States. The name, referring to its shape and the rattle of its seeds, means jingle or sleigh bell in English. It is similar in appearance to the hot cherry pepper but is thin-walled. Its deep, rather nutty flavor is useful in sauces, sausages, and full-flavored dishes.

Cayenne

COLOR: medium bright green ripening to bright red
SIZE: 3 to 8 inches long and ¼ to ¾ inch wide
PUNGENCY: hot to fiery
SUBSTITUTES: serrano, Thai, or jalapeño
OTHER NAMES: finger pepper, ginnie pepper

The cayenne is long, thin, and thin-fleshed. Very often it curls and twists as it grows. It is frequently sold as a finger pepper in the green stage, but is more flavorful and hotter when it is red and mature. This is a very useful pepper fresh or dried. Cayennes are easy to grow: the majority of them in today's market are dried and ground and then sold throughout the world.

Chipotle

COLOR: dried, mottled light and dark brown; en adobo, brick red
SIZE: 2 to 3 inches long and ½ to ¾ inch wide
PUNGENCY: very hot to fiery
SUBSTITUTES: none
OTHER NAMES: dried jalapeño; chipotles en adobo are sometimes called mora

The special flavor of the chipotle comes from the smoke-drying process, the only way to dry the fleshy jalapeño. Chipotles come from Mexico dried, en escabeche (pickled), and en adobo (in tomato sauce). They are often used in chili con carne and barbecue sauces in areas close to the border. They add fire and a subtly smoky flavor to complex dishes and good contrast to lightly seasoned bean or cheese dishes.

Guajillo

COLOR: golden green ripens and dries to golden brownish orange
SIZE: 2 to 3 inches long and ½ to 1 inch wide
PUNGENCY: fairly hot to very hot
SUBSTITUTES: fresh serrano, güero, Santa Fe Grande; dried, cascabel
OTHER NAMES: mirasol, cascabel, puya, ají

Virtually all guajillos are imported dried from Mexico and Peru, where they are very popular. Though the chiles are quite hot, they have a distinctive subtle flavor, fruity and a bit metallic. Other chiles do not really capture this, but may be substituted for a different result. Guajillos are most used in sauces, soups, and stews.

Güero

COLOR: pale yellow to yellow green,
ripening to scarlet
SIZE: 1 to 5 inches long and ½ to 1
inch wide
PUNGENCY: fairly hot to hot
SUBSTITUTES: Hungarian Hot Wax in
yellow stage
OTHER NAMES: Santa Fe Grande (and
cultivars), Caribe, güerito (small cultivars), Fresno

Güero means blond in Spanish; the term is used loosely to refer to
any yellow hot peppers. Güero cultivars are always used fresh or pickled
in relishes, salads, and vegetable dishes. Güeritos en escabeche are as
popular in the Southwest as jalapeños en escabeche.

Hot Cherry

COLOR: medium dark green ripening
to brilliant scarlet red
SIZE: 1½ to 2½ inches in diameter
PUNGENCY: fairly hot to hot
SUBSTITUTES: cayenne, Sandia, Mexico Improved
OTHER NAMES: Hungarian cherry pepper, bird cherry, Creole cherry

Hot cherry peppers may be used green, but have the best flavor when
they ripen to their characteristic color. There are many named cultivars
of the hot cherry in seed catalogs. Sometimes the tomato pepper, a different sweet cultivar, is called the sweet cherry pepper. The peppers are
not dried because of their thick flesh, but make excellent relishes, pickles,
and jams. They are also tasty in salads and as garnishes.

Hungarian Yellow Wax

COLOR: pale yellow green turns orange
then ripens scarlet on the vine
SIZE: 4 to 6 inches long and ¾ to 1
inch wide
PUNGENCY: fairly hot to hot
SUBSTITUTES: Santa Fe Grande, güero, güerito
OTHER NAMES: hot banana pepper

Much important botanical work with capsicums has been done in Hungary, from where this pepper derives its name. The sweet variety is usually sold as the banana pepper and the hot variety as the yellow wax pepper. It is used in sauces, salsas, salads, and pickles. We find this easy-to-grow chile has the best flavor when is it bright yellow or orange.

Jalapeño

COLOR: bright to dark green or purple-black, vine-ripening to vermillion and finally scarlet
SIZE: 2½ to 3½ inches long and ½ to ¾ inch wide
PUNGENCY: fairly hot to fiery
SUBSTITUTES: serrano, cayenne
OTHER NAMES: known as chile gordo in Mexico

Perhaps the best-known capsicum in this country, the jalapeño is most often used when it is green and mature. Tons of jalapeños are commercially pickled each year; some brands of these are fair substitutes for fresh peppers in salsas and as an accompaniment to meals. Fresh jalapeños have recently become available almost year-round, but the best flavor and pungency by far are found in the mid- to late-summer peppers from the Southwest or from the garden. They are good in salsas, sauces, soups, salads, with meat, poultry, fish, and many vegetables, and in jellies and preserves. Very large peppers are occasionally roasted, peeled, and stuffed. The Jalapeño TAM is a fairly new cultivar, developed to retain the flavor but remove the heat for those who don't like pungent peppers.

Mexico Improved

COLOR: medium dark green ripening to dark bright red
SIZE: 3½ to 4½ inches long and 1½ inches wide
PUNGENCY: hot to very hot
SUBSTITUTES: Sandia, Anaheim (for milder flavor)
OTHER NAMES: hot green chile

Large amounts of this chile are grown in New Mexico. It is used green (roasted and peeled) in sauces and salsas; when it is red-ripe, it is dried for use as ground hot red chile. The flavor is full and a little sweet. Because the fruit tapers to a point and grows upright on the plant, it makes a good ornamental pepper.

Mulato

COLOR: dark green ripening to red-brown; deep chocolate brown-black when dried
SIZE: 3 to 6 inches long and 2½ to 4 inches wide
PUNGENCY: mild to fairly hot
SUBSTITUTES: ancho
OTHER NAMES: poblano, ancho

The heart shapes and coloration of the mulato and ancho are very similar in their unripe stage on plants, so that it is difficult to tell them apart. Mulatos are usually larger and once the chiles are dry, the rich chocolate brown of the mulato is clearly different from the brilliant dark red brown of the ancho. The mulato is also used much like the ancho: fresh it is occasionally roasted and peeled and then stuffed or added to soups or stews. Most mulatos are dried and sold whole; in Mexico, where they are favorite mole chiles, they are often ground and sold in paste form. Their toasty chocolate flavor is quite distinct.

New Mexico 6

COLOR: medium bright green; when ripe, scarlet
SIZE: 6 to 7 inches long and 1½ to 2 inches wide
PUNGENCY: mild to slightly hot
SUBSTITUTES: Anaheim, Numex Big Jim
OTHER NAMES: New Mexico 6–4, mild green chile

Another member of the mild green chile cultivar family, the New Mexico 6 is grown extensively for commercial canning and freezing. The chile is smooth-skinned, thick-fleshed, and rather flat, making it a good relleno pepper. It must be roasted and peeled when green, after which it is used in sauces, salsas, soups, stews, with vegetables, eggs, meats, poultry, and fish. It is also dried for ground mild red chile and strung on ristras.

Numex Big Jim

COLOR: medium bright green
SIZE: 7 to 8 inches long and 1½ to 2 inches wide
PUNGENCY: mild to slightly hot

SUBSTITUTES: New Mexico 6, Anaheim
OTHER NAMES: mild green chile
This cultivar was developed several years ago by Dr. Roy Nakayama, a specialist in chile botany, with the help of Jim Lytle, a New Mexico chile farmer. They succeeded in being able to reproduce a chile without too much pungency and with high yields. In New Mexico, a single Big Jim can grow to a foot long and weigh over one-quarter pound. The peppers may be used as any other mild green chile, though they are often stuffed when fresh. The bulk of the crops are grown for commercial canning and freezing.

Pasilla

COLOR: fresh ripe, chocolate brown; dried, very dark raisin brown
SIZE: 5 to 7 inches long and ¾ to 1 inch wide
PUNGENCY: mild to fairly hot
SUBSTITUTES: ancho, mulato
OTHER NAMES: pasilla negro, pasilla negro largo, chile negro, ancho, mulato, black chile
The chile takes its name from *pasa*, raisin, in Spanish. It is very raisin-like when dry, shiny, wrinkled, and almost black with brown and red highlights. The fresh chile, used in Mexico, is often called *chilaca*. The pasilla may be called ancho or mulato and similarly used, but it is very different in appearance and flavor from those. It is long and thin, quite dark, and somewhat earthy in taste.

Pequin

COLOR: fresh, ripens from medium green to scarlet;
dried, bright red-brown
SIZE: about ½ inch long and ¼ inch wide
PUNGENCY: very hot to fiery
SUBSTITUTES: tepin, cayenne, Thai
OTHER NAMES: chiltepiquin, petine,
chile pequeño, bird pepper, chiltecpin

As the number of names indicates, this is a difficult pepper to classify. It is little cultivated, but grows wild in many regions of Mexico and along the Southwestern borders. Because the chile is not harvested in large lots, it is relatively expensive. Very little is needed, fresh or dried, for its role as a seasoning. Commercially, it is used as Tabasco and cayenne are, in vinegared hot sauces.

Poblano

COLOR: very dark green with a black
cast, ripening to deep red-brown
SIZE: 3 to 5 inches long and 2 to 3
inches wide at the stem end
PUNGENCY: mild to fairly hot
SUBSTITUTES: none with the same flavor; other stuffing peppers
may be used
OTHER NAMES: ancho, pasilla

The poblano is a very attractive chile in shape and flavor. It is triangular, wide at the stem end, and tapers rather like a valentine heart. When it is green and mature, it is especially good as a relleno pepper. It is also good in soups, stews, and sauces. It has a thick flesh and skin and must be roasted and peeled when used fresh. The rich rounded flavor deepens as the pepper becomes fully ripe. At this time, poblanos are harvested and dried and called ancho chiles.

Sandia

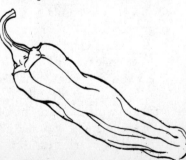

COLOR: medium bright green ripening
to bright red
SIZE: 6 to 7 inches long and about 1½
to 2 inches wide
PUNGENCY: fairly hot to very hot

Substitutes: Mexico Improved, or milder green chiles
Other Names: hot green chile

Like other long green chiles, the Sandia is a good relleno pepper, especially for those who like more heat than the mild varieties provide. The flavor is rich and full-bodied. In the ripe green stage, the Sandia is roasted and peeled and cooked in the spicy chile verde dishes of New Mexico. It is also ripened and hung in ristras or dried and ground for hot red chile powder.

Santa Fe Grande

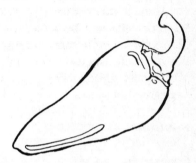

Color: pale yellow green ripening through yellow orange to scarlet
Size: 3 to 4 inches long and 1 inch wide
Pungency: fairly hot to very hot
Substitutes: Hungarian Yellow Wax, güero
Other Names: güero, Caribe

The Santa Fe Grande is a named cultivar of the güero type. It has the best flavor in the pale yellow green stage and is good pickled or fresh, in salsas, vegetable escabeches, and salads. This is a good garden pepper, ripening fairly early, prolific, and handsome.

Serrano

Color: medium bright to dark green, ripening to scarlet red
Size: 1½ to 2 inches long and up to ½ inch wide
Pungency: fairly hot to fiery
Substitutes: jalapeño, Thai, cayenne
Other Names: serranito, chile verde

The serrano is usually eaten in the green mature stage when it has the typical lively, fruity flavor. Jalapeños are the best substitute for serranos, though their flavor is a little duller. Serranos are also available fresh at different levels of ripeness, from green with orange streaks through bright red. In addition, the whole red pods are sold dried. Serranos are used in relishes, salsas, sauces, in many main dishes, and as a garnish accompaniment. They are also home and commercially pickled.

Tepin

COLOR: fresh, bright medium green
ripens to red; dried, bright red-brown
SIZE: about ¼ inch in diameter
PUNGENCY: very hot to fiery
SUBSTITUTES: pequin, cayenne, Thai
OTHER NAMES: chiltecpin, petine, chile
pequeño, bird pepper

This chile and the pequin are very closely related, the difference being
in the shape: the tepin is round while the pequin is oval and longer. The
peppers may be used interchangeably.

Thai

COLOR: fresh, bright medium green
ripening to bright deep red; dried,
glossy deep red
SIZE: ½ to 1 inch long and ¼ inch
wide
PUNGENCY: very hot to fiery
SUBSTITUTES: pequin, tepin, cayenne,
serrano and jalapeño (in larger
amounts)
OTHER NAMES: ornamental pepper

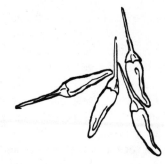

The Thai pepper is no exception to the rule of thumb that ornamental
peppers are very small and very hot. It shares with them another characteristic: the sensation of heat is intense, but fades rather quickly. It is
often found in Oriental markets in all forms, fresh green and red, and
dried. It is principally used to season sauces, soups, stews, in fact any dish
where intense but not lingering heat is desirable.

Glossary of Other Ingredients

Achiote

The richly colored red-orange seeds of the tropical annatto tree are commonly called achiote, occasionally annatto or arnotto. They have come into Southwestern cooking with settlers from the Yucatán region in Mexico where they are used to season and color fish, pork, chicken, and rice or beans. Achiote has a subtle nutty acidic flavor a little similar to green olives. The pulp surrounding the very hard seeds yields a deep orange-yellow color when the seeds are softened in water or oil. They must be softened and ground before using. Achiote is available in an oily paste form as *recado rojo* or *achiotina*; the brands without preservatives have much better flavor. Substitute half the amount of paste for seeds. Achiote can be bought in Mexican and Latin American grocery stores; if the seeds are brown, they are too old to use.

Atole

See Blue Corn.

Avocado

Of the common market varieties, the Hass and the Fuerte, the Hass has the best flavor and texture. It has a blackish-green skin with a very pebbly surface. The Fuerte skin is medium green, shiny, and smooth. Some variety of avocado is available throughout most of the year. A perfectly ripe avocado, with its buttery texture and slightly nutty flavor, is practically a Southwestern staple. Aside from guacamole, they are often used to garnish soups and main courses. If you cannot find them firm, with just slight give when they are gently pressed, you can still ripen them by leaving them at room temperature for two or three days, or hasten the ripening by placing them in a brown paper bag in a sunny spot. Avocados are subject to oxidation; rub or sprinkle the cut flesh with lime or lemon juice. To help keep guacamole from discoloring, save the avocado pit and surround it with the guacamole.

Bell Peppers

These are the sweet relatives of chile peppers. They belong to the capsicum family, but contain no capsaicin. They are available in red, yellow, green, and even purple colors. The flavors are very similar, with the green and purple varieties being a little more acidic and less sweet. If you must use pickled hot peppers because fresh ones are not available, a little chopped bell pepper will add fresh flavor. Bell peppers are chosen, stored, and roasted and peeled like chile peppers.

Beans

Pinto beans, red beans, black beans, and chick-peas are the favored legumes in Southwestern cooking. Pintos are mottled pale brown or reddish-brown and cream. They are called *frijoles* and are the most popular bean, used in soups, stews, burritos, tacos, and tostadas, and as a side dish. Red beans are close in size, shape, and flavor to pintos and may be used interchangeably. Black beans can be called *frijoles negros* or turtle beans. They have a richer flavor than pintos and feature in dishes that came into the region's cooking from the Yucatán and central Mexico. Chick-peas or garbanzos made a reverse migration, from Spain to the New World. They appear in dishes of Spanish origin, especially soups and stews and with chorizo. Their nutty sweet flavor is also good in salads and with rice.

The current year's crop of legumes has by far the best flavor, the shortest cooking times, and the most digestibility. Health food stores or Mexican and Latin American grocery stores usually offer fresh dried beans. Goya is a good brand of legumes that is carried by many supermarkets. Canned beans or chick-peas are not recommended; if you use them, rinse them well to help rid them of the metallic taste. Bean dishes are susceptible to fermentation: refrigerate them as soon as they have cooled to room temperature.

Blue Corn

Blue corn is a native Southwest food, cultivated by the Pueblo Indians for centuries. Much ceremony and tradition attend its sowing and harvest. It is always dried and ground and comes in several forms. *Atole* is roasted blue corn flour, traditionally eaten as a breakfast beverage/porridge, cooked with milk or water, and sweetened with honey, sugar, or chocolate. *Harina maíz azul* is blue cornmeal (actually a steel blue-gray color) and can be substituted for yellow or white cornmeal. *Harinilla* is a finely ground blue corn flour used to make the tortillas that are a northern New Mexican specialty. Blue corn is grown in this country only in the Southwest and is relatively expensive because of hand-cultivation and low yield. It has a more earthy flavor than yellow or white cornmeal.

Cajeta

Cajeta is a syrupy caramel made from sweetened goats' and cows' milk. Perhaps it is an acquired taste, but we fell in love with it on first spoonful in Mexico several years ago. It is available in some border towns, and of course people bring it back from Mexico as a special treat. We give a recipe for making it which yields a close approximation of the Mexican *Cajeta de Celaya*. For further information, see page 245.

Chayote

This pale jade green and delicately flavored member of the squash family tastes just a little like cucumber. It makes a nice change from zucchini and is used in similar ways, frequently stuffed. It is also called custard marrow and vegetable pear; the fruit does have a pear shape, but the skin is tough and deeply ribbed. Chayote must be peeled and cooked before it is eaten. The seed is edible; some people consider it the cook's treat. Choose fruit that is firm with no blemishes; it keeps for two to three weeks in the refrigerator.

Cheese

Many cheeses are used in Southwestern cooking. In general they fall into two categories: melting cheeses, usually mild in flavor, and accent or garnishing cheeses, usually sharp or tangy.

For melting cheeses, Monterey Jack, mild Cheddar, Lappi, semi-soft farmer's cheese, or Muenster may be used, according to the dish. For mild dishes where melting is not so important, farmer's or pot cheese and *queso fresco* are good. Quesco fresco can be found in Mexican or Latin American stores; it is slightly salty and acidic, and is crumbly rather than creamy.

For accent cheeses, aged Monterey Jack, sharp Cheddar, Parmesan, ricotta salata, and *queso cotijo* are used, again according to the dish and the cook's taste. Queso cotijo is a white fresh cheese like queso fresco, but aged a bit so that it has more definite flavor.

Fresh goat cheese is popular and very good with chiles and beans. If you are fortunate enough to find some aged goat cheese for grating, a sprinkling of it can spark rich chile stews or enchiladas.

Colby and longhorn cheese are used throughout the Southwest. We don't think they add much zest (though plenty of artificial color), but they are readily available, and are in a certain sense authentic to a Mexican restaurant style of cooking which parallels the Italian spaghetti, meatballs, and red sauce style.

Chili Powder

We spell chili powder with an *i* at the end to differentiate it from the pure ground red chile, which is also a powder. Chili powder is a blend made of ground dried chiles, toasted and ground chiles, oregano, and cumin. Often ground coriander seed, celery seed, cloves, cinnamon, and paprika are added. Of the many commercial varieties, Gebhardts and Texas Three-Alarm are considered good. We prefer to concoct our own to get a flavor we like with no salt or chemical additives. The recipe for this is in the Condiments & Accompaniments chapter on page 50. Chili powder is added to many Southwestern dishes, especially chile con carne and chili beans. Some people use it almost like salt, sprinkling it into eggs, guacamole, soups, or any savory dish.

Chocolate

The Mexican love for chocolate spread to the Southwest, where it is drunk in the Mexican manner, occasionally added to *moles* (though much less so than in Mexico), and used in desserts. A popular chocolate tablet is imported from Oaxaca; it is quite sweet, grainy from rather coarse sugar and ground almonds, and has cinnamon added. We prefer to add spices and sugar according to the dish, and use semi-sweet or extra-bitter cooking chocolate by Lindt, Tobler, or Callebaut.

Chorizo

This sausage is well-liked in the Southwest where it is served as a companion to eggs, tortillas, and beans. It is also used as a taco filling and cooked in many soups and stews. There are an amazing number of chorizo recipes, each butcher shop and chorizo factory having its variation. The seasonings always include some hot ground chile, the meat is usually pork, and the sausage is usually sold in casings. Beyond this, anything from achiote or almonds to wine is added. Commercial chorizo is very often over-salted. There is a recipe for chorizo in the Meat, Poultry, & Fish Dishes chapter on page 153.

Cinnamon

See Spices.

Cloves

See Spices.

Coriander

Coriander is an essential herb and spice in Southwestern cooking. The leafy herb is called *cilantro* in Spanish, and is usually available in Mexican or Latin American grocery stores. It is also called Chinese parsley and can be found in Oriental markets. Special care should be taken to select fresh coriander leaf because it does not keep well and the flavor is rank if it is old. The leaves should be glossy medium green, with no yellow, and no mold; for best keeping buy whole immature plants, with the roots still on the stems. Store the coriander leaf with the roots and about half an inch of the stems in water in a loosely covered jar in the refrigerator for two or three days. Coriander leaf is used in practically all kinds of savory dishes; its strong, slightly woodsy and oily, grassy flavor goes well with chiles, tomatoes, fish, and chicken. Dried coriander leaf has very little of the fresh leaf flavor; substitute parsley for a different effect.

Coriander seed comes from the same plant as the leaf, but its flavor is quite different and more subtle. It is citrusy, sweet, with a hint of anise and cumin. The seed can be lightly toasted to bring out the best flavor. It is usually ground and used as an accent in stews, sauces, salad dressings, and desserts. It is used whole in pickling.

Corn

Corn is still the staff of life in the Southwest. It is grown in every color, is used fresh in many special dishes, and is dried in several forms to provide the material for tortillas, posole, and tamales. (See Blue Corn, Hominy, and Masa.) Green corn (or *elote verde*) means ripe fresh corn rather than dried in the Southwest; it is not green in color. Chicos are dried whole unhulled corn kernels, used especially in New Mexican and Pueblo Indian cooking. They must be soaked, like dried beans, before they can be cooked. Corn husks (*hojas* in Spanish) are used fresh or dried as wrappers for tamales. In most recipes, frozen corn can be used in place of fresh.

Cumin

See Spices.

Epazote

This strongly-flavored herb is also called Mexican tea, wormseed, and goosefoot. The green leaves have a resinous oily aroma, and taste somewhat like pungent winter savory. It is used in bean dishes, especially with black beans, for its special flavor and the belief that it reduces the flatulence that can accompany bean-eating. The fresh herb is hard to find, but Mexican grocery stores often carry the dried leaves. The resins are concentrated as epazote dries, so use about a third the amount of dried herb when substituting it for the fresh. Epazote *(Chenopodium ambrosioides)* is sometimes mistakenly identified as lambs' quarters *(Chenopodium album)*, called *quelites* in Spanish, a wild green much relished in the high deserts of the Southwest. Occasionally young epazote leaves are added to simply sautéed wild and garden greens. There is no substitute for epazote.

Garlic

Like so many of the world's regional cuisines, Southwestern cooking can hardly be thought of without garlic. Meats, chiles, beans, corn, and tomatoes have strong but single flavors that benefit from garlic in its mellow or pungent modes. Fresh garlic is essential; powder, salt, or garlic packed in oil are sharp and acrid, not sweet and nutty. The first fresh garlic available nationwide comes from Mexico in February or March. It has reddish-purple husks and is a little sharper in the raw state than the white California garlic available in July. Either are good for all recipes in this book. When the recipe calls for a clove of garlic, we mean a good-sized medium to large clove. Toward the end of winter when you must use garlic that has been stored for several months, cut out the green center shoots which give the bitter "garlicky" taste most people find unpleasant.

Ground Red Chile

Most ground red chile comes from New Mexico and is a valuable staple in the Southwestern kitchen. The chiles are whole dried red chiles, usually Sandia, New Mexico 6, and Mexico Improved, and are ground into pure powders. The styles of grinding vary according to the chile processor; some grind the seeds with the flesh. The powders may also be coarsely or finely ground. Pungency depends on the types and combinations of chiles used. Suppliers usually indicate mild, medium, or hot ground red chile. Directions for grinding your own dried chiles are found on page 10.

Harinilla

See Blue Corn.

Herbs

BAY: California and Mexican bay have longer, thinner, and more pointed leaves than European bay. We think the European bay is more flavorful, but the others may be substituted. Fresh bay from *Laurus nobilis* plants may also be used; these are noticeably more aromatic.
MINT: Mint, or *yerba buena* in Spanish, is used in Southwestern cooking in small amounts. Some mint does make a pleasing addition to heavy and

spicy dishes. It appears in soups and stews, with meat, corn, and beans, and sometimes in desserts. Any common garden mint can be used. Wild mint is still gathered in rural regions for use as a medicinal tea.

OREGANO: This is the second most widely used herb in the region's food, after coriander. It has an affinity for tomatoes, onions, chiles, cheeses, meats, and beans. The imported Mexican variety has a stronger flavor than the Italian oregano. Imported Greek oregano can be substituted for the Mexican. Dried oregano is strong: use only one-third the amount of fresh oregano. Buy the whole dried leaves in Mexican or Mediterranean grocery stores. A Southwestern version of *quatres epices* uses one part oregano to one-half part cumin, one-quarter part coriander seed, and one-eighth part cloves for marinating meats, and in stews and sauces.

PARSLEY: Since cilantro is the preferred green herb, parsley is not as common in Southwestern cooking. We do like its fresh, more neutral flavor in some dishes. We always use the Italian flat-leaved parsley for its taste, but any bright green parlsey will do.

Hominy

Dried white or yellow corn kernels are soaked in slaked lime to remove their hulls; then they are rinsed, and redried and frozen or canned to become hominy. Hominy is also called *posole* or *pozole*, though this is really a dish with hominy in it. In the dried state hominy takes hours and hours of soaking and cooking before it is done. Partially cooked frozen hominy has very good flavor; it is available only in the Southwest. Canned hominy, possibly because of its original lime bath, does not pick up the metallic taste that makes so many canned foods unpalatable. Use it after draining and rinsing it.

Jicama

This tropical root vegetable has become popular in the area for its sweet, nutty taste and crisp texture which complement spicy dishes and rich sauces so well. It is eaten slightly cooked as a vegetable, or raw in salads and with other appetizer vegetables to be dipped in salsas and smooth guacamoles. The outer potato-like skin of jícama must be free of blemishes, and the vegetable should be very firm. It can be stored in the refrigerator for a week to ten days. The layers just under the brown skin must be pared as they are very tough. The white flesh inside does not turn dark when cut.

Lard

Although some people consider lard indispensible for authentic flavor in every bean and meat dish, many soups and stews, breads, flour tortillas, tamales, and for deep frying, we do not. Certainly not the preservative-laden commercial lard. Lard was virtually the only cooking fat in the Southwest before refrigeration; now most cooks use oil and butter also, reserving lard for special dishes. Fresh leaf lard, rendered from pork fat, can give a creamy rich flavor to otherwise rather bland beans and tamales. It also creates a flaky texture in pie crusts that no other fat does. Mexican and Latin American butcher shops often sell lard that they render. Use this or the substitute called for in individual recipes.

Limes

Limes are not in the limelight, but taken for granted in Southwestern cuisine. They add a pleasing counterpoint to rich dishes and work well in soups, stews, salads, salsas, desserts, and beverages. They are used as garnish to many dishes. Lemons can be substituted for tartness, but lack, of course, the lime's flavor. Lemons cannot be substituted in margaritas. Lime or lemon zest is the thin, colored, topmost layer of the rind. It contains the essential oils and flavor; the white pith beneath is bitter and should not be used.

Masa

Masa means dough in Mexican-Spanish, usually the dough for corn tortillas and tamales. It can be purchased already mixed in the Southwest in Mexican delicatessens, or tortilla factories. *Masa Harina* is a Quaker Oats trademark name for their lime-soaked and finely ground flour. It makes good tortillas, gorditas, and tamales and is widely available in grocery stores. Masa is simply made and easy to work with. For more information see the introduction to Tortilla & Masa Dishes on page 127.

Nopales

The leaves or pads of the prickly pear cactus are called nopales. They are eaten with some relish in salads and with eggs in the Southwest. We like them grilled, a technique which rids them of their okra-like sliminess. Their flavor is quite tasty, like a green bell pepper with some tartness crossed with a string bean. To choose fresh nopales, be careful. Those in the market or supermarket often have hair-thin cactus prickles still attached. The leaves with best flavor are thin rather than thick. They keep refrigerated for a week to ten days. *Nopalitos* refers to the diced leaves which are often canned. Nopales do not take well to canning in our opinion.

Nuts

Toasting nuts to bring out their flavor is frequently called for in recipes. Small amounts (½ to ¾ cup) can be toasted in a skillet on top of the stove over moderately low heat for 5 or 6 minutes. The nuts should be watched, as their oils will burn and taste bitter if they are left too long. Shake the skillet to ensure even toasting. Larger amounts of nuts should be oven-toasted at 350 degrees for 10 minutes, shaking the pan once or twice for even toasting. Toasted nuts should be used immediately or stored in tight-lidded jars in the refrigerator for a short time.

ALMONDS: Almonds were introduced to the region by the Spanish and figure especially in Spanish-derived desserts. Their flavor is versatile; if you like them, they can be substituted for any nut except pine nuts.

HAZELNUTS: Hazelnuts are grown and eaten in the Southwest, but do not appear in traditional dishes. We like them as a change from pecans.

PECANS: Large crops of pecans are grown in southern New Mexico. They

are prized for their sweet flavor, and used to thicken sauces, stews, and in desserts. Almonds or hazelnuts may be substituted for different flavor.
PINE NUTS: *See* Piñons.
WALNUTS: Many recipes call for walnuts or almonds interchangeably; this is odd considering the strong, slightly bitter flavor of walnuts. They are used like almonds and pecans, in sauces, soups, stews, and desserts.

Oils and Fats

Lard is discussed in a separate entry. Corn, safflower, peanut, and mixed vegetable oils are all used for frying and sautéing. Refined corn oil is by far the most popular. If plain tortillas or gorditas are fried in it, the oil can be strained and used again. Unrefined oils have heavier flavor and lower smoking temperatures, making them hard to use in most Southwestern dishes. We use pure olive oil for sautéing, and in many dishes where a mild olive oil flavor is good. Pure olive oil, whether Italian, Spanish, French, or Greek, is a blend of extra virgin and later pressings of oil. It is light in color and does not smoke at the low temperature of unrefined oil. Extra virgin olive oil is good with salads, but definitely imparts a Mediterranean flavor. We often use vegetable shortening in place of lard; if we don't have lard for tamales, we use a mixture of Crisco and unsalted butter for texture and flavor. Our preference is butter pastry crusts; if you like a lard crust, use your favorite recipe.

Onions

Onions can be very sweet or very pungent, and all the shades between. We like certain varieties for some dishes; this is specified in the recipes. White, yellow, or red, the flavor depends less on variety than on growing conditions and season. Onions are sweeter in spring and early summer; adjust quantities according to your palate and the dish in question. Sliced or diced onions can be made somewhat milder by giving them a cold water bath with a little salt for about 30 minutes. Dry them well before using. White onions are very common in the Southwest. In addition to their standard use as plate garnish, scallions are good in salads.

Panocha

Panocha is flour from sprouted whole wheat grain. It is most used in New Mexico for breads, cakes, puddings, and pastries. It has a definite sweet, nutty wheat flavor; whole wheat flour may be substituted for it.

Pepitas

See Pumpkin Seeds.

Piloncillo

These little pylon-shaped cakes of pressed unrefined brown sugar are imported from Mexico. They give holiday desserts and tamales a special traditional touch. Their flavor is intense, with a hint of molasses and nuttiness. Dark brown sugar, with perhaps a touch of molasses, can be substituted for piloncillo.

Piñons

Piñons, or pine nuts, have been gathered in the desert mesas for at least a thousand years. Because they are hand-gathered and difficult to hull, they are expensive. Their flavor, piney, oily, and sweet, is different from any other nut. There is no substitute for pine nuts, though in some desserts, almonds, pecans, or walnuts could be used for a different flavor. Southwestern pine nuts are available in the area, or through mail order (see Sources). Other sources of closely related pine nuts are Italian, Greek, and Mid-Eastern grocery stores, and health food stores. In Italian stores they are called *pignoli*. Piñons should be stored in the refrigerator.

Pomegranates

Pomegranates are grown all over southern Arizona and California. They are most commonly eaten out-of-hand, but a few Mexican-inspired dishes which use them have made their way into Southwestern cuisine. The ruby-colored, tart-sweet seeds are a nice garnish for custard desserts and rice puddings.

Posole

See Hominy.

Prickly Pear Fruits

The bright red flesh inside the tough skin of these cactus fruits tastes like a watermelon crossed with a mild apple. They are used in the Southwest, where they are native, mainly in jellies and pastes to sweeten desserts. The very hard seeds should be removed by puréeing and straining the pulp. The fruit is usually the size of a large kiwi, and green when unripe, becoming reddish-brown with a green tinge when ripe.

Pumpkin Seeds

The hulled, raw, and unsalted pumpkin seeds are sold as *pepitas*. The seeds are also sold unhulled and salted and hulled, toasted, and salted. In this book, we use only the pepitas. Pepitas have a high oil content; they should be bought from a supplier who sells them regularly, and stored in the refrigerator. They can be found in Mexican grocery stores and in health food stores. Their pretty sage green color and mild nutty flavor have kept them popular in the Southwest and Mexico as snacks, as garnishes for salads, main courses, and desserts and as thickeners in sauces and *moles*.

Rice

Long-grain white rice from the southern states, California, or Texas is the rice used in Southwestern cooking. Some people prefer converted rice; we use unconverted. The important thing is to find a brand of rice you like and learn to cook it. Package directions may need some adjustment. Rice is always cooked in the style of dry and fluffy, with each grain separate. For more information on rice, see the Dried Bean, Corn, & Rice Dishes chapter (page 189).

Salsas

Salsas resemble each other in that they are juicy and spicy. Beyond this, they can be thick or thin, smooth or chunky, hot or mild, green or red. Whatever their texture or taste, they are a class of food which has no counterpart in other areas of this country. The idea of salsa came from the Mexicans; it has taken hold here as strongly as in its homeland. Salsa, or salsas, accompany a traditional meal from start to finish. With tortilla chips they serve as appetizers; with soups, stews, and main courses, a garnish; with any other courses (except desserts), the individual's contribution to seasoning. The essence of salsa is freshness. An extemporaneous attitude helps to make a good salsa: what is especially fresh today in the way of tomatoes, herbs, garlic, and onions; what fresh, dried, or ground chiles will go best. If red summer-ripe tomatoes are out of season, use good quality canned tomatoes. Commercial salsas can be tasty: look for brands that have real ingredients, and no starch, sugar, or preservatives.

Spices

Toasting spices brings out a richer flavor that contributes to the final dish. It takes a few minutes, but a few tablespoons can be toasted and ground at one time, then stored in tightly-lidded jars away from sunlight and heat. Use a small, heavy-bottomed skillet. Put the spice in it over low heat. The commonly toasted spices, coriander seed, cumin, and cloves will be done in a few minutes. Shake the skillet occasionally and remove the spices from the heat when they just begin to release their fragrance. Do not over-toast the spices; they will taste burnt and bitter. Spices can be ground much more easily after they are toasted. When they have cooled a bit, grind them in a mortar and pestle, *molcajete* (Mexican mortar and pestle), spice mill, or clean coffee mill. Measure spices after they are toasted and ground; the yield is a little more than the seed. In some recipes we call for the whole seeds, which are then toasted and ground. This is done to obtain the slightly higher yield.

CINNAMON: Any ground cinnamon can be used. For a more subtle flavor, buy the true cinnamon sticks, pale brown and splintery. These are easily toasted and ground. Cinnamon is used by itself and in combination with other spices to season meats, stews, sauces, desserts, breads, and drinks.

CLOVES: Cloves accent meats, stews, soups, and desserts. They are usually used in combination with other spices. Cloves sometimes appear in chili powders. They are one of the best-keeping ground spices, and can be bought that way, or whole, and then toasted and ground.

CUMIN: Cumin is the predominating spice in Southwestern and Mexican cuisine. It is widely used, and over-used, in savory dishes. The spicy, nutty flavor goes well with meats, beans, and chiles. For this reason, it is an essential ingredient of chili powder. Store-bought ground cumin is a pale imitation of freshly ground cumin, as the flavor oils are very volatile. Buy the raw seed and toast and grind it in small amounts.

VANILLA: Look for pure vanilla extract; the flavor is much superior and the extra expense is measured in pennies per use. Vanilla beans are used in some recipes for really intense flavor. Directions for their use is given as needed. Vanilla beans should be pliable; the stiff ones are old. Store them in tightly-lidded jars away from sunlight and heat.

Tomatillos

The tomatillo is a Mexican native, often called green tomato or *tomate verde*, though it belongs to an entirely different family than the common tomato. Fresh tomatillos are becoming much more available in supermarkets, a good thing, since canned tomatillos are a poor substitute. If you must use canned tomatillos, drain and rinse them, then blanch them for 30 seconds before proceeding with the recipe. Fresh tomatillos are very tart. A sweeter dimension to their flavor is brought out by the technique of roasting them in their husks on an ungreased skillet or comal over medium heat for a few minutes. Turn them frequently until they have little brown spots and begin to sizzle. Cool and remove the husks before further cooking. Tomatillos store well in the refrigerator for a week to ten days. In the market, choose very firm tomatillos, pale green not yellow in color. They are best if the husks are just beginning to split, but remain firmly attached.

Tomatoes

Many Southwestern dishes, especially salsas, depend on flavorful tomatoes. Red, ripe, summer tomatoes are the ones called for in this book. In some areas of the country, ripe tomatoes from Mexico, Chile, or Israel are available in the winter. If fresh ripe tomatoes cannot be found, use good quality, red canned tomatoes.

Tortillas

Both corn and flour tortillas are available in most supermarkets. They can be used wherever tortillas are needed, but we do urge you to try homemade tortillas. The commercial varieties have a stiff texture that makes them especially unsuitable as breads, but they do work well when they are fried as tortilla chips, or in *chilaquiles*. For further information see the Breads chapter (page 91).

Vanilla

See Spices.

Vinegar

White wine and distilled vinegars are too strong for most Southwestern dishes. Dilute them by about one-third with water. We often use rice wine vinegar; its mild flavor and acetic acid level taste right in most salad dressings, *escabeches*, and marinades. It is available in supermarket gourmet sections and in Oriental food stores. Red wine and apple cider vinegars are called for occasionally. The kind and strength of vinegar is specified in each recipe.

Yerba Buena

See Herbs, Mint.

CHAPTER TWO

Beverages

A lot of liquid is consumed in the Southwest and not all of it comes from a margarita pitcher, though the standard restaurant list does evoke the image of tequila wells like oil wells. Sometimes, when the evening is hot, the dinner is a big burrito, and the makings are ready, a margarita can go beyond its excellent function as an aperitif and accompany the meal. The choice of beverages is greater, however, than stereotypical margaritas and beer. For thirst-quenching, the tropical fruit coolers, originally from Mexico, and iced tea, often sun-brewed, are popular. Some regional twists are given to sangrías, sangritas, and a concoction called a wine margarita. Something about citrus acid and sugar added to wine sets our taste buds on edge and leads us to other waterholes. Our version of a sangrita, a fruit juice and chile drink with or without liquor, is the Tequila Diablo. For tequila drinks, good tequila is essential. A "nail in the head" usually accompanies inferior (read cheap) tequila. We like the gold tequilas, particularly Sauza and José Cuervo.

It's not all alcohol though, or large drafts of iced tea and fruit or soft drinks in the Southwest. *Atole,* a hot cornmeal beverage/food usually consumed at breakfast, came from Mexico so long ago that it is quite firmly established as a New Mexican specialty. Mexican-style hot chocolate, with a little spice, is drunk at breakfast, for a snack, or as an after-dinner drink.

Beer is considered by many to be the best complement to chile-laden and spicy dishes, but as the cuisine encompasses lighter foods and more seafood, wine is being drunk more frequently. California wines are the most natural partners to Southwestern food, but we find that some Spanish, French, and Italian wines fit remarkably well.

Any beer with some body can be drunk with many of the appetizers, dishes such as enchiladas, burritos, chile rellenos, and some of the poultry and meat dishes. Light, thin beers do not stand up to the full flavors of this food. Imported beer from almost anywhere, Europe, Asia, and of course Mexico, is a treat with a Southwestern meal. We are partial to Modelo, Modelo Negro, Bohemia, and Corona from Mexico.

Very generally, white wines are better with Southwestern food than red wines. California Sauvignon or Fumé Blancs, French white Burgundies, Italian Pinot Grigios, and Spanish white Riojas can be excellent with fish, poultry, egg, and pasta dishes, and dishes which use fresh and briefly-cooked chiles. Red wine and red chiles do work well together in some hearty dishes, but the heat of the chiles tends to flatten red wines as they are drunk. We like California Cabernet Sauvignons (though not the exceptional vintages) and Spanish red Riojas. The wines mentioned here are by no means the only wines that can be enjoyed with this cuisine. There is always plenty of room for individual preference when matching food and wine. Some like Zinfandels with chile and meat dishes, for example, though we think that the flavors of both Zinfandel and chiles are so intense and definite that they fight one another. Still, we have enjoyed an occasional Zinfandel or Pinot Noir with a chile dish. Experimentation is part of the fun. The wines do need to be full, not thin, and red or white, they will have plenty of acid, fruit, and flavor in good balance.

Atole

≡ Atole is a thin gruel made from ground blue corn. It is hearty and nourishing, much recommended by the Pueblo peoples and northern New Mexico farmers as a healthy food and a restorative.

Serves 2

¼ cup atole (page 24)
1½ cups cold water
2 pinches of salt
1 tablespoon packed light brown sugar, or to taste
1 tablespoon unsalted butter

1. Dissolve the atole in cold water with the salt in a heavy-bottomed saucepan. Bring to a simmer over medium heat. Lower the heat slightly and simmer for 5 minutes, stirring with a wooden spoon. Add the brown sugar about halfway through the cooking time.

2. Remove from the heat and stir in the butter until it has completely melted. Pour into two cups and serve with spoons.

Corn Shake

Serves 4

3 cups milk
¼ cup sugar
½ vanilla bean, split lengthwise, or 1 teaspoon pure
    vanilla extract
2½ cups fresh sweet corn kernels
Ice

1. Scald the milk with the sugar and vanilla bean. (If using the extract, do not add it until the milk has cooled a bit.) Remove from the heat and add the corn. Let stand until cooled to room temperature. Remove the vanilla bean.

2. Purée the milk and corn mixture in a blender in batches. Strain the puréed mixture through a sieve and discard the pulp. There should be about 4 cups of liquid.

3. Fill a blender half full of ice, a generous 2 cups, and add 2 cups of the corn liquid. Blend until smooth and pour into two glasses. Repeat the process to make the other two drinks and serve immediately. The corn milk can be prepared ahead of time and refrigerated; it will keep for 48 hours.

Mexican-Style Hot Chocolate

≡ Serves 2

2 cups milk
1 tablespoon plus 1 teaspoon sugar
1 tablespoon unsweetened cocoa powder
⅛ teaspoon cinnamon, preferably freshly ground
¼ teaspoon pure vanilla extract

1. Heat the milk with the sugar in a saucepan over medium heat. Whisk in the cocoa powder and cinnamon.
2. Heat the mixture until it is hot but not simmering. Remove it from the heat and stir in the vanilla. Pour into two cups and serve hot.

Iced Vanilla Coffee

≡ We like a nice bit of ritual with our coffee drinking; this coffee satisfies that as well as summer thirst. The coffee is best steeped in a cloth bag. These bags are worth trying if you do not have one; they are inexpensive and are found in coffee specialty stores. The coffees should be served with straws so that each person can stir some creamy patterns into the frosty brown.

Serves 3

½ vanilla bean, split lengthwise, or 1 teaspoon pure
    vanilla extract
½ tablespoon sugar
6 tablespoons freshly ground coffee
2 cups water, barely at the boil
3 tablespoons heavy (whipping) cream

1. Put the vanilla bean and sugar in a coffee pot. Put the coffee in a coffee bag or sock and pour the water over the coffee. Steep the coffee for 5 minutes.
2. Remove the coffee bag and let the coffee stand for 5 minutes. Stir to dissolve the sugar and remove the vanilla bean.

3. Pour the coffee into tall glasses filled with ice cubes. Stir the coffee well.

4. Hold a tablespoon so that the rim of the spoon is level with the top of the coffee. Fill the spoon with a tablespooon of cream and slip the spoon carefully out of the glass. The cream should float. Repeat with the other drinks. Serve immediately.

Sun Tea

Because the sun is so intense in the Southwest, the tea is often brewed in an hour. This method gives the tea a fine clarity of color and flavor, especially when it is made without additions, as is often done. In other parts of the country, it may need 8 hours of strong sunshine to steep correctly. There are many variations; experiment with different types of tea, substitute a lemon or an orange for the lime, or vary the sweetness.

Makes about ½ gallon

2 quarts cold water
¼ cup Darjeeling or black tea leaves
3 sprigs fresh mint, about 5 to 6 inches long
1 lime, thinly sliced
⅓ cup sugar

1. In a large jar combine all of the ingredients and stir well. Cover and let sit in bright sunlight for 8 hours.

2. Strain the tea and serve over ice garnished with a mint sprig or a slice of lime. The recipe can easily be doubled to make a gallon.

Pineapple Cooler

This is an extremely refreshing and energizing summer drink, and a pleasant change from lemonade.

Serves 4

1 handful fresh mint sprigs
¼ cup sugar
1 cup boiling water
2 cups finely diced fresh pineapple
2 cups ice cubes
Fresh mint leaves for garnish

1. Bruise the mint sprigs. Put them in a bowl with the sugar. Pour the water over them and steep for 15 to 20 minutes.

2. Remove the leaves, pressing them to extract the liquid. Put the syrup and pineapple in a blender and add the ice cubes. Blend until completely smooth, about 1 minute. Serve immediately, garnished with mint leaves, if desired.

Tangerine Sunrise

Serves 4

3 cups fresh or frozen tangerine juice
6 ounces tequila
2½ tablespoons fresh lime juice
Crushed ice
4 teaspoons grenadine

1. Combine the tangerine juice, tequila, and lime juice in a pitcher and stir well.

2. Fill four glasses half full of crushed ice. Pour the drinks over the ice.

3. Slowly pour 1 teaspoon of grenadine into each glass; it will sink to the bottom. Serve the drinks with a bar straw so that the guests can stir the grenadine.

Frozen Mango Rum Punch

≡ Serves 6

1 mango (about 8 ounces)
2½ cups unsweetened pineapple juice
5 ounces rum
1 ounce Triple Sec
Ice

1. Peel and seed the mango and cut it into chunks. Put half of the chunks in a blender. Add half of the pineapple juice and purée.
2. Add half of the rum and Triple Sec and fill the blender with ice. Hold the lid and blend until smooth.
3. Place a few ice cubes in each glass and pour the drinks over them. Serve immediately. Repeat the process with the remaining ingredients.

Tequila Diablo

≡ Serves 4

½ red hot cherry pepper, or 1 fresh red serrano pepper,
    stemmed and seeded
3 cups V-8 juice
¾ cup tequila
Juice of ½ lime, or to taste
Salt
Ice cubes
Lime wedges for garnish

1. Purée the pepper with the V-8 juice, tequila, and lime juice in a blender. Season lightly with salt.
2. Refrigerate the drink for 30 minutes before serving. Adjust the seasoning and stir in several ice cubes. Pour the drinks into chilled glasses and garnish with lime wedges.

Margaritas de Tomaso

≡ Serves 4

 2½ cups limeade, frozen or homemade (If using the
   frozen concentrate use only 3 cans of water to mix,
   rather than 4⅓ as instructed on the can.)
 6 ounces gold tequila, preferably José Cuervo or Sauza
 3 ounces Triple Sec
 Ice
 Fresh lime wedges
 Margarita salt

1. In a blender, combine the limeade, tequila, and Triple Sec. Fill the blender with ice and blend until smooth. If your blender pitcher holds less than 6 cups, make this in two batches.

2. Prepare four glasses by rubbing a lime wedge around each rim; then press the rim lightly into the salt and shake gently to remove any excess salt.

3. Squeeze a wedge of lime into each glass and fill with the blended margarita. A few cubes of ice can be added to each glass, if desired. Serve immediately.

Margarita Suprema

≡ Serves 4

 1 cup boiling water
 ½ cup sugar
 ⅔ cup fresh lime juice
 4 ounces gold tequila
 1½ ounces Cointreau
 Margarita salt
 Crushed ice

1. Pour the boiling water over the sugar, and stir well to dissolve. Add the lime juice to the sugar syrup, stir, and allow to cool.

2. Mix the limeade in a pitcher with the tequila and Cointreau. Pour into four salt-rimmed glasses that are half-filled with crushed ice. Serve immediately.

Honeydew Margarita

≣ Serves 6

3 cups diced ripe honeydew melon
4 ounces gold tequila
2 ounces Triple Sec
¼ cup fresh lime juice
12 to 14 large ice cubes
6 lime wedges

Blend the melon, tequila, Triple Sec, lime juice, and ice cubes in a blender to a fine icy purée. Pour the margaritas into the glasses and garnish with the lime wedges. Serve immediately.

Kahlua Alexander

≣ This is a rich ice-cream drink that could be served as a dessert. Vary the ice-cream flavor to suit your taste—it is also good with coffee ice cream.

Serves 4

6 scoops ice cream, 3 vanilla and 3 chocolate, or all
      vanilla
¾ cup milk
2 ounces Kahlua or other coffee-flavored liqueur
2 ounces brandy
Freshly grated nutmeg

1. In a blender, combine the ice cream with the milk, Kahlua, and brandy. Blend until smooth.
2. Pour the drinks into cocktail glasses and serve with a pinch of nutmeg on top.

CHAPTER THREE

Condiments & Accompaniments

So many of the sauces, uncooked or bottled, are used as accompaniments or condiments, we call them *salsas* as they are called in the Southwest and reserve the term sauces for the cooked preparations which nap finished dishes or are incorporated into them. The practice of individual seasoning and garnishing is very strong and there are as many firm convictions about cooked table salsas, raw table salsas, and commercial salsas as there are varieties. (We think some people in Tucson make two fine, pungent, vinegary bottled salsas, red and green, under the label *Poblano*.) A good fresh salsa can make the plainest bowl of beans or Southwestern quesadilla a purely satisfying dish.

Really good fresh salsas are made with vine-ripened summer tomatoes or tomatillos, just-picked chiles, and just-snipped fresh herbs. Winter salsas can be tasty if made with a little care. Lacking seasonal tomatoes with summer flavor, it is best to use a good-quality canned plum tomato. If you have access to, and money for, Mexican or Chilean tomatoes in midwinter, these do nicely of course. If the cilantro is not bright and clean, it is better to leave it out, or use another herb, such as dried oregano or sage. Pickled or frozen chiles may also be used when the fresh ones are not available.

Salsas are essential to most traditional meals, but other, more relish-like accompaniments are very common. Fresh or cooked vegetables are the main ingredients of these. They are usually put on the table like salsas and left there for the entire meal; their vinegary spiciness serves to stimulate the appetite and refresh the palate as a salad does.

During the past twenty years chile jellies have become something of a fad in the Southwest. Beyond their usual cream cheese-and-cracker context, the homemade varieties are very good with grilled meats and on muffins or corn bread. There are many commercial jalapeño jellies, often too sweet, with the bright greens from food coloring. We find more flavor and brilliant natural color in the fresh red chile jellies.

Three pantry "condiments" we consider indispensable: a personal chili powder and hot pepper and herb vinegars. We invite modifications to the chili powder recipe offered, but we do believe that making your own makes a difference. Some hot pepper vinegar, whether jalapeño, cayenne, or Thai, is very handy. Sage and oregano vinegars suit some dishes very well, especially elaborate tostadas and sautéed vegetables. Skirt or flank steak can be thinly sliced, marinated in a spicy vinegar with a little fresh oregano for 30 minutes or so and quickly grilled or seared for a fast, flavorful main course. Mundane egg or potato salads benefit from a sprinkling of these vinegars. A few drops are good on plain steamed vegetables. A little dish of flavored vinegar on the table is nice to garnish bean dishes, soups, stews, or salads.

Chili Powder

≣ Most commercial chili powders do not have enough chile flavor for our palates. We like this version which is not searing, but has enough pungency to be interesting. Add 3 or 4 more chipotle chiles, or more cayenne, if you prefer really hot chili powder. Oregano, a common ingredient in many preparations is, we think, best added to individual dishes.

Makes about 2 cups

6 large New Mexico hot dried chiles
6 dried chipotle chiles
3 large pasilla negro chiles
2 large mulato chiles
6 tablespoons cumin seed
6 tablespoons coriander seed
1 tablespoon whole cloves
3 tablespoons celery seed
6 tablespoons paprika
2 tablespoons ground cayenne

1. Break the New Mexico, chipotle, pasilla, and mulato chiles. Remove the stems and shake most of the seeds loose. Toast the chiles in two or three batches on an ungreased skillet, griddle, or comal over medium heat for about 30 seconds. The chiles should just begin to release their aroma. Do not let them darken or they will become bitter-tasting. Let the chiles cool to room temperature on a platter.

2. Toast the cumin, coriander, and cloves on a large ungreased skillet, griddle, or comal over low heat until they release their fragrance and become lightly toasted, about 3 minutes. Let the spices cool to room temperature on a plate.

3. Break the chiles up further by hand or in a food processor. Grind them in small batches in a spice grinder or clean coffee mill.

4. Grind the toasted spices and celery seed in small batches in a spice grinder or coffee mill.

5. Mix the ground chiles and ground spices together. For a fine powder, which is best, grind the mixture in small batches.

6. Stir in the paprika and cayenne. Store the chili powder in tightly-sealed glass jars away from the heat and light.

Oregano or Sage Vinegar

≡ Makes about 1½ pints

> 30 to 35 fresh oregano or sage sprigs, about 4 inches long
> About 1 quart white wine vinegar or distilled white vinegar
> 1 fresh oregano or sage sprig

1. Cut the herbs on the morning of a sunny day and rinse them. Pack them loosely in a quart jar. Fill the jar with vinegar to just above the tops of the herbs. There should be about 1 inch of space to the topmost of the jar.

2. Close the jar tightly and set it in the sun for 2 to 4 weeks. If the sun is very hot and shines continuously, 2 weeks will be enough time to flavor the vinegar well. (Leaving the jar outside all night will not affect the vinegar.)

3. Remove the herbs and decant the vinegar into a clean bottle if you like. Add a fresh herb sprig to the jar or bottle.

Hot Pepper Vinegar

≡ Any fresh, small, really hot pepper will make good vinegar. Jalapeños, serranos, güeros, red or green cayenne, even Thai, tepins, and pequins could be used. The hotter the pepper, of course, the hotter the vinegar.

Makes 1 quart

1 quart distilled white vinegar or white wine vinegar
4 ounces fresh hot peppers, washed and stems
    removed.

1. Add the vinegar and peppers to a heavy stainless steel or enameled pan. Bring to a boil, lower the heat, and simmer for about 5 minutes. Remove from the heat and cool to room temperature.

2. Pour the vinegar and peppers into a sterilized 1-quart canning jar and seal. Let it stand in a cool, dark place for a week before using. The longer the vinegar ages, the more pungent it becomes.

Jalapeño Mayonnaise

≡ **Makes about 1 cup**

1 jalapeño pepper, stemmed, seeded, and finely diced
1 garlic clove, finely minced
1 extra large egg yolk
¾ cup corn oil, or corn oil and olive oil mixed
1 tablespoon fresh lime juice, or to taste
Salt and freshly ground white pepper

1. Put the jalapeño and garlic in a mortar and bruise them well with a pestle. Stir in the egg yolk.

2. Add the oil, drop by drop, then in a fine stream, until the mayonnaise emulsifies.

3. Stir in the lime juice and season with salt and pepper. The mayonnaise should be tart.

Jalapeño Mustard with Lime Zest

≡ **Makes 2 ½-pint jars**

¾ cup yellow mustard seed
¼ cup black mustard seed
1¼ cups water
⅓ cup hot pepper or white wine vinegar
2 or 3 jalapeño peppers, finely minced
½ teaspoon salt
1 tablespoon finely minced lime zest

1. In a spice grinder or mortar and pestle, combine and finely grind the mustard seeds except for 2 tablespoons. Coarsely grind the remaining 2 tablespoons.

2. Transfer all the mustard to a small bowl. Add the water and vinegar and stir with a fork. Add the jalapeño peppers, salt, and zest and blend well.

3. Pack the mustard into sterilized jars and seal. Store in a cool place. The mustard will be quite hot at first; it is best to let it mellow for at least 2 weeks before using. Store the mustard in the refrigerator after it has been opened.

Cilantro Butter

≡ A particularly good butter on corn, this is also tasty on fish, summer squash, carrots, and new potatoes.

Makes about ½ cup

½ cup unsalted butter, softened
¼ cup chopped fresh cilantro leaves
½ teaspoon ground mild red chile
Pinch of salt

Combine the butter, cilantro, chile, and salt and blend well. Pack the butter into a small crock or ramekin and chill for at least 30 minutes before using.

Tomatillo Butter

Makes about 1½ cups

½ pound tomatillos, roasted, husked, and finely diced
½ cup unsalted butter, softened
1 garlic clove, finely minced
Salt and freshly ground white pepper

Drain the tomatillos in a sieve for about 10 minutes to rid them of excess liquid. Combine the tomatillos, butter, and garlic in a small bowl with a fork. Season with salt and pepper. The butter can be used immediately or it can be kept in the refrigerator, covered, for 2 to 3 days.

Guava Jelly

Makes 4 to 5 ½-pint jars

1 pound guavas
Water
¾ cup sugar for every cup of juice
1 tablespoon grenadine for every cup of juice

1. Wash the guavas and cut them into ⅜-inch slices. Put them in an enameled or stainless heavy-bottomed saucepan and barely cover them with water. Bring the liquid to a boil, lower the heat, and simmer for 20 minutes, or until the guavas are tender.

2. Pour the contents of the pan through a jelly bag or a strainer lined with cheesecloth. Let it drip, for 30 to 45 minutes, until most of the liquid has gone through. Squeeze gently once to extract any extra liquid.

3. Measure the guava juice and return it to the saucepan. For every cup of juice add ¾ cup sugar and 1 tablespoon grenadine. Stir well.

4. Bring to a boil and simmer, stirring, for about 20 minutes, or until the jelly reaches the setting stage or a candy thermometer registers 220 degrees. Ladle into hot sterilized ½-pint jars and seal.

Kumquat Jalapeño Marmalade

≣ Makes about 4 ½-pint jars

1 pound kumquats, trimmed and sliced (about 3 cups)
3 cups water
3 cups sugar
3 ounces jalapeño peppers, stemmed, seeded, and cut
    into rings

1. In a large enameled or stainless heavy-bottomed pot, soak the sliced kumquats in the water with 1 cup of the sugar for 24 hours.
2. Add the rest of the sugar and the jalapeños to the pot with the kumquat slices and stir well. Place the pot over medium-high heat and bring to a boil, stirring occasionally.
3. Keep the marmalade simmering, stirring occasionally, for about 30 minutes. When the marmalade reaches the setting stage, or 220 degrees on a candy thermometer, ladle into hot sterilized jars and seal.

Sandia or Red Pepper Jelly

≣ Makes about 6 ½-pint jars

1½ pounds Sandia, Mexico Improved, or red hot cherry
    peppers
1 pound red bell or paprika peppers
1½ cups water
1½ cups apple cider or distilled white vinegar
1 1¾-ounce package powdered pectin
5½ cups sugar

1. Stem and seed peppers and purée them as finely as possible in a food processor, about 1 minute; there should be about 5 cups of purée.
2. Transfer the pepper purée and the water to a heavy-bottomed stainless or enameled pot. Place over moderately high heat. When the liquid comes to a simmer, lower the heat to medium and simmer slowly for about 12 minutes, stirring occasionally.
3. Transfer the cooked pepper purée to a jelly bag or a strainer lined

with dampened cheesecloth and let the juice drip for 45 minutes to 1 hour, or until cool. Stir the purée occasionally with a spoon but do not squeeze the bag.

4. Pour the strained juice into a large heavy-bottomed pot; there should be about 2½ cups of liquid. Add water to equal this amount, if necessary; then add the vinegar and pectin, stirring well.

5. Bring the contents of the pot to a full boil, add the sugar all at once, and bring to a boil that can't be stirred down; boil and stir for 1 minute. Pour into sterilized jars and seal.

Avocado and Tomatillo Salsa

Makes about 2½ cups

2 medium-sized California avocados
¾ pound fresh tomatillos, roasted and husked
½ medium-sized onion
2 large garlic cloves
3 or 4 fresh or canned jalapeño peppers
⅓ cup packed fresh cilantro leaves
1 teaspoon chopped fresh marjoram leaves, or
    ¼ teaspoon dried marjoram leaves
Salt

1. Peel and pit the avocados. Cut the tomatillos in half. Rough chop the onion. Peel and rough chop the garlic. Stem and seed the jalapeños.

2. Combine all the ingredients, except the salt, in the bowl of a food processor. Purée to a smooth sauce. Season with salt. Allow the sauce to stand about 30 minutes before serving.

Fresh Green Chile Salsa

Uncooked green chile salsa makes a good topping sauce for enchiladas, tostadas, rellenos, or eggs. It can also be served as is, or mixed with a little sour cream to accompany tortilla chips.

Makes about 2½ cups

1 pound green chiles, roasted, peeled, seeded, and
    roughly chopped
½ pound tomatillos, roasted, husked, and roughly
    chopped
1 small red onion, cut into chunks
3 garlic cloves, peeled
¼ teaspoon cumin seed, toasted and ground
Salt to taste

Combine all the ingredients in a food processor and process to a chunky purée. Scrape down the sides and process for 2 seconds more. Or chop the chiles, tomatillos, onions, and garlic finely by hand. Let the salsa stand for at least an hour before serving.

Jalapeño Salsa

Makes about 6 cups

2½ pounds ripe tomatoes
2 large garlic cloves
1 medium-sized onion
8 medium-to-large jalapeño peppers, halved, stemmed,
    and seeded
2 tablespoons chopped fresh coriander leaves
½ teaspoon salt, or to taste

1. Peel and core the tomatoes. Peel the garlic and onion.
2. Chop the vegetables finely by hand or in a food processor. The sauce should have some texture with small bits of vegetables. Stir in the chopped coriander and salt to taste. Let the flavors develop for an hour before serving. Serve as a relish or dipping sauce.

Salsa Colorado

≡ This is a very versatile sauce; we use it as a marinating sauce for meats, shrimp, fish, and poultry that are going to be grilled, as well as a binding sauce for impromptu tacos or burritos. For the latter use, add a little water and simmer the sauce for 15 minutes. The finished consistency should be the same as when the sauce came from the blender. Toss the sauce with whatever leftover poultry, pork, or beef you have and roll the mixture in warm corn or flour tortillas. Salsa Colorado keeps well in the refrigerator for 5 or 6 days and in the freezer for a month. The recipe may be doubled; in that case you will need to blend it in two batches.

Makes about 1½ cups

2 large pasilla chiles
1 large ancho chile
4 dried cascabel or cayenne chiles
1 cup boiling water
3 garlic cloves, chopped
1 small onion, diced
Salt

1. Stem and seed the chiles. Break or cut them into pieces about 1 inch square. Put the chile pieces in a bowl and pour the boiling water over them. Soak them for 30 minutes.

2. Pour the chiles and their liquid into a blender. Add the garlic and onion. Purée the sauce for about 45 seconds; it should be smooth, although there will be some bits of chile. Season the sauce lightly with salt.

Salsa Fria with Sage

≡ **Makes about 3 cups**

1¼ pounds ripe tomatoes
2 or 3 serrano or jalapeño peppers
1 small yellow or white onion
1½ teaspoons dried sage leaves
1½ teaspoons white wine vinegar
1½ teaspoons corn oil
Salt

1. Peel and core the tomatoes and cut them into med
and stem the chiles and cut them into thin half-rings. Pee
cut it into medium dice. Combine the vegetables in a bowl. It is possible
to chop the vegetables in the food processor, taking care not to overpro-
cess them.

2. Crumble the sage leaves and add them to the vegetables with the
vinegar and oil. Salt lightly and toss well. Let the salsa stand an hour before
serving. If necessary, season with additional salt and vinegar. Serve with
tortilla chips or with grilled nopales, lamb, or beef.

Salsa Verde with Pepitas

≡ **Makes about 2½ cups**

1½ cups loosely packed fresh cilantro leaves
½ cup loosely packed fresh parsley leaves
½ cup finely chopped onion
1 garlic clove, minced
⅓ cup pepitas
⅓ cup olive oil
⅓ cup water
3 medium-sized Anaheim peppers, or other mild green
     chiles roasted, peeled, and seeded
2 to 3 tablespoons fresh lime juice
Salt

1. Combine all the ingredients, except the lime juice and salt, in a
food processor. Purée to a smooth texture.

2. Season with lime juice and salt. Allow the salsa to stand an hour
before serving. Serve as a dipping sauce or with grilled chicken, fish, or
vegetables.

Tomato and Tomatillo Salsa

Makes about 3½ cups

1½ pounds ripe tomatoes
½ pound fresh tomatillos, roasted and husked
1 medium-sized red onion
3 garlic cloves
4 serrano or jalapeño peppers, stemmed and seeded
1 tablespoon ground hot red chile
Salt

1. Core the tomatoes and chop them medium-fine. Chop the tomatillos medium-fine. Chop the onion medium-fine and the garlic very fine.

2. Chop the peppers very fine. Combine all the ingredients in a bowl and stir in the ground red chile. Season with salt and allow the salsa to stand for an hour before serving. Serve the salsa as a dipping sauce for tortilla chips or as an accompaniment to grilled foods.

Beets and Onions en Escabeche

Serves 8; makes about 1½ quarts

1 pound small red beets
2 cups water
½ cup apple cider vinegar
1½ teaspoons toasted coriander seed
¾ teaspoon toasted cumin seed
1 3-inch cinnamon stick
2 bay leaves
1 tablespoon plus 1 teaspoon sugar, or to taste
1 large onion, halved and sliced into ¼-inch-thick slices
¾ teaspoon salt

1. Scrub and trim the beets, leaving 1-inch tops and stems. Place in an enameled or stainless saucepan with a tight-fitting lid and add the water, vinegar, coriander, cumin, cinnamon, bay leaves, and sugar.

2. Cover and place over high heat. Bring to a boil, lower the heat, and cook until the beets are just tender, 15 to 20 minutes.

3. Reserve the beet juice and plunge the beets into cold water, rubbing off their skins and stems. Set the beets aside.

4. Add the onion and salt to the pan with the reserved beet juice and toss well. Bring to a boil, cover, and remove from the heat.

5. If the beets are not small, halve them. Slice them into ¼-inch-thick slices and add them to the pan with the onions.

6. Stir the vegetables and the marinade occasionally as they cool. Serve the beets and onions at cool room temperature.

Cabbage en Escabeche

☰ Serves 6 to 8

4 cups finely shredded green cabbage
½ medium-sized red onion, thinly sliced
1 small red bell pepper, julienned
3 large jalapeños, stemmed, seeded, and julienned
2 garlic cloves, minced
1 tablespoon chopped fresh oregano leaves, or ½ tea-
    spoon dried oregano, leaves crumbled
5 tablespoons white wine vinegar mixed with 2 table-
    spoons water
½ cup olive oil
½ teaspoon salt
½ teaspoon sugar
½ teaspoon cumin seed, toasted and ground

1. Toss the vegetables and herbs together. Mix the vinegar, water, olive oil, salt, sugar, and cumin together.

2. Toss the dressing with the vegetables. Cover and refrigerate for 2 hours. Remove from the refrigerator and allow to come to cool room temperature before serving.

Summer Fruits and Vegetables with Lime and Red Chile

≣ Serves 4 to 6

1 cucumber, peeled, cut in half across, and cut lengthwise into ⅜-inch slices
1 ripe mango, peeled and cut into ⅜-inch-thick slices
1 ripe avocado, peeled and cut lengthwise into ⅜-inch
slices
1 ripe papaya, peeled, seeded, and cut lengthwise into
⅜-inch slices
3 tablespoons fresh lime juice
2 to 3 teaspoons ground hot red chile

Arrange the sliced fruits and vegetables on a platter. Sprinkle them
with the lime juice. Dust them with the ground chile. Serve at cool room
temperature.

Whole Pickled Peppers

≣ We have made good pickled peppers from Santa Fe Grande, Hungarian hot, red hot cherry, jalapeño, and serrano chiles.

Makes about 6 pints

1 gallon red, green, and yellow chile peppers
1 quart water
3 cups distilled white vinegar
2 teaspoons salt

1. Wash the peppers and cut the stems from the large chiles. Make
a slit with a sharp knife in all of the peppers. For larger peppers make
about a 1-inch slit, and for smaller peppers make about ½-inch slit.
2. Bring the water, vinegar, and salt to a boil in a large enameled or
stainless pot. Add the peppers and return to a simmer. Let them simmer
for 2 to 3 minutes.
3. Remove from the heat and pack in hot sterilized jars. Pack peppers

to 1 inch from the top and add boiling liquid to ½ inch from the top. Seal the jars.

4. Process in a boiling water bath for 25 minutes or in a pressure cooker for 15 minutes. Wrap in towels to cool slowly. The peppers may be eaten immediately, and they will keep until the next season.

Vegetables en Escabeche

≡ If jalapeños are not in season, it is better to make this escabeche with pickled jalapeños to ensure a good hot flavor.

Makes about 2 quarts

1½ cups white wine vinegar
2 cups water
½ teaspoon sugar
Salt to taste
1 pound cauliflower, trimmed and broken into bite-sized flowerets
1 large white onion, halved lengthwise and cut into slivers
2 medium-sized carrots, cut into 3-inch-long slivers
1 small red bell pepper, seeded and cut into ¼-inch slivers
1 green bell pepper, seeded and cut into ¼-inch slivers
8 jalapeño peppers, seeded and cut into slivers
1 teaspoon dried sage leaves
2 teaspoons chopped fresh oregano leaves, or 1 scant teaspoon dried oregano leaves
2 tablespoons olive oil
Freshly ground black pepper

1. Bring the vinegar, water, sugar, and salt to a boil in a stainless or enameled pan. Put the cauliflower in a large bowl and pour the vinegar solution over it. Let it stand while preparing the rest of the ingredients.

2. Add the rest of the vegetables to the cauliflower. Add the herbs, oil, and freshly ground pepper. Toss well to coat the vegetables evenly.

3. Cover and let the vegetables marinate for at least 3 hours. Stir occasionally and taste for salt. The escabeche can be prepared in advance and will keep for a day or two in the refrigerator. Serve at cool room temperature.

Canned Hot Peppers en Escabeche

☰ Traditionally, this kind of escabeche has a little oil in it, but for long-term storage we feel it is better left out. The hot peppers may be stemmed and seeded if you like. We usually don't, except when the peppers have very thick stems, such as hot cherry peppers. We do stem and seed the bell peppers. The hot peppers are sliced lengthwise in quarters, halves, or whatever is appropriate to provide ⅜- to ½-inch thick slices.

Makes 8 pints

1 quart distilled white vinegar

6 cups water

2 tablespoons sugar

1 tablespoon salt

2 teaspoons cumin seed

4 cups carrot sticks cut 2½ inches long by ⅜ inch wide (4 to 5 medium carrots)

8 cups sliced hot peppers, about 35 to 40 mixed jalapeños, hot Hungarian, hot cherry, Fresno, or other hot peppers

4 green and red bell peppers, cut in ⅜-inch-wide strips

3 large onions, peeled, cut in half from stem to root, and then into ⅜-inch-wide strips

8 garlic cloves, slivered

8 4-inch-long fresh oregano sprigs, optional

1. Bring the vinegar, water, sugar, salt, and cumin seed just to a boil, lower the heat, and simmer for 10 minutes.

2. Add the carrot sticks and bring the liquid to a vigorous simmer. Cook the carrots for 3 minutes. Add the hot peppers, green peppers, onions, and garlic and cook for 3 minutes.

3. Ladle the escabeche into hot sterilized canning jars, putting the oregano sprigs in each first, if you are using them. Leave ½-inch head space and seal the jars.

4. Process the jars in a water bath for 20 minutes from the time the water starts to boil. Or pressure can according to directions with your pressure canner.

CHAPTER FOUR

Appetizers

≡

Botanas, antojitos, or appetizers, however they are called, they form an extremely important category in Southwestern cooking. Many of the specialties, tostadas, and tamales, are made small to be eaten before the main course. Vegetable relishes serve as appetizers as well as salads, and are left on the table to cleanse the palate at any time during the meal. The hearty nature of the region's cooking and its influences from Mexico encourage making whole meals from a selection of appetizers.

In the flavorful merry-go-round of appetizers, main courses, salads, and vegetables, there is considerable place-changing. *Carne asada*, a main course of quickly-grilled, large thin, beef steak can be first cut into strips, then grilled and served in small portions to become *fajitas*. Conversely, *chile con queso* is often served as a brunch or lunch main course. *Rajas*, sautéed fresh chile and pepper strips, are served before the meal or as a vegetable accompaniment. Fish and shellfish appetizers are usually tangy with lime juice or vinegar, fulfilling their role of perking up the appetite, but we enjoy them as summer suppers with tortillas or, perhaps, corn fritters on the side. Often, good light meals can be composed of one substantial appetizer with a fitting bread, vegetable, or salad. The tortilla-based snacks, nachos, tostadas, and quesadillas, are less versatile in this regard because they are simple; while they can be quite filling, they are not as palate-satisfying.

Guacamoles comprise an appetizer class by themselves. Almost infinitely variable, simple to make but full of flavor, they customarily precede the meal, but appear as salads, garnishes, and components of complex *topopo* and tostada structures.

Appetizers can be rustic (Southwestern quesadillas), informal (tortilla chips and salsa), elegant (crêpes or ceviche), or elaborate (guacamole with ceviche). Whichever style, the cooking acknowledges that people like (and sometimes *need*) to nibble or take up the first fork before settling to the pleasureful task of fulfillment.

Simple Guacamole

≣ This is a dish for early summer when the nutty Hass avocados from California are at their peak. A little chopped fresh coriander leaf is a good variation, or cream or sour cream can be stirred in to thin the guacamole to a more sauce- or dip-like texture.

Makes about 1½ cups

2 ripe avocados
2 tablespoons fresh lime juice
1 large garlic clove, finely minced
Salt and freshly ground black pepper to taste

Peel the avocados and remove the pits. Mash the avocado meat in a bowl. Add the lime juice and garlic and blend well. Add salt and pepper. Serve with tortilla chips or on salad greens.

Annie's Guacamole

≣ Because of its smooth texture and mild flavor, this is a good guacamole to serve with raw vegetables, such as jícama, red, yellow, and green sweet peppers, cucumbers, mild onion rings, scallions, and radishes. If you are making the guacamole ahead, reserve one of the pits and add it to the guacamole—it seems to help the guacamole from turning dark.

Makes about 3½ cups

3 large ripe California avocados
4 ounces natural cream cheese, cut into chunks
1 large ripe tomato, cored and cut into wedges

¼ cup chopped onion
2 pickled jalapeños, stemmed, seeded, and minced
1 tablespoon plus 1 teaspoon hot pepper vinegar
1 teaspoon toasted and ground cumin seed
1 garlic clove, pressed
Salt and freshly ground black pepper

1. Peel and pit the avocados and put them in a food processor with the cream cheese and tomato. Add the onion, jalapeños, vinegar, cumin, garlic, and salt and pepper. Process, until smooth, stopping once to scrape down the sides.

2. Transfer to a serving bowl and serve immediately or cover and refrigerate. Thirty minutes before serving, let the guacamole stand at room temperature.

Guadalajara-Style Guacamole

Serves 4 to 6

1 large ripe tomato
1 small onion
2 medium-sized garlic cloves
3 ripe Hass avocados
Juice of 1 lime, or to taste
3 large jalapeño peppers, stemmed, seeded, and diced
Salt

1. Seed and core the tomato and cut it into medium dice. Peel the onion and garlic and mince them.

2. Peel and pit the avocados and cut them into medium dice. Toss the avocado with the lime juice. Gently stir in the jalapeños, tomato, onion, and garlic. Season with salt.

Black Beans with Goat Cheese and Jalapeños

When we serve these as an appetizer with tortilla chips, even people who don't like bean dips are impressed. They are also good with soft tacos and simply grilled meats.

Serves 10 to 12

1 pound black beans, sorted and rinsed
3 garlic cloves, peeled
2 large epazote leaves, or ½ teaspoon dried epazote, or 1 large bay leaf
Salt
4 jalapeño peppers, stemmed, seeded, and finely diced
2 garlic cloves, finely minced
½ teaspoon cumin seed, toasted and ground
12 ounces mild goat cheese
2 bunches scallions

1. Soak the beans overnight in 2 to 3 quarts of water. Drain and cover them with 2 inches of water. Add the 3 garlic cloves and the epazote. Cover and cook until the beans are done, 1 to 2 hours.

2. Salt the beans and let them stand covered for about 10 minutes. Drain the beans and reserve the cooking liquid. Mash the beans well, adding liquid as necessary to make a fairly loose paste.

3. Preheat the oven to 350 degrees. Mix the peppers, minced garlic, and cumin with the beans. Season with salt if necessary.

4. Crumble the goat cheese. Trim the scallions to 2 inches of green and slice them thinly.

5. Layer about one-third of the beans in an ovenproof casserole. Cover with about one-third of the cheese, then one-third of the scallions. Layer another one-third of the beans, goat cheese, and scallions.

6. Cover with the remaining beans and bake for 15 to 20 minutes, or until the beans are heated through. Just before serving, sprinkle with the remaining goat cheese and scallions.

Anaheim Chile Timbales

Serves 12 as an appetizer, 6 as a lunch or supper course

3 tablespoons unsalted butter
3 tablespoons unbleached white flour
1 cup milk
¼ teaspoon salt
⅛ teaspoon freshly ground black pepper
2 egg yolks
1 large jalapeño pepper, stemmed, seeded, and finely
    diced
1 cup *cooked* brown rice
½ cup grated Monterey Jack cheese
1 tablespoon chopped fresh coriander leaves
Salt and freshly ground black pepper
About 3 tablespoons unsalted butter
12 Anaheim chiles, roasted, seeded, peeled, and halved
    lengthwise
3 egg whites

1. Melt the 3 tablespoons of butter in a saucepan over low heat. Stir in the flour and cook for 2 to 3 minutes. Add the milk and stir vigorously. Add the ¼ teaspoon salt and ⅛ teaspoon black pepper and cook the béchamel for about 5 minutes. Remove from the heat and cover. Cool to room temperature.

2. Stir the egg yolks into the béchamel. Transfer the béchamel to a bowl and stir in the jalapeño, brown rice, cheese, and coriander. Season with salt and pepper.

3. Preheat the oven to 350 degrees. Using 3 tablespoons of butter, generously butter 12 ½-cup timbale molds or baking cups. Line the sides of the molds with the roasted Anaheim peppers.

4. Beat the egg whites until they are stiff but not dry. Fold the egg whites into the béchamel mixture. Spoon the mixture into the lined molds and place the molds in a large baking dish. Pour very hot water to come halfway up the sides of the molds.

5. Bake the timbales for 20 minutes. Remove the molds from the dish and unmold onto a warm serving platter or plates. Serve with Salsa Fria with Sage (page 58) or Tomato and Tomatillo Salsa (page 60).

Crêpes with Squash Blossoms and Mushrooms

≡ Makes 12 crêpes, 6 of each kind

1 recipe Roasted Garlic Cream Sauce (page 86)

CRÊPE BATTER
 ⅔ cup unbleached white flour
 ¼ teaspoon salt
 3 extra large eggs, lightly beaten
 ¾ cup milk
 2 tablespoons unsalted butter, melted and cooled

MUSHROOM FILLING
 8 large mushrooms, about 2 inches in diameter
 3 tablespoons unsalted butter
 1 tablespoon finely chopped shallot
 Salt and freshly ground black pepper to taste

SQUASH BLOSSOM FILLING
 8 to 10 large squash blossoms, carefully rinsed and
   patted dry
 3 tablespoons unsalted butter
 1 tablespoon finely chopped shallot
 Salt and freshly ground black pepper to taste

1. To make the crêpes, combine the flour and salt in a bowl and make a well. Add the eggs to the well and whisk them into the flour until smooth. Add the milk and butter and whisk until smooth.

2. Strain the batter into another bowl. There should be about 2 cups. Cover and chill the batter for at least an hour before cooking.

3. To cook the crêpes, brush a small amount of butter in a 7-inch crêpe or omelet pan and heat the pan over medium-high heat. Using a ladle or spoon that measures 2 tablespoons, pour the batter into the pan, swirling to distribute it evenly. Cook the crêpe for 30 to 40 seconds, or until the edges begin to curl. Turn the crêpe and cook for 30 seconds on the other side. Stack the crêpes on a plate and continue cooking. At this point the crêpes can be prepared, cooled, and refrigerated until ready to use or kept warm in a 250-degree oven, covered with a damp tea towel until ready to assemble. There will be a few extra crêpes.

4. To prepare the mushroom filling, remove the stems and cut the mushrooms into fine dice. Melt the butter over medium-low heat in a small skillet and sauté the shallot for 2 to 3 minutes.

5. Add the mushrooms and sauté 2 to 3 minutes more. Remove from the heat and season lightly with salt and pepper.

6. To prepare the squash blossom filling, cut the blossoms in half lengthwise and then in fine crosswise strips. Melt the butter over medium-low heat in a small skillet and soften the shallots in the butter for 2 to 3 minutes.

7. Add the blossoms and stir gently until they are just wilted. Remove from the heat and season lightly with salt and pepper.

8. Preheat the oven to 250 degrees. The sauce should be hot and the crêpes and filling should be warm. Serving plates should also be warm.

9. Divide the mushroom filling equally onto 6 of the crêpes, placing it on a quarter of the crêpe. Fold the crêpe in half and then in quarters. Keep these in a warm dish in the oven while repeating the same procedure with the squash blossom filling.

10. Spoon a little sauce onto each warm plate. Place one of each kind of crêpe on the plate. Spoon the sauce evenly over the crêpes and serve immediately.

Chile con Queso with Corn

≣ In addition to its usual place as an appetizer, this is a good brunch dish. It goes well with dry white wines with pronounced fruit, such as Fumé Blanc.

Serves 4

1 to 1½ cups fresh white corn kernels
½ cup finely diced onion
1 garlic clove, finely minced
2 tablespoons corn oil
⅔ cup light cream (18 to 20 percent butterfat)
½ pound Monterey Jack cheese, shredded
1 medium-sized ripe tomato, peeled, seeded, and diced
¾ to 1 cup roasted and peeled green chiles, chopped,
    or a mixture of roasted and peeled chiles and fresh
    serranos or jalapeños
Salt

1. Stew the corn with the onion and garlic in the oil over low heat until the onions and garlic soften, about 10 to 12 minutes. An earthenware casserole which can be put on top of the stove is the best pan for this dish, as the chile con queso can be served directly from it. Transfer the vegetables to a blender or food processor and add the cream. Blend or process to a medium-smooth purée.

2. Return the mixture to the pan and add the cheese, tomato, and chiles. Heat through over very low heat for 10 to 15 minutes, stirring occasionally to dissolve the cheese. Do not increase the heat; this dish will separate if cooked too quickly. Serve the chile con queso hot with warm flour or corn tortillas.

Snapper en Escabeche with Tomatoes

≡ **Serves 6**

ESCABECHE

¼ cup rice wine vinegar
2 to 3 pickled jalapeños, stemmed, seeded, and finely
   chopped
¼ cup juice from the jalapeños
½ cup finely chopped onion
½ cup finely chopped red or green bell pepper
2 garlic cloves, finely minced
3 tablespoons chopped fresh coriander leaves
1 medium-sized ripe tomato, peeled, seeded, and finely
   diced
Salt
¼ teaspoon freshly ground cumin, optional

FISH

2 pounds snapper fillets, skinned
Salt and freshly ground black pepper
½ cup all-purpose flour
Vegetable oil for frying

1. Mix the escabeche ingredients together in a bowl. Let the flavors meld while you prepare the fish.

2. Cut the fish into 1½-inch pieces on a diagonal so that they are of equal thickness. Salt and pepper the fish lightly.

3. Dredge the fish in flour and pat it free of excess flour. Pour a ½-inch layer of oil into a large frying pan and heat it over medium-high heat. Fry the fish in one layer, in two batches if necessary, until it is light golden brown on both sides, 3 to 5 minutes altogether.

4. Remove the fish as it is done to a large serving dish. When half of the fish is on the platter, pour half of the escabeche over it. Cover with the remaining fish and escabeche. Let the dish stand at room temperature for an hour before serving. Or, after an hour, cover and refrigerate for 2 to 24 hours. Allow the Snapper en Escabeche to warm slightly before serving. The flavor is best after 2 to 3 hours in the refrigerator.

Crab and Scallop Ceviche

≡ Serves 6 to 8

1 2-pound Dungeness crab, or 1 pound fresh cooked
    lump crab meat
1 recipe Fish Broth (page 111)
1 pound sea scallops
4 or 5 limes
½ small red onion, diced
2 jalapeño peppers, stemmed, seeded, and cut into slivers
2 tablespoons chopped fresh coriander leaves
Salt and freshly ground black pepper
About ½ cup extra virgin olive oil
2 ripe Hass avocados
2 jalapeño peppers, stemmed, seeded, and diced
1 large ripe tomato, cored and diced
2 garlic cloves, finely minced

1. Boil the Dungeness crab in the fish broth for about 12 minutes. Cool the crab on a rack; then crack it and remove the meat. Or pick over the lump crab meat. Trim the scallops and cut them into ¼-inch rounds.

2. Put the shellfish in a large glass or ceramic dish in one layer. Squeeze the juice of 3 limes over the fish. Scatter the onion, slivered jalapeños, and coriander over the fish and season lightly with salt and pepper.

3. Drizzle about ⅓ cup of the olive oil over the fish and toss the ceviche. Marinate, covered, in the refrigerator for 4 hours, turning occasionally. Season with lime juice, salt, and pepper.

4. Peel and pit the avocados and cut them into ⅜-inch dice. Toss the avocado meat with some salt and pepper, the juice of half a lime, and olive oil to coat thoroughly.

5. Toss the diced jalapeños, tomato, and garlic with the avocados. Add a little more olive oil and season with lime juice, salt and pepper. Cover and refrigerate from 1 to 4 hours. Serve the salads side by side on a large serving platter or on individual serving plates.

Shrimp in Salsa Colorado

Serves 6

2 pounds large (16 to 20 count) shrimp
1 recipe Salsa Colorado (page 58)

1. Shell and devein the shrimp, leaving the tails on if possible. Arrange the shrimp in a dish just large enough to hold them in one layer. Pour the Salsa Colorado over the shrimp and toss to coat the shrimp.

2. Cover with plastic wrap and refrigerate for 24 hours. Turn the shrimp two or three times. Remove the shrimp from the refrigerator 1 to 2 hours before cooking.

3. Grill the shrimp over a medium-hot wood or wood-charcoal fire until they are just firm. Serve hot. The shrimp may be oven-broiled. Place them on a baking sheet 5 inches from the broiler heat. Broil 2 to 3 minutes on each side, or until the shrimp are just firm.

Oysters to Accompany Southwestern Meals

Oysters are considered very new to Southwestern eating, though Huntley Dent, in *The Feast of Santa Fe*, notes that they were shipped to the area packed in barrels of ice in the 1880s. Certainly oysters are still uncommon in parts of Arizona, Colorado, New Mexico, and Texas. We think that they make a perfect prelude to some elegant menus. When we serve them before Grilled Leg of Lamb with Sandia Jelly or Duck Stuffed with Chorizo with Red Wine and Red Chile Sauce, we do as follows.

4 to 6 oysters per person
1 or 2 limes, cut into small wedges
Small amounts of one or more of these salsas:
    Fresh Green Chile Salsa (page 56); Hot Pepper
    Vinegar (page 52) with a little chopped fresh
    oregano; Jalapeño Salsa (page 57); Tomato and To-
    matillo Salsa (page 60)

Shuck the oysters and place them on packed crushed ice on a pretty platter. Surround them with the lime wedges. Serve the salsas in small pottery or glass bowls.

Nachos with Goat Cheese and Pepitas

In the past few years, nachos have proliferated rather wildly and inappropriately on restaurant menus. Good things can be said about mass food, but nachos exemplify the worst slide into mediocrity and even badness that occurs when food crazes meet marketing brainstorms. A good nacho is direct, piping hot, simple, with the ingredients on top complementing, never overwhelming, the tostaditos. Many restaurants lay claim to having devised the original nachos: a few shreds of *queso fresco* or good quality Cheddar and a slice of pickled jalapeño on the restaurant's homemade tostaditos. These are good if you are lucky enough to find them, rather than thin, soggy corn chips under a gooey blanket of processed or totally inapt cheese, such as domestic mozzarella, topped with anything from hot dog slices to canned pinto beans. Our recipe starts with the best foundation, homemade stale tortillas, and offers some tasty and workable variety in the topping.

Serves 4 to 6

8 or 10 6- or 4-inch stale Corn Tortillas (page 92)
Oil for frying
Salt
5 ounces mild California or French goat cheese
4 or 5 fresh red and green hot peppers, such
    as, serranos, jalapeños, red hot cherry, cayenne
2 tablespoons pepitas
1 teaspoon ground hot red chile, optional
2 or 3 scallions with some green, thinly sliced, optional

1. Cut the tortillas into quarters. Heat about ½ inch of oil in a frying pan. When the oil is very hot, but not smoking, fry the tortillas in batches of 4 to 6.

2. Turn the tostaditos once and cook them for about 30 seconds, or until they are just starting to turn pale golden brown. The cooking time will vary according to the temperature of the oil and thickness of the tortillas. It is important to remove the tostaditos from the oil before they color too much, as they taste bitter if browned too long. Remove the tostaditos to paper towels to drain and sprinkle them lightly with salt.

3. Crumble the goat cheese. Stem, seed, and cut the peppers into thin rings or half-rings.

4. Line some baking sheets with foil and preheat the broiler. Arrange the tostaditos on the baking sheets. Sprinkle the crumbled goat cheese over them. Drop a piece or two of red and green peppers on each nacho. If you don't have fresh red peppers, use a little red chile powder. Put 2 or 3 pepitas on each nacho.

5. Place the baking sheets 8 inches from the broiler heat, in batches if necessary, and broil for 2 to 3 minutes, or until the cheese just melts and pepitas roast a bit. Watch the nachos carefully and remove them from the oven when they begin to brown. Sprinkle the scallions over the nachos, if desired, and serve them immediately.

Quesadillas with Roasted Peppers

≡ Serves 8

8 Whole Wheat Tortillas (page 98)
4 cups grated Monterey Jack, queso fresco, or Colby
    cheese
1 medium-sized green bell pepper, roasted, seeded,
    peeled, and cut into very thin strips
1 medium-sized red bell pepper, roasted, seeded, peeled,
    and cut into very thin strips
2 large jalapeño or Santa Fe Grande peppers, halved,
    seeded, and cut into slivers

1. Heat a griddle over medium-low heat. Place a tortilla on the griddle
and cover it with about 1 cup of cheese. Arrange about a quarter of the
green and red pepper strips evenly over the cheese, and then scatter
about a quarter of the hot pepper slivers over the top. Cover with another
tortilla and let the bottom tortilla cook for 20 to 30 seconds.

2. Carefully turn the quesadilla and cook for about 1 minute on the
other side. It should be cooked just long enough to melt the cheese.

3. Place on a cutting board, cut into pie-shaped slices, and serve hot
with salsa.

4. Repeat the process with the rest of the ingredients. If desired, the
quesadillas can be prepared on the skillet and then placed on baking
sheets and held for a short time in a warm oven.

Tostadas with Chipotle and Chorizo

≡ Serves 6

12 ounces Chorizo (page 153)
3 or 4 chipotle peppers en adobo
3 scallions with about 2 inches of green
3 10-inch Flour Tortillas (page 96)
½ pound Muenster or Monterey Jack cheese, grated

1. Fry the chorizo over low heat until it is cooked through, about 10
minutes. Cut the chipotles in slivers. Slice the scallions very thinly.

2. Heat the tortillas, one at a time, over medium-low heat on an ungreased griddle or in a frying pan. Turn the tortillas once, and cook them until they begin to crisp, about 2 minutes altogether. Preheat the oven to 500 degrees.

3. Place the tortillas on a baking sheet (or sheets) and divide the chorizo among them. Divide the cheese and sprinkle it over the tortillas. Arrange the chipotles on the cheese.

4. Bake until the cheese melts and bubbles, about 5 minutes. Remove from the oven and garnish with the scallions. Serve very hot.

Tostadas with Egg Salad

Makes 12 3½- to 4-inch tostadas

6 hard-cooked extra large eggs
A generous ⅓ cup sour cream
¼ cup pimiento-stuffed olives, thinly sliced
¼ cup thinly sliced scallions
2 tablespoons coarsely chopped fresh cilantro leaves
2 dashes of bitters
¼ teaspoon salt
Freshly ground black pepper
1½ cups Jícama Guacamole (page 217)
Vegetable or corn oil for frying
12 3½- to 4-inch Corn Tortillas (page 92)
About 1½ cups shredded garden lettuce, such as ruby,
    salad bowl, oak leaf, or buttercrunch

1. Using an egg slicer, slice the eggs across; then turn them a quarter turn and slice them again; or dice them into small pieces. Place them in a small mixing bowl.

2. Add the sour cream, olives, scallions, cilantro, bitters, and salt. Season well with salt and pepper and toss gently until mixed. Taste for seasoning. Cover and refrigerate until ready to use. At this point both the egg salad and the Jícama guacamole can be made in advance and refrigerated for a few hours. When ready to assemble the tostadas, the salads should be taken out of the refrigerator and allowed to come to cool room temperature.

3. Pour the oil to about ½ inch deep in a small skillet and heat until

hot, but not smoking. Fry the tortillas until they are just crisp, about 30 seconds on each side; do not let them brown too much. Drain on paper towels.

4. Assemble the tostadas by spreading the egg salad evenly over the crisp tortillas, mound about 2 tablespoons of the guacamole in the center of each tostada. Surround the guacamole with shredded lettuce and serve immediately.

Southwestern Pizza

Serves 4 to 6 as an appetizer, 2 to 3 as a main course

PIZZA DOUGH
2 teaspoons active dry yeast
3 tablespoons warm water
1¾ cups unbleached white flour
¼ cup whole wheat flour
¼ cup stone-ground cornmeal
⅔ cup warm water
1 tablespoon olive oil
½ teaspoon salt

PIZZA TOPPING
6 jalapeño peppers, stemmed, seeded, and cut into dice
1 large or 2 medium-sized red bell peppers, stemmed, seeded, and diced
1 tablespoon olive oil
About 1 teaspoon fresh lemon juice
Salt and freshly ground black pepper
1 small onion
6 ripe Roma tomatoes, or 1 pound ripe tomatoes
1 pound queso cotijo, or ¾ pound Monterey Jack and ¼ pound ricotta salata cheese
2 tablespoons chopped fresh parsley leaves
1 tablespoon chopped fresh oregano leaves
Olive oil for brushing
3 garlic cloves, finely minced
1½ teaspoons cumin seed, toasted and ground

1. Dissolve the yeast in the 3 tablespoons of warm water. When the yeast is active, add it to a well of the mixed flours. Let the sponge rise with the flour for 10 minutes or so. Gradually add the ⅔ cup warm water. About halfway through adding the water, stir in the olive oil and salt. Incorporate as much flour as the sponge will take and still be a bit sticky, though very lively. Knead the dough for about 5 minutes on a well-floured surface.

2. Let the dough rise for 45 minutes, or until doubled in bulk. Punch it down and divide it in half. Roll each half into a ball on a floured surface and rest the dough, covered, for at least 15 minutes before forming into pizza shapes. Preheat the oven to 500 degrees with a baking tile on the bottom shelf.

3. To make the topping, sauté the peppers in the olive oil over medium heat for 5 minutes. Sprinkle with lemon juice and season lightly with salt and pepper. Remove the peppers to a plate.

4. Cut the onion in half lengthwise; then cut it into thin slices. Slice the Roma tomatoes crosswise into rounds. Or slice the round tomatoes crosswise; then halve the slices.

5. Coarsely grate the cheeses. Mix the chopped parsley and oregano together.

6. Sprinkle a pizza peel or wooden board lightly with flour or corn-meal. Stretch one ball of dough by hand and shape it into a 9- or 10-inch round on the peel.

7. Brush the dough lightly with oil and sprinkle half of the minced garlic over it, leaving about a ½-inch border. Scatter half of the sliced onion over the pizza and sprinkle about one-third of the cumin over the onions. Arrange half of the sliced tomatoes on the pizza, and arrange half of the sautéed peppers on top of the tomatoes.

8. Slide the pizza onto the preheated baking tile and bake for 4 to 5 minutes. Slide the pizza out and sprinkle about one-third of the chopped herbs over it; then scatter half of the grated cheeses on top. Return the pizza to the oven and bake for another 2 to 4 minutes, or until the cheese is well melted and bubbly, but not browned.

9. Slide the pizza onto a cutting board and garnish with a little ground cumin and chopped herbs. Cut the pizza and serve hot. Make the other pizza in the same way with the remaining ingredients.

CHAPTER FIVE

Sauces

Cooked sauces based on chiles are the traditional heart of the region's cuisine. Hand-ground chiles, toasted or untoasted chiles, and secret recipes all have their passionate advocates. The key, we think, is to find the best-quality chiles; if red, clean, brilliant, whole, and the current crop of dried fruit; if green, fully mature and fresh garden peppers do make the best sauces. Unpleasantly bitter chile sauces can be avoided by selecting the chiles carefully and cooking them with attention. If the dried chiles are toasted, they should be toasted on a heavy griddle until they just begin to release some fragrance; over-toasting will leave the chiles burned-tasting. Green chiles, likewise, should be roasted for peeling just until the skins can be scraped or pulled loose. Over-blistering results in loss of flavor. Onions and garlic, essential for rich, rounded sauces, should be sweated very slowly in fat to release their full sweetness.

We consider red and green chile sauces basic preparations, as important as broths and stocks. Before refrigeration they were made fresh for each dish, often twice a day. The quantities of our cooked red and green chile recipes make enough for one or two dishes, with a little left over for improvisations. The red sauce keeps well in the refrigerator for a week; it can also be frozen for up to two months. Green chile sauces are more perishable, keeping two or three days refrigerated, or frozen for up to a month.

Modern cooks in the Southwest make adventurous use of untraditional ingredients, such as crème fraîche, though even this has some precedent in the soured cream of Mexico. Sauces are also being used out of their original enchilada, chile colorado con carne, or chile verde con carne contexts, often with good results. A swirl of green chile sauce in a summer vegetable soup is a pleasant change from a pesto garnish. Roasted chicken has a subtle Southwestern flavor when red chile sauce is rubbed under and over the skin. Combining chile sauces with tomato or tomatillo sauces opens another realm of possibilities: lightening the intensity of the chiles and cutting the acidity of the tomatoes increases the number of foods which can be enhanced by the sauces. Fish, potatoes, even pasta work well with the judicious use of these hybrid sauces.

Crème Fraîche and Jalapeño Sauce

≡ If you cannot buy crème fraîche, you can easily make it; it takes from 24 to 48 hours to grow the culture, so plan accordingly. Exact time varies because of temperature and culture differences. For 2 cups of crème fraîche, shake 2 cups heavy cream with 1 tablespoon buttermilk in a pint jar. Set the mixture in a warm place, such as an oven with a pilot light, or a yogurt maker. Check after 24 hours; the crème fraîche should be slightly thicker than heavy cream, and should taste tangy. It keeps in the refrigerator for up to a week, becoming a little thicker and tangier.

This sauce is especially good with Red Chile Pasta (page 182), but we also like it as an accompaniment to pan-fried fish and steamed cauliflower or as a garnish for plain black beans.

Makes about 2 cups

2 cups crème fraîche
1 cup heavy (whipping) cream
2 or 3 jalapeño peppers, stemmed, seeded, and finely
    diced
1 garlic clove, finely minced
Salt and freshly ground black pepper

Heat the crème fraîche and heavy cream in a deep heavy-bottomed saucepan with the jalapeños and garlic over medium-low heat for about 10 minutes, or until the creams have reduced by about one-third. Season the sauce with salt and pepper. Toss with pasta or serve hot.

Green Chile Sauce

≣ The variety of chiles used in this sauce determines how hot it will be. In New Mexico, where the piquant varieties are grown under optimum conditions, it can be very hot. Sandia, New Mexico 6 (or 6–4), and Mexico Improved chiles will provide the hottest sauce. Anaheims and Numex Big Jim chiles make a milder sauce. If only mild varieties are available, roast and peel some jalapeños for added bite. The sauce may be made with canned or frozen green chiles, but the flavor will be very different and not as lively. Bueno brand frozen chiles from New Mexico are very good if you can find them. This sauce has many uses: with enchiladas, eggs, tostadas, seafood, potatoes, and as a base for chile verde stews. It keeps for two or three days, covered tightly, in the refrigerator.

Makes about 1 quart

2½ to 3 pounds fresh green chiles; the amount depends
    on the fleshiness of the chiles
1 cup diced onion
2 garlic cloves, finely chopped
2 tablespoons corn oil
2 teaspoons chopped fresh oregano leaves, or ½ tea-
    spoon dried oregano, crumbled leaves
½ teaspoon toasted and ground cumin seed, or to taste
½ teaspoon toasted and ground coriander seed
1½ cups broth or water
Salt and freshly ground black pepper
1 tablespoon chopped fresh coriander leaves, optional

1. Roast the chiles. Peel, seed, and dice them. There should be 3 cups diced chiles.
2. Soften the onion and garlic in the oil over low heat, covered, for 15 minutes or so. Stir in the chiles, oregano, cumin, coriander, and broth. Season lightly with salt and pepper. Add the fresh coriander, if desired.
3. Simmer the sauce, covered, for 15 minutes. Adjust the seasoning and use the sauce as needed.

Green Chile Sauce with Sage

≡ If the green chiles are mild, add 2 finely minced serranos or jalapeños to this sauce; it should have a little fire to it.

Makes about 1 quart

3 tablespoons corn oil
1 medium-sized onion, chopped
3 garlic cloves, minced
2 medium-sized celery stalks, thinly sliced
2 cups green chiles, roasted, peeled, and chopped
½ pound tomatillos, roasted, husked, and puréed
1 cup water or broth
2 tablespoons minced fresh sage leaves, or 2 teaspoons
    dried sage, crumbled leaves
1 teaspoon Chili Powder (page 50)
Salt

1. Heat the oil over medium heat in a skillet and add the onion, garlic, and celery. Cook for 5 minutes. Add the chile, tomatillos, and water and stir well. Cook for a few minutes.

2. Add the sage and chili powder and cook over low heat for 25 minutes, stirring occasionally. Season with salt.

3. The sauce can be served as is; or, if a smoother texture is desired, part or all of the sauce can be puréed in a food processor or in a blender in batches.

Green Chile Tomatillo Sauce

≡ This is a quick sauce, an especially good way to use leftover green chile sauce, and quite good on fresh fettuccine noodles.

Makes about 3 cups, enough for 6 servings of pasta

1 tablespoon olive oil
½ cup chopped onion
2 or 3 garlic cloves, finely minced
2 cups roasted, husked, and finely chopped tomatillos
1 cup Green Chile Sauce (page 83)
Salt and freshly ground black pepper

1. Heat the oil in a large skillet and sauté the onion and garlic in it for 2 to 3 minutes. Add the tomatillos and cook over low heat for 5 minutes, stirring occasionally.

2. Add the green chile sauce and salt and pepper and cook for 5 minutes more. Taste for seasoning and serve hot over *al dente* egg pasta.

Red Chile Sauce

Red and green chile sauces figure in many Southwestern dishes. This is used as is for enchiladas, burritos, and tacos. Meat, especially cubed beef or pork, is browned or poached and then simmered in it with some broth. A little may be mixed with tomato sauce and used to flavor chicken or rice dishes.

Makes about 5 cups

1 cup finely chopped onion
1 garlic clove, minced
2 tablespoons corn oil
½ cup New Mexico ground mild chile
½ cup New Mexico ground hot chile
6 cups water
Salt

1. Completely soften the onion and garlic in the oil over low heat. About 20 minutes in a heavy, covered pan is necessary to bring out the sweetness. Do not brown.

2. Add the chile powders and water. Simmer for 30 to 40 minutes over medium heat, until the sauce is a medium-thin consistency. Season lightly with salt.

3. The sauce may be used as is, or puréed for a more refined finish in some dishes. The sauce keeps well, tightly-covered and refrigerated for a week; or it may be frozen with good quality for 2 months.

Roasted Garlic Cream Sauce

≡ **Makes about 1 cup**

1 head fresh garlic
¼ cup olive oil
1½ cups heavy (whipping) cream
1 bay leaf
10 whole black peppercorns
Salt and freshly ground black pepper

1. Preheat the oven to 200 degrees. Break the garlic into cloves. Remove any extra skin but do not peel the cloves. Put the cloves in a small heavy ovenproof pan and pour the olive oil over the garlic. Roast in the oven for about 45 minutes, or until the garlic is very soft and slightly caramelized.

2. Squeeze the garlic from its skin into the cream in a saucepan. Mash the garlic a little with a wooden spoon. Add the bay leaf and peppercorns and reduce the cream by almost half over medium heat, about 20 minutes. Strain the sauce and season it with salt and pepper.

Roasted Tomato Sauce

≡ Many foods, especially steamed or grilled vegetables, grilled fish, and pasta, go well with this sauce. The tomatoes may also be grilled over a wood or wood-charcoal fire; core them but leave them whole and turn them to blacken evenly.

Makes about 2½ cups

2 pounds ripe tomatoes
½ cup chopped onion
1 garlic clove, minced
2 tablespoons olive oil
1 teaspoon chopped fresh oregano leaves, optional
Salt and freshly ground black pepper

1. Wash the tomatoes and core them. Cut them in half crosswise and place them skin side up on a rack in a roasting pan.

2. Broil in the oven 4 to 5 inches from the heat for 6 to 8 minutes, or until the tomatoes are completely blackened.

3. Soften the onion and garlic in the oil for about 10 minutes over low heat in a heavy-bottomed pan. Add the tomatoes and oregano, if desired.

4. Cook the sauce over medium heat for 15 minutes. Pass the sauce through a food mill and season with salt and pepper.

Sesame Chile and Tomato Sauce

☰ Moisten shredded turkey or chicken with this sauce for flavorful tostadas or tacos. We use it with duck and chicken burritos and serve a little as a pan sauce for sautéed rabbit.

Makes about 3½ cups

1 recipe Salsa Colorado (page 58)
1 pound ripe tomatoes, peeled, seeded, and diced, or
    1 14-ounce can whole tomatoes, seeded and chopped
3 tablespoons sesame seed, toasted and ground
½ teaspoon coriander seed, toasted and ground
¼ teaspoon cumin seed, toasted and ground
About ½ cup water
Salt and freshly ground black pepper
Ground hot red chile, optional

1. Pour the Salsa Colorado into a heavy-bottomed saucepan. Add the tomatoes, sesame, coriander, cumin, and about ¼ cup water.

2. Simmer the sauce for 30 minutes, adding more water, if necessary, to maintain a medium-thick consistency. Season the sauce with salt and pepper and chile powder, if desired.

Simple Tomato Sauce

☰ This is an extremely useful sauce, light yet capable of imparting a definite Southwestern flavor to many dishes. Use it with rice, vegetables, chicken, fish, or wherever a tomato sauce is desired. It is delicious blended with any number of fresh or dried red chiles or red chile sauces. The recipe may be tripled for canning except for the onion, oregano, and cloves. These should be doubled.

Makes about 2½ cups

2 pounds ripe tomatoes, cored and chopped, or 1
    28-ounce can whole tomatoes, cored and chopped
1 medium-sized onion, diced
2 garlic cloves, minced
1 tablespoon chopped fresh oregano leaves, or ¾ tea-
    spoon dried oregano leaves
½ teaspoon toasted and ground coriander seed
¼ teaspoon toasted and ground cumin seed
2 large pinches of ground cloves
Salt and freshly ground black pepper

1. Put all the ingredients, except the salt, pepper, and cloves, in a heavy-bottomed saucepan. Bring the sauce to a boil, lower the heat, and simmer, uncovered, for 30 minutes.

2. Put the sauce through a food mill and season it with salt and pepper and cloves. Or purée the sauce carefully in a food processor; it should have some texture. Season after puréeing.

3. For canning, return the sauce to the kettle after it is puréed. Bring it to a simmer and cook for 5 minutes. Pack in sterilized jars and process in a hot water bath or pressure cooker following manufacturer's directions for processing tomato sauce.

Southwestern Barbecue Sauce

≡ This is an all-purpose marinating and basting sauce, much less sweet and salty than commerical sauces. It is best with meat and poultry.

Makes about 1 quart

3 pounds ripe tomatoes, or 1 35-ounce can plum
    tomatoes
1 cup coarsely chopped onion
2 or 3 cloves garlic, coarsely chopped

2 chipotle chiles en adobo, finely chopped
2 tablespoons Chili Powder (page 50)
¼ cup red wine vinegar
Salt
Sugar

1. Put the tomatoes, onion, garlic, chipotle chiles, chili powder, and red wine vinegar in a heavy saucepan. Season lightly with equal amounts of salt and sugar.

2. Bring the sauce to a simmer and cook for about 40 minutes. Adjust the seasoning with salt and sugar. Pass the sauce through a food mill or purée it in a food processor.

3. The sauce will keep tightly closed in the refrigerator for about 3 weeks. You may pack it into 1- or 2-cup freezer containers for up to 6 months.

Tomatillo Sauce

Makes about 3 cups

1½ pounds fresh tomatillos, roasted and husked
1 medium-sized onion, chopped
3 garlic cloves, chopped
¼ cup lightly packed whole coriander leaves
2 tablespoons corn oil
Salt

1. Rough chop the tomatillos. Purée them with the onion, garlic, and coriander to a sauce of some texture in a food processor or blender.

2. Heat the oil over medium heat and sauté the sauce for 5 minutes. Season with salt.

CHAPTER SIX

Breads

≡

One of the truly indigenous breads of the Southwest is *piki* bread, made by the Pueblo Indians, especially the Hopis. They use a specially prepared blue cornmeal made into a gruel with water, large flat smooth igneous stones which will not crack or explode when they are heated, and a sheep's brain for greasing the stone. The gruel is applied to the stone by hand in a very thin layer and allowed to cook dry; it is then peeled from the stone and rolled, or stacked and rolled, depending on the size of the piki. The bread is called paper bread in English, a much simpler translation than the cooking procedure. As any modern home cook's version of this bread is very far from the original and the flavor is an acquired one, we urge you to eat the bread when you are in the Southwest, rather than supplying a recipe for it here. The *Pueblo Indian Cookbook*, edited by Phyllis Hughes, gives a fascinating recipe for this, as well as for many other Pueblo specialties. Yeast bread from the Pueblos is called *horno* bread after the clay ovens in which it is baked. Again, the special crust and chewy texture cannot be duplicated in modern ovens, though if you have a wood-burning oven you could use our recipe for Ranch Bread with the modifications noted.

Other breads, though they may have come from Mexico, or with Anglo settlers, are still recognizable as Southwestern breads: corn and flour tortillas, corn breads, ranch or camp breads. Cross-cultural breads, Indian, Mexican, Spanish, and Anglo, are the Navajo and Pueblo fry breads, blue corn breads, and blue corn tortillas. There are many skillet or griddle breads, yeasted or not, since open-fire cooking was prevalent even among the early Anglo settlers, who did not often bring heavy iron stoves with them. Dutch ovens were popular for breads, which sometimes took the form of biscuit-dumplings dropped on top of stews.

Breads are the most change-resistant foods in any cuisine. The process is so complicated, from the planting of the right grain, through harvesting and milling, then devising the most tasty and nourishing cooking method available in the environment, that the accretion of very old methods and tastes becomes cultural and even religious. The Indians in the region recognized the pleasant advantages of yeast, and learned to make tortillas from the Mexicans, yet kept their own blue cornmeal. A salient feature of Southwestern bread history is that whole grain breads have remained popular during the last four hundred years, long before the modern interest in high-fiber diets.

Corn Tortillas

Hand-patted tortillas require a dexterity that takes years to acquire. It is fascinating to watch tortilla-makers at work, and to eat those tortillas which have both lightness and substantiality. Very good pressed or rolled tortillas are easily perfectible with some practice at home. Enchiladas, home-fried tostaditos, warm tortillas to accompany a meal, and tostadas are incomparably better with fresh tortillas. The packaged varieties available in supermarkets are cardboardy and lifeless. If you live in an area with tortilla factories, you can purchase good tortillas. Whether purchased or homemade all tortillas—corn, blue corn, or flour—must be served hot. Reheating cold tortillas is best done on a griddle over medium-high heat for a few seconds on each side. Wrap the tortillas well in a tea towel or large cloth napkin and keep them in a tortilla basket or on a plate with a bowl over it. If you don't have a tortilla basket (which has a cover), serve the tortillas wrapped and in a basket with another cloth napkin draped over the top.

We use the Quaker Masa Harina for the dough because it makes a good tortilla and is readily available. The wetness of the dough is the important thing to establish. It should not be so dry that the tortillas crack or crumble when they are pressed or rolled, and not so wet that they stick to the plastic and are soggy when they are cooked. A little extra water or Masa Harina is easily worked into the dough. It may be pressed together and reworked without harm, but should not stand more than an hour before the tortillas are formed and cooked. The dough should always be covered with plastic wrap.

Tortillas may be rolled out with fine results if you do not have a press. An even-diameter rolling pin is necessary, the old-fashioned American kind, not the tapered French type. Roll the dough between thick plastic; trimmed pieces from zip-close food storage bags are perfect for this. After you have divided the masa into balls, cover them with plastic wrap and flatten one. Put this between thick plastic and roll it lightly with the pin. Turn the dough one-quarter turn and roll lightly again to form a circular shape. To keep a round shape, roll lightly from the center out in a clockwise (or counterclockwise if that is easier) fashion. If the tortilla starts to get very out of round, use quarter-turns and light rolls to bring it back. The tortillas should be a little less than ¹⁄₁₆ inch thick and of even thickness. One or two sessions of rolling tortillas will make these techniques clear and develop a sense of rhythm for the rolling and cooking steps. It is simpler to master the procedures than to write about them.

Using a tortilla press is even easier and a little faster. There are slight variations in the way people like to press tortillas. We get the best results by flattening the masa balls a little between the thick plastic and placing them slightly toward the back of the press away from the handle. Then we press with some firmness, raise the top of the press, and turn the dough to be sure the tortilla will be evenly thick. Turning the dough is more important when making large tortillas. We press again firmly, but not enough to squash the tortilla or end up with very thin edges.

Whether rolling or pressing, it is handy to have four sheets of thick plastic. You can then have three tortillas ready to cook by removing the top sheets from the first two tortillas and rolling or pressing another one. Some exposure to the air seems to help the tortillas cook in the right amount of time. We like the rhythmic motions and pauses in making tortillas. You will find your own pace to form a tortilla, cook the first side, then the second side, form another tortilla or two, cook the first side again, put the next tortilla on the comal, and slide the finished one into the basket.

We had been making tortillas with a press for several years, but it was not until Diana Kennedy's *The Cuisines of Mexico* came out that we heard the invaluable suggestion of cooking the tortillas over two fires. This can be done with two griddles, or with one large comal; the important thing is the two levels of heat. Experimentation with other methods has convinced us that the two-fire technique is the best for corn and blue corn tortillas. The contrast in heat puffs the tortillas more than any other factor. A press and twist motion with a tea towel on the tortilla surface also encourages puffing. Tortillas which puff are lighter, but this is not really necessary unless you are stuffing them.

Tortillas may be made ahead and stored in the refrigerator for two days if they are used in enchiladas, tostadas, or served warm with meals. They should be made at least one day ahead for home-fried tostaditos and chilaquiles. If they are stored in the refrigerator for longer than two days, they will still be good for these last two dishes. In our opinion, tortillas do not freeze well. Since it takes only about 30 minutes, start to finish, for 12 to 16 tortillas, we do not recommend freezing tortillas.

For 12 to 16 corn tortillas

2 cups Masa Harina
1¼ cups water

1. Put the Masa Harina in a bowl and add the water all at once. Stir with a fork to incorporate the water. Knead the dough together in the bowl.

2. Divide the dough into 12 portions for 5½- to 6-inch tortillas. Divide the dough into 14 to 16 portions for 3½- to 4-inch tortillas.

3. Cover the dough with plastic wrap. Heat two ungreased griddles, cast-iron frying pans, comals, or one large comal over two burners. One pan is heated over medium-low to medium heat, the second over medium-high heat. Press or roll the tortillas as described above.

4. Remove the plastic from a tortilla and carefully lay the tortilla on the pan over the lower heat. If the tortilla is slapped on the griddle, air pockets, which cause uneven cooking, will form. If air pockets do form, press them down lightly with your fingers or with a spatula. Too much heat will also cause air bubbles with cracks in them so that steam escapes. Lower the heat slightly in this case. Cook the tortilla for 30 to 40 seconds, or until the edges just begin to dry and become lighter in color.

5. Turn the uncooked side of the tortilla onto the hotter pan and cook until the tortilla has brown speckles, about 40 to 50 seconds. Turn the tortilla over, still on the hotter pan and cook for 10 to 20 seconds. The tortilla should puff immediately upon being turned over. This is the time to press with a towel if the tortilla has not puffed in 2 to 3 seconds. Total cooking time for the tortillas is close to 2 minutes.

6. The side which is on the griddle now is the best side if the presentation of the tortillas is important. For immediate use, or use in an hour's time, hold the tortillas well-wrapped in a tea towel or large thick cloth napkin in a basket. A tortilla basket is handy to have for this purpose.

7. If the tortillas are to be used later in the day or the next day, wrap them in a tea towel until they are all cooked; then unwrap them and let them cool a bit before storing them in a zip-close bag in the refrigerator.

Blue Corn Tortillas

≡ Blue corn tortillas are a specialty of northern New Mexico. We think the blue cornmeal gives them a deeper, earthier flavor, and, certainly, they are impressive-looking with their slate gray-blue color. They are usually used for enchiladas or served as a bread. Occasionally they are fried into tostaditos. You will need to have blue corn *harinilla* to make the tortillas. Blue corn *harina* is a coarser grind of cornmeal, suitable for breads and pancakes. Any kind of blue corn (also called *maíz azul*) is hard to find outside of New Mexico; refer to the Sources section (page 251) to locate suppliers of blue corn.

Read the recipe for Corn Tortillas (page 92) before making blue corn tortillas. These tortillas are more difficult to master because the dough must be slightly drier and more crumbly if the tortillas are to be perfectly cooked. Slightly higher heats and cooking times are best for blue corn tortillas, and they do not puff as well as masa tortillas. In any case, they are not as limber. They are wonderful in the traditional, flat northern New Mexico Green Chile Enchiladas (page 136) and a good bread with Hopi-Style Lamb and Hominy Stew (page 123) or Rabbit Adovada (page 159). Blue corn tortillas do not keep as well as masa tortillas; we recommend using them on the day they are made, or the day after. They make rather heavy, but deliciously flavored tostaditos or chilaquiles after two or three days in the refrigerator.

For 14 to 16 blue corn tortillas

1 cup Masa Harina
1 cup blue corn harinilla
⅛ teaspoon salt
1⅛ cups water

1. Mix the Masa Harina, harinilla, and salt together in a bowl. Add the water all at once and stir well with a fork. Knead the dough together; it will be a little crumbly.

2. Divide the dough into 14 to 16 portions for 3½- to 4-inch tortillas. It is difficult to make larger blue corn tortillas; smaller ones are traditional. Cover the dough with plastic wrap.

3. Heat two ungreased griddles, cast-iron frying pans, comals, or one large comal over two burners. One pan is heated over medium heat, the second over medium-high heat. Press or roll the tortillas as described in the Corn Tortilla recipe (page 92). Cook one tortilla first and adjust the heat under both pans, if necessary.

4. Remove the plastic from a tortilla and carefully lay the tortilla on the pan over medium heat. If the tortilla is slapped on the griddle, air pockets, which cause uneven cooking, will form. Cook the tortilla for 40 to 50 seconds, or until the edges just begin to dry and become lighter in color.

5. Turn the uncooked side of the tortilla onto the hotter pan and cook until the tortilla has brown speckles, about 50 to 55 seconds. Turn the tortilla over, still on the hotter pan and cook for 10 to 20 seconds. The tortilla should show some puffing immediately upon being turned over. Encourage this by pressing the tortilla with a towel.

6. The side which is on the griddle now is the best side if the presentation of the tortillas is important. For immediate use, or use in an hour's time, hold the tortillas well-wrapped in a tea towel or large thick cloth napkin in a covered basket. A tortilla basket is handy to have for this purpose.

7. If the tortillas are to be used later in the day or the next day, wrap them in a tea towel until they are all cooked; then unwrap them and let them cool a bit before storing them in a zip-close bag in the refrigerator.

Flour Tortillas

≡ Every reason for making corn or blue corn tortillas—flavor, texture, and freshness—applies with the same force to flour tortillas. Burritos, of which there are many battered, bruised, and even frozen examples, are just not wonderful simple food unless they are made with fresh flour tortillas. Burrito fillings are hearty and rich and really need the substantial, yet puffy, texture of homemade flour tortillas. Fresh flour tortillas served as bread are downright satisfying, with the same slight chewiness and immediacy that all homemade flat breads possess. Some tortilla factories and bakeries in the Southwest make fresh flour tortillas and these can be good if used the same day on which they are purchased.

The only part of making flour tortillas that requires some technique is the rolling of them. Perfect rounds need some concentration; we never make perfectly perfect rounds, but we like the slightly uneven edges that show our tortillas were not made by machine. For burritos, the edges are all tucked in anyway, so you may want to use your first few batches to make burritos. To make round tortillas, use an even-diameter rolling pin, not a tapered pin. After the dough balls have been flattened slightly and rested, take one portion of dough and flatten it lightly with the pin in one direction. Turn the dough one-quarter turn and flatten again. Make two more quarter-turns, flattening each time. You should have a circle about 3 inches in diameter. Begin stretching the dough by pushing it out from the center with the pin in a clockwise (or counterclockwise if that is easier) motion. The end of the pin in the center makes a slight push out, then stays lightly anchored while the end near the edges makes the circular movement. Turn the dough over if it sticks, or if you have a radically elliptical shape. Keep pushing the dough out from the center and around the edges in a circular motion until it is very thin (about ⅟₃₂ inch) and 9 to 10 or 11 to 12 inches in diameter. If the dough springs back at any time, let it rest for 2 or 3 minutes and go on to partially rolling out another tortilla.

As with corn tortillas, you will develop a rhythm for rolling and cooking the tortillas. The flour tortillas cook much more quickly, so you can have three or four rolled and ready to cook. Only one griddle or comal is needed to cook the tortillas, but it should be a large, flat round one. When you become proficient, you will be able to roll the big 11- or 12-inch tortillas and these should be cooked on a 13- or 14-inch griddle so that the circumference stays flat and cooks evenly.

For 6 11- or 12-inch or 8 9- or 10-inch tortillas

2 cups unbleached white flour
1 teaspoon baking powder
½ teaspoon salt
4 tablespoons vegetable shortening or lard
½ cup warm water

1. Mix the flour, baking powder, and salt together in a bowl. Cut the shortening in with a pastry blender or with two knives. Add the water and stir the dough with a fork.

2. Press together a small ball of dough. If it clings and is moist, turn the dough out to knead it. Otherwise, sprinkle in another tablespoon of water.

3. Knead the dough for 5 minutes; then cover with plastic wrap and let it rest for 30 to 40 minutes.

4. Divide the dough into 6 or 8 portions and flatten them slightly. Cover with plastic and let them rest for 10 minutes. Roll the dough out according to the directions above.

5. Heat a large ungreased griddle, cast-iron frying pan, or comal over medium-high heat. The griddle should be at least 1 inch larger than the tortillas.

6. Carefully transfer a tortilla to the griddle, being careful not to stretch it or to place it on the griddle so that air pockets form. This takes a little practice. If air pockets do form, press them down lightly with your fingers or a spatula.

7. The tortilla should sizzle slightly when placed on the griddle. The tortillas cook very quickly. The first side should speckle in 20 to 30 seconds. Turn it and cook about 15 seconds on the other side. The tortillas should not stay on the griddle too long or they will become stiff. Adjust the heat slightly higher, if necessary, to brown and cook them quickly.

8. As the tortillas are done, wrap them in a well-wrung damp towel for immediate use. Otherwise, wrap them in a dry towel until all the tortillas are cooked; then spread them to cool a bit before refrigerating them in zip-close bags. The tortillas will be stiff, but can be reheated to pliability on a griddle for a few seconds on each side. Burritos are best made from very fresh tortillas, but if you are careful in the reheating, you can still roll them after the tortillas have been refrigerated for 2 days. Flour tortillas freeze marginally better than corn tortillas. They do not attract the ice crystals, but they do lose limberness. They should be defrosted for an hour or so and then heated briefly on the griddle to serve as bread, or heated to crispness to use for tostadas.

Whole Wheat Tortillas

≡ Read about Flour Tortillas (page 96) before making these; they are not more difficult than flour tortillas.

For 6 11- or 12-inch or 8 9- or 10-inch tortillas

1 cup whole wheat flour
1 cup unbleached white flour
1 teaspoon baking powder
½ teaspoon salt
4 tablespoons vegetable shortening or lard
½ cup warm water

1. Mix the flour, baking powder, and salt together in a bowl. Cut the shortening in with a pastry blender or with two knives. Add the water and stir the dough with a fork.

2. Press together a small ball of dough. If it clings and is moist, turn the dough out to knead. Otherwise, sprinkle in another tablespoon of water.

3. Knead the dough for 5 minutes; then cover with plastic wrap and let it rest for 30 to 40 minutes.

4. Divide the dough into 6 or 8 portions and flatten them slightly. Cover with plastic and let them rest for 10 minutes. Roll the dough out according to the directions above.

5. Heat a large ungreased griddle, cast-iron frying pan, or comal over medium-high heat. The griddle should be at least 1 inch larger than the tortillas.

6. Carefully transfer the tortilla to the griddle, being careful not to stretch it or to place it on the griddle so that air pockets form. This takes a little practice. If air pockets do form, press them down lightly with your fingers or a spatula.

7. The tortilla should sizzle slightly when placed on the griddle. The tortillas cook very quickly. The first side should speckle in 20 to 30 seconds. Turn it and cook about 15 seconds on the other side. The tortillas should not stay on the griddle too long or they will be stiff. Adjust heat slightly higher, if necessary, to brown and cook them quickly.

8. As the tortillas are done, wrap them in a well-wrung damp towel for immediate use. Otherwise wrap them in a dry towel until all the tortillas are cooked; then spread them to cool a bit before refrigerating them in zip-close bags. The tortillas will be stiff, but can be reheated to pliability on a griddle for a few seconds on each side. Burritos are best made from very fresh tortillas, but if you are careful in the reheating, you can still roll them after the tortillas have been refrigerated for 2 days. Flour tortillas freeze marginally better than corn tortillas. They do not

attract the ice crystals, but they do lose limberness. They should be defrosted for an hour or so and then heated briefly on the griddle to serve as bread, or heated to crispness to use for tostadas.

Blue Corn Pancakes

Serves 2 to 4

½ cup unbleached white flour
1 cup blue cornmeal
1 tablespoon sugar
2 teaspoons baking powder
½ teaspoon salt
3 tablespoons dry milk powder
2 extra large eggs
1¼ cups milk
2 tablespoons vegetable or corn oil

1. Blend the dry ingredients in a mixing bowl. In a separate bowl, beat the eggs; then add the wet ingredients and blend well. Add the wet ingredients to the dry and blend well. The batter will be a bit thin.

2. Heat a griddle over medium heat. Brush it with a little oil and cook the pancakes in whatever size desired.

3. Serve the pancakes hot. They are good with maple syrup and butter or Sandia Jelly (page 55); some people like them with a fried egg, salsa, or sour cream.

Buttermilk Biscuits with Chiles

Makes about 16 biscuits

1 tablespoon active dry yeast
2 tablespoons warm water
Pinch of sugar
1½ cups unbleached white flour
½ cup stone-ground yellow cornmeal

1½ teaspoons baking powder
½ teaspoon baking soda
1 teaspoon salt
2 tablespoons unsalted butter
¾ cup buttermilk
1 large green chile and 1 large red chile, roasted, peeled,
    and diced (about ¼ cup)
About 2 tablespoons unsalted butter
1 tablespoon plus 1 teaspoon sesame seeds

1. Dissolve the yeast in the water with a pinch of sugar. Let the yeast proof.

2. Meanwhile, mix all the dry ingredients together in a large bowl. Cut 2 tablespoons of butter into the dry ingredients with a pastry blender or two knives.

3. Stir the buttermilk, chiles, and yeast into the dry ingredients. Turn the dough onto a lightly floured board and knead for about 2 minutes. Sprinkle a little flour into the dough if it seems sticky.

4. Divide the dough into 16 pieces. Roll the pieces into balls about 1¾ inches in diameter.

5. Spread 1 tablespoon of the butter in a 9½- or 10-inch skillet or baking pan. Sprinkle 1 tablespoon of the sesame seeds on the bottom of the pan. Arrange the dough in the pan and cover with a lightly damp towel. Let the dough rise until almost doubled in bulk, 30 to 40 minutes. Preheat the oven to 425 degrees.

6. Melt 1 tablespoon of butter over low heat. Just before baking the biscuits, drizzle the melted butter over them and sprinkle with the remaining sesame seeds.

7. Bake the biscuits for 18 to 20 minutes, or until they are light golden brown. Serve the biscuits hot.

Green Corn Muffins

Makes about 1 dozen muffins

¾ cup fresh corn kernels
1 large green chile, roasted, peeled, and seeded
½ cup grated Monterey Jack or Cheddar cheese
3 extra large eggs

½ cup milk
⅓ cup stone-ground cornmeal
⅓ cup whole wheat pastry flour
⅓ cup unbleached white flour
2 teaspoons baking powder
¾ teaspoon salt

1. Preheat the oven to 375 degrees. Purée the corn, chile, and cheese in a food processor fitted with a steel blade. Add the eggs and milk and process until just blended. Add the dry ingredients and process until just blended, stopping to scrape down the sides once or twice.

2. Spoon the batter into generously buttered large muffin pans and bake for 20 to 25 minutes, or until a cake tester comes out clean and the tops of the muffins are golden brown.

Panocha Coffee Cake with Pecan Topping

Serves 8 to 16

1 cup panocha flour
1 cup unbleached white flour
2 teaspoons baking powder
¼ teaspoon salt
¾ cup packed light brown sugar
8 tablespoons unsalted butter, melted and cooled slightly
¾ cup milk
2 extra large eggs, lightly beaten
¾ cup pecans, roughly chopped
¼ teaspoon ground cinnamon
¼ teaspoon freshly grated nutmeg

1. Preheat the oven to 350 degrees. Butter an 8- by 8-inch baking pan. Combine the panocha, flour, baking powder, salt, and ½ cup of the brown sugar in a large bowl and mix well.

2. Pour 6 tablespoons of the melted butter into the flour mixture. Add the milk and eggs and blend until combined. Pour the batter into the prepared pan.

3. In the pan with the reserved butter, combine the pecans, remaining ¼ cup of brown sugar, cinnamon, and nutmeg. Swirl half of the pecan mixture into the batter with a knife. Distribute the rest of the pecan mixture evenly over the top of the batter.

4. Place the pan in the center of the oven and bake for 30 minutes, or until a cake tester comes out clean. Let the cake cool on a wire rack for at least 10 minutes before serving. Serve warm or at room temperature.

Yeasted Corn Bread

Makes 2 loaves

2 tablespoons active dry yeast
¾ cup warm milk
1 tablespoon honey
4 cups stone-ground cornmeal
2 cups whole wheat flour
4 cups unbleached white flour
¾ cup dry milk powder
2 teaspoons salt
2½ cups warm water
¼ cup corn oil
2 teaspoons dried oregano or sage leaves, crumbled,
    optional

1. Dissolve the yeast in the milk with the honey until it is foamy. Mix the cornmeal, flours, milk powder, and salt together in a large bowl. Make a well in the center.

2. Pour the yeasted milk mixture into the well and incorporate a little of the flours. Add the water, 1 cup at a time, mixing until just combined. Add the oil along with the last cup of water. Form the dough into a mass.

3. Turn the dough onto a lightly floured board. Knead the dough for about 10 minutes, incorporating unbleached flour, if necessary, until the dough feels smooth and elastic. Knead in the dried herb, if desired.

4. Place the dough in a large oiled bowl and cover with a damp towel. Place the bowl in a warm spot and let the dough rise until it is doubled in bulk, about an hour. The dough may take longer to rise because of the high proportion of cornmeal.

5. Punch down the dough and divide it into two parts. Knead each portion for a minute or so and shape them into loaves. Place the loaves on a baking sheet that has been lightly sprinkled with cornmeal, or in two oiled 9- by 5-inch loaf pans. Cover the loaves with a damp towel and let them rise about 20 minutes, or until almost doubled in bulk. Preheat the oven to 375 degrees.

6. Bake for about 40 minutes, or until the loaves are golden brown. Remove from pans or baking sheets after 5 minutes and cool on wire racks.

Panocha Cinnamon Bread

Makes 2 small loaves

2½ cups unbleached white flour
1 cup panocha flour
⅛ teaspoon ground cloves
1 tablespoon active dry yeast
¼ cup warm water
6 tablespoons unsalted butter
⅔ cup milk
¼ cup packed light brown sugar
½ teaspoon salt
1 extra large egg
2 tablespoons cinnamon, preferably freshly ground
½ cup sugar

1. Mix the flour, panocha, and cloves together in a large bowl. Make a well in the flour. Add the yeast and water to the well and mix a little of the flour into it.

2. Melt the butter and stir in the milk, sugar, and salt. When the mixture is lukewarm, add the egg, stirring well. Add the milk and egg mixture to the flour and yeast and mix well.

3. Turn out onto a lightly floured board and knead well for 5 minutes, adding up to another ¼ cup of flour, if necessary. The dough should be soft but not sticky. Place it in an oiled bowl, cover with a damp tea towel, and let rise until doubled in bulk.

4. Butter two 9- by 5-inch loaf pans. Mix the cinnamon and sugar together.

5. Punch the dough down and knead it for a minute; then divide it in half. Flatten one portion of the dough into a large rectangle about ½ inch thick. Spread half the cinnamon and sugar over the dough and roll it into a cylinder shape. Pinch the loaf along the seam and tuck the ends under, pinching them firmly. Repeat with other portion of dough.

6. Place the loaves in the pans, seam side down. Cover them with a tea towel and let them rise until almost doubled in bulk, about 15 to 20 minutes. Preheat the oven to 350 degrees.

7. Bake the breads for 45 to 50 minutes. They may need to be covered with foil toward the end of baking if the tops are browning too quickly. Let them cool in the pans for 10 minutes; then turn them out onto a wire rack to cool completely.

Ranch Bread

To approximate *horno* bread, build a good hardwood fire in the center of a brick oven. It should be hot enough that the brick mass is well heated. Judge the timing of the fire so that the oven is about 400 degrees and has no fire but hot coals when the dough has risen. Make the dough, increasing the salt to 2 teaspoons and cutting the yeast back by 1 teaspoon. Form the dough into a round loaf and let it rise covered with a tea towel on a baker's peel or board so that it can be slid onto the oven floor. Bank the coals around the edges of the oven and sweep the center clear of excess ash. Slide the bread into the oven and bake for about an hour. You may need to turn the bread around for even browning during the baking.

Makes 1 large loaf
_____

1½ pounds unbleached white flour (about 5 cups)
1 teaspoon salt
1 tablespoon plus 1 teaspoon active dry yeast
2 cups warm water
2 tablespoons lard or vegetable shortening, melted

1. Combine the flour and the salt in a large mixing bowl. Make a well in the flour. Put the yeast in the well along with 1 cup of the warm water. Stir the water and yeast lightly with a fork, incorporating a small amount of flour. Let the mixture stand for about 5 minutes, or until the yeast becomes active and foams.

2. Begin to combine the flour and yeast mixture with a fork. When the mixture starts to get stiff add the remaining water and the melted fat. Continue mixing with the fork until the dough is very stiff; then finish the mixing by hand. When the dough is together in a mass, turn it onto a floured board and knead for about 10 minutes, or until the dough is smooth. If the dough is a little sticky, knead in a bit more flour.

3. Place the dough in a lightly oiled 8- or 9-inch skillet, with an ovenproof handle and cover it with a towel. Let it rise until doubled in bulk, about 40 minutes. Check on the rising and preheat the oven to 400 degrees 10 to 15 minutes before the dough is ready to bake.

4. Place the skillet in the oven and bake for 50 to 60 minutes, or until the top is golden brown. Remove the bread from the oven. After 5 to 10 minutes take the bread out of the skillet and cool it on a wire rack.

Sopaipillas

Sopaipillas cover a lot of territory in Southwestern cuisine. They are served for dessert with honey and cinnamon almost everywhere. In New Mexico, they appear as a main course, split and stuffed with beans and cheese or meat and covered with red chile sauce. They can be large or small, round, triangular, or square. When we make them for dessert, we usually add a teaspoon of freshly ground anise seed to the dough. Kids like them sprinkled with confectioner's sugar.

Makes 12 medium sopaipillas

1½ cups unbleached white flour
2 teaspoons baking powder
½ teaspoon salt
Pinch of sugar
1 tablespoon plus 2 teaspoons vegetable shortening
½ cup water
Corn or vegetable oil for frying

1. Mix the dry ingredients together in a mixing bowl. Cut the shortening in with a pastry blender. Add the water and blend with a fork.

2. Turn the dough onto a lightly floured board and knead for a minute or so to bring the dough together. Continue kneading by gently flattening the dough, folding it, turning it a quarter turn, and flattening it; repeat

this process about 10 times. Wrap the dough in plastic wrap and let it rest for 20 to 30 minutes.

3. Roll the dough into a large rectangle about ³⁄₁₆ inch thick. Trim the uneven edges and cut the dough into 12 equal-sized triangles or rectangles.

4. Pour the oil into a skillet until it is ½ to ¾ inch deep. Heat the oil until it is very hot but not smoking. Test the oil by dropping a piece of the dough trimmings into the skillet. It should immediately bubble, sizzle, and puff.

5. Drop the sopaipillas, one at a time, into the oil and hold them under with a slotted spoon until they puff. Spoon the hot oil over the top side and turn after 30 or 40 seconds. Cook the other side for about the same amount of time. The sopaipillas should be golden brown. Serve immediately or hold in a 150-degree oven until all the sopaipillas are cooked. The sopaipillas can be held for a few hours uncovered at room temperature; they will not be as light. To reheat them, wrap them very well in an aluminum foil package and put them in a 300-degree oven for 10 minutes or so.

CHAPTER SEVEN

Soups
& Stews

As the fundaments of early Southwestern cooking were dried foods, soups and stews held large importance in the region and still do. Long simmering over carefully-conserved wood fires was necessary to make parched or dried corn, dried beef, or beans digestible and to render these simple ingredients palatable. This transmutation was brought about mainly from the necessary slowness of the fire, and was aided by dried or semi-dried seasonings: chiles, yerba buena, garlic, and juniper berries.

Even today, people cook long-simmered stews on the back of the stove or in crockpots. An Arizona cowboy gave us a recipe for jackrabbit stew as follows: "Put your jackrabbit hide hair 'n all in a crockpot. Throw in an onion, some salt pork, a handful of jalapeños and cover the whole thing with water. Cook *real* slow for 24 hours then throw the jackrabbit out and eat the stew." Simple and a timesaver for the camp cook.

We think full-flavored soups owe more to good broth than any other ingredient; consequently, we offer recipes for chicken, fish, and vegetable broth. To our knowledge, no stews or soups of the Southwest use specially prepared meat stock in the French manner. Apparently beef was always too expensive and cooking fuel too hard to get for this method to have found a place in the region's cooking.

Instead, beef bones with meat (never veal—cattle had to grow to a minimum weight on the sparse ranges before they could be profitably eaten) were added to water, with the resulting broth and meat consumed together, a bit like the Italian *bollito misto* or French *pot au feu*.

As fresh vegetables became widely available in this century, they were more frequently added to soups and stews. Currently, the traditional dishes are lightened considerably by reducing the use of lard, using lighter broths, and adding even more vegetables. We have been impressed by some restaurant versions of soups and stews; our Frijoles Borrachos was developed after tasting a very fine soup in Tucson. All the regional elements are here, but the precision in cooking methods and timing gives the dish a new freshness. The use of garnishes, part of the Mexican heritage of the Southwest, remains important in the presentation and enjoyment of soups or stews. Table-served garnishes are almost a ritual; each person has the pleasure of adding his or her touch to the dish.

Several soups in this chapter are of the rustic variety that benefits by being made ahead and left to mellow. Black Bean Soup with Jalapeño Sherry, Caldo de Res, Chick-Pea and Hominy Stew, Hopi-Style Lamb and Hominy Stew, Menudo, Tortilla Soup, and Vegetable and Rice Soup are good on the day they are made and take on extra flavor if they are kept.

Chicken Broth

Makes about 2 quarts

3 to 4 pounds chicken bones, parts, necks, and backs
8 to 10 quarts water
1 medium-sized carrot
1 medium-sized onion
1 garlic clove
2 whole cloves
½ celery stalk
2 to 3 fresh coriander sprigs
1 teaspoon whole black peppercorns
½ teaspoon dried oregano leaves

1. Place the chicken in a stock pot and add about 8 quarts of water. The chicken should be covered with water by about 1½ inches. Bring the water almost to a boil and begin to skim the broth. Lower the heat to a simmer.

2. Cook the broth for about 45 minutes, skimming it carefully. Meanwhile, peel the carrot, onion, and garlic. Cut the carrot into 5 or 6 pieces and halve the onion.

3. Stick the cloves in the onion and add the onion, carrot, garlic,

celery, and coriander to the stock pot. Add more water to completely cover the vegetables and chicken. Put the black peppercorns and oregano in a bouquet garni bag and add them to the stock pot.

4. Simmer the broth another 45 minutes to an hour, skimming occasionally. Strain the broth through rinsed cheesecloth in a colander into a clean pot. Allow it to drain for 30 minutes; then press on the cheesecloth to extract all the juices.

Fish and Shrimp Broth

≣ **Makes about 1½ quarts**

1½ to 2 pounds nonoily fish frames
Shells from 1 to 1½ pounds shrimp
½ medium-sized onion, peeled
½ celery stalk
1 bay leaf
6 to 8 whole black peppercorns
½ teaspoon sea salt
2 quarts water
Salt and freshly ground white pepper

1. Clean the fish frames very well. Remove the gills and rinse away any blood.

2. Combine all the ingredients in a stock pot. Bring to a simmer. Simmer and skim the broth for 20 to 30 minutes. Strain the broth through rinsed cheesecloth in a colander into a clean pot. Season with salt and pepper. Use as a broth or soup base.

Vegetable Broth

≣ **Makes about 2 quarts**

1 medium-sized onion, cut into quarters
1 large carrot, cut into 3 pieces
1 large celery stalk, cut into 3 pieces
1 medium-sized potato, cut into quarters
¼ of a small cabbage

Handful of fresh parsley sprigs
10 whole black peppercorns
1 bay leaf
2 quarts water

1. Combine all of the ingredients in a large stock pot, cover, and bring to a boil. Remove the lid, lower the heat, and simmer for 1 hour, stirring occasionally.

2. Strain the broth through rinsed cheesecloth in a colander into a clean pot. Use the broth as desired; it can be refrigerated for a few days or frozen.

Menudo

This soup is very popular in southern Arizona and southern California. It has been imported with little variation straight across the border; its reputation as a hangover cure came with the soup from Sonora. We have found that people who don't know or don't like tripe are pleased with this menudo. The soup should always be cooked at a bare simmer. This brings out the best flavor and softens the tripe to a fine consistency.

Serves 4 to 6

2 pounds lamb tripe
2 veal knuckles, split
4 to 6 quarts water
1 quart Chicken Broth (page 110)
Salt and freshly ground black pepper
1 medium-sized onion, diced
2 garlic cloves, finely diced
2 fresh oregano sprigs, or ½ teaspoon dried oregano leaves
1 26-ounce can hominy, drained and rinsed
1 fresh hot green pepper, halved, stemmed, and seeded, optional

GARNISHES
Lime wedges
Thinly sliced scallions, or diced onion
Crushed dried red hot peppers, or diced fresh hot red peppers
Dried or fresh chopped oregano leaves
Red or green salsa

1. Rinse the tripe and cut it into small pieces. Put it in a pot with the veal knuckles and cover with water by about 3 inches. Bring the liquid just to a simmer; then lower the heat to a bare simmer. Skim the broth as necessary and cook for 2 hours.

2. Strain the broth through cheesecloth in a colander into a clean pot. Remove the knuckles and let them cool. Remove any meat from them. Return the strained broth, tripe, meat, and chicken broth to a pot.

3. Season the broth lightly with salt and pepper and add the onions, garlic, and oregano. Cook at a bare simmer for 30 minutes.

4. Add the drained and rinsed hominy and the hot green pepper, if desired. Cook the soup for about 30 minutes at a bare simmer. Remove the pepper and serve the soup very hot with the garnishes.

Tortilla Soup

≡ Serves 6 to 8

1 medium-sized onion, diced
3 garlic cloves, finely chopped
2 tablespoons corn oil
1 pound ripe tomatoes, peeled, seeded, and diced, or
    1 14-ounce can whole tomatoes, seeded and
    chopped
1 tablespoon ground hot red chile
1 tablespoon ground mild red chile
6 to 8 cups Chicken Broth (page 110)
Salt and freshly ground black pepper
6 to 8 stale tortillas
Corn or vegetable oil for frying
2 to 3 cups shredded leftover chicken meat
Chopped fresh coriander leaves for garnish
Grated Monterey Jack, Lappi, or Muenster cheese for
    garnish

1. Soften the onion and garlic for 10 to 15 minutes in the 2 tablespoons of corn oil in a soup pot or casserole. Add the tomatoes, ground chiles, and chicken broth to the pot. Simmer for 30 minutes and season with salt and pepper.

2. Meanwhile, cut the tortillas in half; then cut them into ¼-inch-wide strips. Fry the tortilla strips in very hot oil until they just become leathery, about 20 seconds. Remove them to a paper towel to drain as they are done.

3. Add the chicken to the soup and heat it through. Divide the tortilla strips among warm soup plates and ladle the soup over them. Serve the soup hot, accompanied by the garnishes.

Shrimp Albóndigas

Serves 4 to 6; makes about 36 albóndigas

1¼ pounds large shrimp (16 to 24 count)
2 large garlic cloves
Salt and freshly ground black pepper
1 extra large egg, lightly beaten
¼ cup fine dry bread crumbs
1 recipe Fish and Shrimp Broth (page 111)
½ celery stalk, finely diced
½ onion, finely diced
1 tablespoon olive oil
Fresh coriander sprigs, optional

1. Shell and devein the shrimp. Reserve the shells to make broth. Mince the garlic very finely. Purée the shrimp in a food processor to a medium-smooth purée. Stir in the garlic and season well with salt and pepper.

2. Remove the mixture to a bowl and vigorously stir the egg into it. Stir in the bread crumbs.

3. Moisten your hands with cold water and form the mixture into 1-inch balls. Place on wax paper on a platter and keep chilled until ready to use.

4. Heat the broth over medium heat. Soften the diced vegetables in the oil. When they are soft, add them to the broth.

5. Poach the albóndigas in the broth until just done, about 4 minutes. Serve in warm bowls, garnished with coriander sprigs, if desired.

Black Bean Soup
with Jalapeño Sherry

≡ Serves 6 to 8

1 cup dry sherry
1 jalapeño pepper, seeded and cut into slivers
1 pound black beans, sorted and soaked overnight in
    2 to 3 quarts of water
1½ quarts water
4 tablespoons olive oil
1 teaspoon salt
1 cup chopped red onion
3 garlic cloves, slivered
2 teaspoons toasted and ground cumin seed
1 cup Chicken or Vegetable Broth (pages 110 and 111)
Salt
About ½ cup grated Monterey Jack cheese

1. Combine the sherry and the jalapeño in a small saucepan, place over low heat, and bring to a boil. Remove from the heat and cool.

2. Drain the beans and transfer them to a pressure cooker and add the water. Stir in 2 tablespoons of the oil and the salt. Cover and cook for 12 minutes after the pressure gauge is up.

3. Heat the remaining 2 tablespoons of oil and sauté the onion and garlic for about 4 minutes. Add the cumin and sauté 1 minute more.

4. Purée the beans and their liquid in a blender in batches. Pour the purée into a pan. Blend the last batch of beans with the sautéed vegetables and add them to the pan. There will be some bits of vegetable.

5. Stir in the broth and salt. Bring the soup to a simmer. Turn the heat to low, add ½ cup of the jalapeño sherry, and cook for about 7 minutes, stirring occasionally. Taste for salt and sherry.

6. Ladle the soup into warm bowls. Garnish each serving with about 1 tablespoon of cheese. Pass the remaining sherry with the soup.

Frijoles Borrachos

≡ Serves 4 to 6

4 cups cooked pinto beans
1½ cups bean stock
12 ounces mild beer, such as Miller or Michelob
1 jalapeño pepper, seeded and thinly sliced
1½ cups chopped ripe tomatoes
1 cup thinly sliced scallions, with some green
½ cup roughly chopped fresh coriander leaves
Salt and freshly ground black pepper

1. Combine the beans, stock, and beer in a heavy saucepan. Cook over medium-high heat for about 5 minutes.

2. Add the jalapeño, tomatoes, scallions, and coriander. Season lightly with salt and generously with pepper. Cover, lower the heat, and cook for 3 to 4 minutes.

3. Taste the soup for seasoning and serve very hot in warm soup plates or bowls.

Chayote Piñon Soup

≡ Serves 4 to 6

6 ounces pine nuts
1 pound chayote squash, peeled and cut into ¾-inch dice
½ guajillo chile, stemmed, seeded, and cut into slivers
3 cups Vegetable or Chicken Broth (pages 111 and 110)
2 tablespoons unsalted butter
2 tablespoons finely minced shallots
1 teaspoon coriander seed, toasted and ground
1½ cups milk
¾ teaspoon salt, or to taste
Freshly ground white pepper to taste
2 pinches of freshly ground nutmeg
Chopped fresh parsley leaves for garnish

1. Combine the pine nuts, chayote, guajillo, and broth in a large soup pot and bring to a simmer. Lower the heat and cook, covered, barely simmering for 25 minutes.

2. Sauté the shallots in the butter in a small skillet over low heat for 4 to 5 minutes. Add the shallots and coriander to the soup pot, stir well, and cook for 2 to 3 minutes.

3. Purée the soup with the milk in a blender in batches. Return the puréed soup to the pot. Add the salt, pepper, and nutmeg and heat gently. When thoroughly hot, taste for seasoning; do not allow the soup to simmer. Serve hot, garnished with a little chopped fresh parsley.

Cheddar Cheese and Red Chile Soup with Cauliflower

≡ Serves 6

2 tablespoons corn oil
1 medium-sized onion, diced
1 medium-sized red hot cherry or New Mexico red
    chile, stemmed, seeded, and diced
¾ pound potatoes, peeled and cut into ½-inch dice
1 pound cauliflower, washed, trimmed, and broken into
    bite-sized flowerets
4 cups Chicken or Vegetable Broth (pages 110 and 111)
2 cups milk
2½ cups grated, loosely packed, mild or mild and sharp
    Cheddar cheese
1 teaspoon toasted and ground cumin seed
Salt and freshly ground black pepper
Tortilla chips for garnish, optional

1. Heat the oil in a large heavy-bottomed soup pot over medium heat. Add the onion and chile and sauté for a minute or so. Add the potatoes and sauté for 3 to 4 minutes. Add the cauliflower and cook for another 2 minutes or so, stirring occasionally.

2. Stir in the broth, cover, and cook over medium heat for about 15 minutes. Add the milk to the soup.

3. Purée about half of the soup in a blender in batches, adding a

handful of cheese to each batch, and reserving one handful of cheese for garnish.

4. Return the puréed soup to the pot, add the cumin, and season with salt and pepper. Heat over low heat for 5 minutes. Ladle the soup into warm bowls and garnish with the rest of the cheese and a handful of crumbled tortilla chips, if desired.

Gold and Green Soups

≡ This combination of soups is handsome in both appearance and flavor. The soups can be made ahead of time and gently reheated. If you make them the day before, do not add the cream until you are ready to reheat and serve the soups. Nasturtium or squash blossoms make an elegant garnish.

Serves 4 to 6

GOLD SOUP

3 tablespoons unsalted butter
1 heaping cup diced yellow onion
¾ cup diced red bell pepper
3 cups fresh corn kernels
3 cups Chicken or Vegetable Broth (see pages 110 and 111)
¼ teaspoon saffron threads
½ cup heavy (whipping) cream
Salt

GREEN SOUP

1½ pounds zucchini, sliced ¼ inch thick
1 jalapeño pepper, peeled, seeded, and minced
2 garlic cloves, minced
2 cups Chicken or Vegetable Broth
1 tablespoon olive oil
1 cup peas cooked until tender in ¼ cup Chicken or
   Vegetable Broth
½ teaspoon dried oregano leaves
½ cup heavy (whipping) cream
Salt

Nasturtium or squash blossoms for garnish, optional

1. To make the gold soup, melt the butter in a heavy-bottomed soup pot over medium heat. Add the onion and red pepper and sauté for 2 minutes. Add the corn, stir well, and sauté for 5 minutes, stirring occasionally so it does not stick.

2. Add the broth and saffron and simmer over low heat for 15 minutes. Purée the soup in batches in a blender and return it to the pot.

3. Add the cream and salt, stir well, and heat gently for 5 minutes. Taste for seasoning.

4. To make the green soup, cook the zucchini, jalapeño, and garlic in the broth with the olive oil in a heavy-bottomed soup pot until tender, about 8 to 10 minutes.

5. Purée the cooked vegetables with the broth in a blender in batches and return to the pot. Purée the peas and broth and add them to the pot.

6. Add the oregano, cream, and salt and stir well. Cook over low heat for 5 minutes. Taste for seasoning.

7. Heat both soups over low heat until completely hot. Ladle the green soup into warm bowls.

8. Gently ladle the gold soup into the center of the green soup. Garnish each bowl with a nasturtium or squash blossom and serve hot.

Green Chile Soup

≡ **Serves 4 to 6**

3 tablespoons unsalted butter
¾ pound waxy red or white potatoes, peeled and diced
1 cup chopped white onion
2 garlic cloves, minced
1½ cups roasted, peeled, and diced mild green chiles
4 cups Chicken or Vegetable Broth (pages 110 and 111)
¾ teaspoon chopped fresh thyme leaves, or ¼ teaspoon dried thyme leaves, crumbled
Salt and freshly ground black pepper

1. Melt the butter in a heavy-bottomed stock pot. Add the potatoes, onions, and garlic and sauté for 3 to 4 minutes. Add the chiles and sauté another 5 minutes.

2. Add the broth to the pot and bring it to a simmer. Lower the heat and cook for about 15 minutes.

3. Add the thyme and season with salt and pepper. Cook for 10 to 15 minutes over low heat. Adjust the seasoning and serve hot.

Pumpkin Soup with Roasted Red Pepper and Pasilla Chile

≣ Serves 6

½ dried pasilla chile, seeded
1 cup boiling water
1 small pumpkin (about 2 pounds)
4 garlic cloves, peeled
1 medium-sized red bell pepper, roasted, peeled, seeded,
   and diced
½ cup half-and-half
½ cup heavy (whipping) cream
Salt and freshly ground white pepper
Dash of bitters
Pinch of ground cayenne, optional

1. Soak the pasilla in 1 cup of boiling water for 30 minutes. Cut the pumpkin in half and scrape out the seeds. Peel the pumpkin and cut it into 1-inch chunks. Put 2½ cups of the diced pumpkin in a pan with the garlic and barely cover with water. Reserve the rest of the pumpkin for another use. Bring the water to a boil, lower the heat to a simmer, and cover the pan.

2. Remove the pasilla from the soaking liquid and strain the liquid. Cut the chile into small pieces. Add the pasilla and strained liquid to the pumpkin after 10 minutes. Cook the pumpkin until it is tender, about 25 minutes. Add the red pepper.

3. Purée the soup in batches in a blender or food processor. Return it to a pan and add the half-and-half and cream. Season with salt, pepper, bitters, and cayenne. Heat the soup until it is just hot and serve immediately.

Roasted Pepper Gazpacho

≡ The croutons we like with this soup are made as follows: cut some Ranch Bread (page 105) or other plain bread into cubes about ⅝ inch square. Peel and crush one or two garlic cloves and heat them in a little olive oil or butter. Add the bread and fry until it is golden brown. Sprinkle the croutons with ground red chile and chopped fresh oregano or dried crumbled oregano and toss to evenly distribute the seasonings. Garnish each bowl with a small handful.

Serves 4 to 6

3 large ripe tomatoes
1 medium-sized cucumber
2 garlic cloves
1 small onion
1 red bell pepper, roasted, peeled, and seeded
1 green bell pepper, roasted, peeled, and seeded
1 red Hungarian or hot cherry pepper, stemmed and seeded
1 jalapeño or serrano pepper, stemmed and seeded
3 tablespoons olive oil
Juice of ½ lime, or to taste
2 dashes of bitters
Salt

1. Seed the tomatoes. Peel the cucumber and seed it, if desired. Peel the garlic and onion.
2. Chop all the vegetables very finely and save the juice. Put the vegetables and juice in a serving dish and stir in the olive oil, lime juice, and bitters; season with salt.
3. Cover and refrigerate the gazpacho for 2 hours before serving. Adjust the seasoning and serve cold. Garnish with croutons, if desired.

Caldo de Res

☰ This is one of those homey delicious soup-stews that for many Mexican–American families still holds its traditional place as a Sunday supper.

Serves 6

MEAT AND BROTH

  5 pounds beef short ribs
  Water
  1 teaspoon salt
  ½ teaspoon dried oregano leaves
  ½ teaspoon coriander seed
  ½ teaspoon whole black peppercorns
  2 pinches of cumin seed

VEGETABLES

  1 pound potatoes, peeled and cut into large pieces
  4 medium-sized carrots, peeled and cut into large pieces
  1 medium-sized onion, cut into wedges
  1 celery stalk, cut into small pieces
  2 large ears of shucked corn, each cut into 6 or 8 pieces
  ½ pound green cabbage, cut into 1½-inch-thick wedges
  Salt and freshly ground black pepper

1. Trim the ribs of excess fat. Blanch them in lightly salted, gently boiling water for 15 minutes. Drain them and put them in a clean stock pot and cover with 2 inches of water. Simmer and skim carefully for 1 hour.

2. Add 2 or 3 cups of water; the meat should be well covered. Add the salt, herbs, and spices. (Removing the herbs and spices is easier if they are in a bouquet garni bag or cheesecloth, but they may be added loose.) Simmer for 1½ hours, skimming as necessary.

3. Strain the broth through rinsed cheesecloth in a colander into a clean soup pot. Remove the bouquet garni bag, or pick most of the spices from the meat. Add the meat to the broth.

4. Add the potatoes, carrots, onion, and celery to the broth and meat. Cover and simmer for 20 minutes. Add the corn and then the cabbage. Cover and cook for 10 minutes.

5. Taste the broth for seasoning. Ladle the meat and some of each vegetable into warm soup bowls or plates. Ladle the broth over and serve hot.

Vegetable and Rice Soup

Serves 6 to 8

3 tablespoons olive oil
1½ cups chopped onion
½ pound snap beans, topped, tailed, and snapped into
    1-inch lengths
1½ cups fresh or frozen corn kernels
1 cup fresh or frozen peas
8 cups Chicken or Vegetable Broth (pages 110 and 111)
1 bay leaf
1 medium-sized ripe tomato, peeled, seeded, and diced
3 cups shredded cabbage
2 teaspoons Chili Powder (page 50)
1½ cups *cooked* long-grain white rice
Salt and freshly ground black pepper

1. Heat the olive oil in a large heavy-bottomed soup pot and add the onion. Sauté about 1 minute. Add the beans, cover, and cook for 2 minutes more.

2. Add the corn and peas, cover, and cook for about 2 minutes. Add the broth and bay leaf, cover, and bring to a simmer. Add the tomato, cabbage, and chili powder, cover, and cook about 5 minutes more.

3. Add the rice and season with salt and pepper. Simmer for a few minutes longer. Taste for seasoning and serve hot.

Hopi-Style Lamb and Hominy Stew

Elemental and flavorful, this soup is a version of one we ate while visiting Second Mesa on the Hopi reservation.

Serves 6 to 8

4 pounds bone-in lamb shoulder and neck meat
About 6 quarts water
1 medium-sized onion, peeled and quartered
6 juniper berries
2 garlic cloves, peeled

1 teaspoon salt
½ teaspoon whole black peppercorns
1 large fresh sage sprig, or ½ teaspoon dried sage leaves
1 26-ounce can hominy, rinsed and drained
½ cup finely diced onion for garnish
¼ to ½ cup finely diced fresh green chiles, (depending
    on the heat of the chiles) for garnish

1. Trim the lamb of excess fat and connective tissue. Place the meat in a large stock pot and cover with cold water by 4 inches.

2. Bring to a boil and skim. Lower the heat to a medium simmer and skim frequently. Add more water to keep the level about 3 inches above the meat. Simmer for 1 hour.

3. Add the onion, juniper, garlic, salt, peppercorns, and sage to the stock pot. Simmer for another hour, skimming occasionally.

4. Strain the broth through a rinsed cloth in a colander into a clean pot. Pick vegetables, herbs, and spices off the meat and return the meat to the broth.

5. Add the hominy and simmer, covered, for 30 minutes. Serve hot in soup plates or bowls and pass the diced onions and chiles at the table. Serve with warm tortillas or bread.

Southwestern Fish Stew

≡ Serves 4 to 6

FISH
3 pounds snapper or Pacific rockfish
1 pound medium-sized (26 to 30 count) shrimp
1 tablespoon ground mild red chile
½ lime, sliced
½ teaspoon salt

STEW
2 large dried hot New Mexico chiles
1 recipe Fish and Shrimp Broth (page 111)
1 cup chopped onion
2 large garlic cloves, minced
2 tablespoons corn oil

½ cup roasted, peeled, and diced hot green chiles
1 medium-sized red bell pepper, seeded and diced
1½ cups fresh corn kernels
Salt
Lime wedges for garnish
Crushed pequin or tepin chiles for garnish

1. Fillet and skin the snapper or have the fishmonger do this for you. Cut the gills from the frame and rinse the frame very well. Put it in a stock pot and reserve to make the broth.

2. Steam the shrimp with the ground chile, lime slices, and salt in a small amount of water for 1 to 3 minutes, or until the shrimp are just firm. The timing will depend on the size and freshness of the shrimp.

3. Shell and devein the shrimp, adding the shells to the stock pot for the broth. Prepare the Fish and Shrimp Broth.

4. Remove any bones from the fish fillets and cut the flesh into even-sized pieces.

5. Simmer the New Mexico chiles in the broth for 20 to 30 minutes. Skim the pods and seeds from the broth.

6. Meanwhile soften the onion and garlic in the oil over low heat for about 15 minutes. Add the green chiles, red pepper, and corn and cook over low heat for 5 minutes.

7. Add the vegetables to the broth and cook for 3 to 4 minutes over medium heat. Add the fish and cook for 2 minutes. Add the shrimp and heat through.

8. Serve the stew hot in soup plates or bowls. Pass the lime wedges and a small bowl of crushed chiles at the table.

Chick-pea and Hominy Stew

≡ Serves 6 to 8

1 30-ounce can hominy, drained and rinsed
3 cups water
2 tablespoons olive oil
1 cup chopped onion
5 dried red serrano or 2 dried cayenne peppers, stemmed
    and seeded

2 large cloves garlic, chopped
3 cups cooked chick-peas
2 cups chick-pea stock
2 large tomatoes, peeled, seeded, and chopped
¼ cup packed chopped fresh parsley leaves
1 tablespoon chopped fresh epazote leaves, or 1 tea-
    spoon dried epazote leaves, crumbled
Salt and freshly ground black pepper
Lime wedges

1. Combine the hominy and the water in a pot. Cover and simmer over low heat for 30 minutes. While the hominy is cooking, heat the oil in a small skillet and sauté the onion, serranos, and garlic lightly for about 5 minutes.

2. Add the sautéed vegetables, chick-peas, stock, and tomatoes to the hominy. Stir the stew and simmer, uncovered, for about 10 minutes.

3. Add the parlsey, epazote, and salt and pepper. Stir, cover, and cook over low heat for another 5 minutes or so. Taste for seasoning and serve hot with a lime wedge to garnish each bowl.

CHAPTER EIGHT

Tortilla & Masa Dishes

Tortillas are the building blocks of the edifice which is Southwestern cooking. In the new cooking especially, the rooms may be variously furnished, but without tortillas there would be no structure. They are cornerstones for simple and elegant meals. Soft, they can be stacked for enchiladas, rolled for soft tacos or enchiladas, tucked and rolled for burritos, simply folded for quesadillas, or eaten as bread. Crisp-fried, they are cut into wedges for tortilla chips (tostaditos) and their fancy nacho cousins, folded for tacos, rolled for flautas, or left flat as the foundations for tostada and topopo towers.

The ancient basic material for tortillas, tamales, sopes, gorditas, chalupas, and a hundred other foods is masa. It is the wet dough ready to be shaped, made from ground lime-treated corn. If you live in the Southwest, you can often buy masa from tortilla factories or Mexican delicatessens. Just seeing the big blocks of it brings out the potter in us as well as the cook. The masa traditions came several centuries ago with immigrants from Sonora, central Mexico, the Yucatán, and other regions of Mexico. Many of the elaborate dishes and those which depended on ingredients no longer available did not become part of the amalgamating cuisine of the Southwest. The love for masa remained, however, and spread to other settlers.

Today the thick masa dishes which are formed into little containers and named sopes, gorditas, or chalupas according to their shape, are rather uncommon, but well worth trying for their texture and concentration of flavor. Sometimes a doubly thick tortilla is fried and then split and stuffed with beans and cheese or meat and served as a gordita. Tamales are prepared regularly at tortilla factories and delicatessens, less frequently in home kitchens. The big tamale season is Christmas, when large batches of sweet, savory, and sweet and savory tamales are made to eat as snacks, to accompany meals (with or without chile gravy), or as desserts. The combinations of fillings are practically endless and are based on dried and fresh fruits, nuts, any kind of meat from chicken to lamb, chorizo, picadillo, and chile sauces. Green corn tamales are a summer treat, made with fresh corn, cheese, and usually green chiles.

All the tortilla and masa dishes are nourishing and filling, something to keep in mind when menu-planning. They are often served as main courses, accompanied simply by salsa, shredded lettuce, and chopped tomato and onion, or with vegetables en escabeche. The textural, flavor, and color contrasts can be very satisfying even in such a simple meal. The small amount of beans and cheese or meat combined with the grain provides a balanced sustenance which is also inexpensive.

Tacos

Tacos come in so many good forms that we don't like to limit ourselves to specific recipes. They are best eaten as appetizers, even doled out one at a time, because their fragile nature cannot stand oven-holding or plate-fussing. The two main taco categories are soft or crisp. Soft tacos can be made with corn or flour tortillas. Corn tortillas are by far the most popular. The important thing is to have good homemade or factory-made tortillas with some texture. The best fillings for soft tacos are shredded, not ground meats, or whole, not mashed beans. The filling should have some bite to contrast with the soft tortilla. Seasonings can be anything you like, but the taco should be a bit dry rather than juicy. Vegetables, such as shredded lettuce or cabbage, chopped tomatoes or avocados, do not traditionally appear in soft tacos, though chopped onions and chiles often do. The tortillas are rolled around the fillings to make a cylinder shape.

Southwestern crisp-fried tacos are always made with corn tortillas and come in the half-moon shape, or rolled, in which case they are usually called *flautas*. For these we think that commercial tortillas are a good choice. The layered fresh tortillas make a quite leathery taco, though many people prefer this texture. Taco shells or flautas should be fried in abundant very hot oil for just a few seconds. The easiest way to make the half-moon shape is to hold the tortilla in that shape with tongs and deep-fry it. With a little practice, tortillas can be fried flat in a skillet, removed from the fat, and bent immediately into shape. In either case, the taco shells are fried before filling and should be well-drained and kept warm.

Fillings for crisp tacos are practically limitless. Ground meat preparations, such as chorizo and picadillo, are often used. Any soft taco filling can go into a crisp taco. The half-moon tacos often have a little bean, meat, and cheese in the center of the taco, and then any combination of the chopped raw vegetables mentioned above. Flautas, because they are rolled first and then fried, use the fillings for soft tacos. Whatever the style of the tacos, they are always served as hot as possible. Everything should be at hand, with the fillings warm, so that the tacos can be put together and eaten quickly. No taco, as far as we know, is ever eaten without salsa.

Tostadas Compuestas

☰ Tostadas compuestas can be quite wonderful if you have some garden vegetables. Marbled-sized new potatoes, fingerling carrots, pencil-thin green beans, and thumb-sized summer squash make this dish special. Amounts are adjustable and the recipe is easily doubled. Beans and chicken are equally good here.

Makes 3 to 6 tostadas

1 tablespoon unsalted butter
⅓ cup finely chopped red bell pepper
⅓ cup fresh corn kernels
⅓ cup tender sweet garden peas
3 tablespoons Jalapeño Mayonnaise (page 52), or a
    vinaigrette made of equal parts Hot Pepper Vinegar
    (page 52) and olive oil
3 6-inch or 6 4-inch corn tortillas
1½ cups beans, simple or refried, or 1½ cups shredded
    cooked chicken
¾ cup grated Monterey Jack or Cheddar cheese
2 cups roughly chopped mixed garden greens, such as
    lettuce, rocket, and spinach
Red or green salsa

1. Melt the butter in a small skillet and stir in the pepper, corn, and peas. Cook for about 3 minutes over medium heat. Remove from the heat to cool. Toss the vegetables with the mayonnaise or vinaigrette.

2. Heat the tortillas on an ungreased comal or in a skillet until crisp. Heat the beans or chicken gently and spread them evenly over the tortillas. Sprinkle them with the cheese. Place the tostadas on warm plates.

3. Mound a generous handful of greens on each tostada. Divide the vegetables among the tostadas and serve with salsa.

Tostadas with Cabbage Escabeche and Goat Cheese

Serves 4 to 8

3 cups cooked pinto or black beans, or shredded cooked
    chicken, turkey, or dried beef
About ½ cup corn oil for frying
8 4- to 5-inch Corn Tortillas (page 92)
5 ounces mild goat cheese, crumbled
2½ cups Cabbage en Escabeche (page 61)

1. Preheat the oven to 350 degrees. Heat the beans, chicken, or turkey gently. The dried beef should be at room temperature.

2. Cover a baking sheet with aluminum foil. Heat the oil in a skillet to hot but not smoking. Fry the tortillas, one at a time, for 20 seconds. Drain them on paper towels.

3. Spread about ⅓ cup of the beans or meat on each tortilla. Place the tortillas on the baking sheet. Sprinkle about 2 tablespoons of the goat cheese over each tostada. Place the baking sheet in the oven for 8 to 10 minutes, or until the goat cheese just starts to melt.

4. Remove the tostadas from the oven and mound about ¼ cup of escabeche in the center of each one. Serve immediately on warmed plates.

Gorditas

≣ Gorditas are not as common as tortillas in the home kitchens or even in restaurants in the Southwest. They give a toothsome and different dimension to masa. We think they are excellent informal party food, especially when some of the party likes to help with the cooking. With two or three people, a nice rhythm can be established for the setting of the masa and forming of the gorditas, the frying, and the filling. The gorditas can then be served one at a time, as hot from the pan as the guests can eat them.

Serves 4 to 8

1 recipe Corn Tortilla dough (page 92); make the recipe with 1½ cups water
Corn or vegetable oil for frying
About 2 cups shredded cooked chicken, pork, beef, or picadillo, chorizo, or diced avocado
About 1½ cups grated queso cotijo, queso fresco, or Monterey Jack cheese
About 2 cups shredded lettuce
About ⅓ cup sliced red radishes
Red or green table salsa

1. Divide the dough into eight parts and pat them into rounds. Roll each round between thick plastic wrap with a rolling pin to a 5-inch diameter circle, about ³⁄₁₆ inch thick. You may press the dough with a tortilla press, but be sure that the outer circumference is not thinner than the center dough. Roll out two or three rounds and remove 1 sheet of plastic from each.

2. Cook the gorditas on an ungreased comal or griddle, one at a time, over medium heat for 40 seconds to 1 minute on each side. The masa should be set but still quite pliable.

3. As each piece of dough is set, place it on a board so that the first side cooked is down. Pinch up the edges to between ¾ and 1 inch high, pressing down to seal the rim to the base of the gordita. The rims will overlap a bit to form the cup shape. Set and form all the gorditas and keep them warm in a 150-degree oven.

4. Meanwhile heat 1 inch of oil in a heavy skillet to very hot. Fry the gorditas, one at a time, hollow side up, for about 30 seconds. Spoon hot fat continually into the center of the gordita.

5. The gorditas should be light golden brown all over. The amount of cooking time varies as to the heat of the oil. Invert the gorditas on paper towels and keep them warm in the oven.

6. Have the filling ingredients at hand and fill the gorditas with the meat or avocado, cheese, and lettuce and garnish with radishes. Serve immediately with the salsa on the table.

Turkey Enchiladas

Serves 6 to 12

3 guajillo chiles, or 3 dried hot New Mexico chiles and
   1 cascabel chile
2 cups hot turkey, chicken, or duck stock, or water
1 medium-sized onion, diced
2 garlic cloves, finely diced
1 cup peeled, seeded, and diced ripe tomatoes, or whole
   canned plum tomatoes, seeded and diced
Salt
2 tablespoons unsalted butter
2 tablespoons all-purpose flour
2 cups milk
3½ to 4 cups coarsely shredded cooked turkey meat
1 medium-sized green bell pepper, seeded and diced
2 tablespoons corn oil
12 4-inch or 8 6-inch Corn Tortillas (page 92)
1 bunch scallions, trimmed with 2 inches of green and
   sliced for garnish, optional
3 tablespoons grated dry Monterey Jack cheese, or dry
   goat cheese for garnish, optional

1. Seed and stem the dried chiles and cut them into pieces. Soak them in the hot stock or water for 30 minutes. Put the chiles and liquid in a blender with the onion, garlic, and tomatoes and blend the mixture to a medium-smooth purée.

2. Cook the blended sauce over medium-high heat for 20 to 25 minutes. It should reduce and thicken slightly. Season with salt.

3. Melt the butter over medium-low heat in a small heavy saucepan. Add the flour, blend well, and cook for 5 minutes. Add the milk and blend well. Cook for 10 minutes over low heat.

4. Stir half of the chile sauce into the béchamel. Season the sauce with salt. Stir the turkey and green pepper into the other half of the chile sauce. Butter a baking dish large enough to hold the enchiladas. The enchiladas should fit snugly; you may need to use two dishes. Preheat the oven to 375 degrees.

5. Heat the oil in a frying pan over medium-low heat. Soften the tortillas, one at a time in it for 4 to 5 seconds on each side. As a tortilla is softened, dip it in the béchamel sauce and put it in the baking dish. Spread about ⅓ cup of the turkey mixture on the small tortillas, or ½ cup on the large tortillas. Roll the enchiladas and place them seam side down.

6. Continue until the enchiladas have been assembled. Cover the enchiladas with the béchamel sauce. Bake for about 15 minutes, until the enchiladas are heated through. Garnish enchiladas with cheese and scallions if desired and serve hot, one per person as a first course or two per person as a main course.

Enchiladas with Sweet Potatoes and Tomatillo Sauce

Serves 6 to 12

3 medium-sized dark orange sweet potatoes (about 1½ pounds total)

2 tablespoons corn oil

3 jalapeño peppers, stemmed, seeded, and finely diced

1 medium-sized onion, finely diced

1 tablespoon chopped fresh oregano leaves, or ¾ teaspoon dried oregano leaves, crumbled

3 tablespoons sesame seeds

12 ounces queso fresco, or 6 ounces *each* Monterey Jack and sharp Cheddar cheese

12 6-inch Corn Tortillas (page 92)

1 recipe Tomatillo Sauce (page 89)

1. Bake the sweet potatoes in a preheated 375-degree oven for about 20 minutes, or until they are tender but not soft. Cool the potatoes, peel them, and cut them into ½-inch dice.

2. Heat the oil over medium heat and sauté the sweet potatoes, peppers, and onion for 5 minutes. Stir in the oregano and sesame seeds and let the mixture cool.

3. Grate the cheese and toss it with the vegetable mixture. Warm the tortillas, for a few seconds on each side, on an ungreased griddle or comal. Wrap them and keep them warm. Preheat the oven to 375 degrees.

4. Oil two 9- by 13-inch baking dishes. Dip the warm tortillas, one at a time in the tomatillo sauce, then fill and roll them with the sweet potato mixture. Place the enchiladas in the baking dishes as they are rolled. Pour the tomatillo sauce over the enchiladas and cover each dish loosely with aluminum foil. Bake for 20 to 25 minutes and serve hot.

Black Bean Enchiladas with Red Chile Sauce

Serves 3 to 8

½ recipe Black Beans (page 190)
3 cups Red Chile Sauce (page 85)
About ½ cup corn oil
6 6-inch or 8 4-inch Corn Tortillas (page 92)
2 cups grated queso fresco or Monterey Jack cheese
1 cup sliced scallions
Sour cream for garnish, optional

1. Mash the beans if they are not already mashed. Add a little cooking liquid or water to heat them. Heat them well over low heat.

2. Heat the red chile sauce over low heat. Heat the oil in a frying pan and soften the tortillas, one at a time, for 15 to 20 seconds. As a tortilla is softened, dip it in the sauce and put it in an oiled baking dish large enough to hold the enchiladas. Preheat the oven to 375 degrees.

3. Fill the enchiladas, one by one, with the beans, cheese, and ¾ cup of the scallions. Roll them and place them, seam side down, in the baking dish.

4. Spoon the remaining sauce over the enchiladas. Bake for about 15 minutes, or until the enchiladas are heated through. Serve hot, garnished with the remaining scallions and sour cream, if desired. Serve one per person as a first course or two per person as a main course.

Sonoran-Style Cheese Enchiladas with Red Chile Sauce

Sonoran enchiladas are made with flat tortillas, filled and stacked, rather than by rolling the tortillas around the filling. They are often served with a fried egg on top.

Serves 4 as a main course

2 cups Red Chile Sauce (page 85)
12 4- to 5-inch Corn Tortillas, white or blue (pages 92 and 95)
2 cups grated Monterey Jack or Lappi cheese
1 cup chopped onion
4 extra large eggs, optional
Shredded lettuce for garnish, optional

1. Heat the red chile sauce over low heat. Generously oil a baking sheet. Preheat the oven to 350 degrees.

2. If the tortillas are freshly-made, use them directly to make the enchiladas. If the tortillas have been refrigerated, warm them for a few seconds on each side on an ungreased griddle or comal and keep them warm.

3. Dip 4 of the tortillas in the sauce and place them on the baking sheet. Cover them equally with half of the cheese and half of the onion. Repeat the layering, ending with tortillas.

4. Bake the enchiladas for 10 to 15 minutes, or until the cheese has begun to melt. Meanwhile fry the eggs, if desired.

5. Remove the enchiladas from the oven and divide the remaining sauce over them. Place the fried eggs on top of each one now. Serve immediately on warmed plates or keep them in the oven for a short while until ready to serve. Just before serving, garnish the plates with shredded lettuce, if desired.

Green Chile Enchiladas with Blue Corn Tortillas

≡ Serves 3 to 6

3 cups Green Chile Sauce (page 83)
1 to 1½ cups broth or water
Salt
About ½ cup corn oil for frying
12 4-inch Blue Corn Tortillas (page 95)
2 cups grated Monterey Jack cheese
1 cup chopped onion

1. Combine the green chile sauce and 1 cup of broth or water in a saucepan. Heat over low heat until just hot. The sauce should be a medium-thin consistency. Add more broth or water and season with salt, if necessary.

2. Preheat the oven to 350 degrees. Heat the oil in a frying pan over medium heat and soften the tortillas, one at a time, in it. As a tortilla is softened, dip it in the sauce and put it on a well-oiled baking sheet large enough to hold 6 enchiladas. Spoon 3 or 4 tablespoons of sauce over the tortilla and sprinkle it with about 2 tablespoons of the grated cheese and about 1 tablespoon of the onion. Cover with another softened and sauce-dipped tortilla and layer as before.

3. Continue until the enchiladas have been assembled. Bake for about 15 minutes, or until the enchiladas are heated through. Serve hot, one per person as a first course or two per person as a main course.

Chilaquiles with Chorizo

≡ Serves 4 to 6

1 pound Chorizo (page 153)
12 4-inch or 10 6-inch stale or frozen and thawed Corn
    Tortillas (page 92)
Corn or vegetable oil for frying
½ cup Red Chile Sauce (page 85)
2 cups grated Monterey Jack cheese, Muenster, or queso
    fresco

1 cup Chicken Broth (page 110)
2 güero or 3 serrano peppers, seeded and cut into
    slivers for garnish

1. Cut the chorizo into small pieces or crumble it and fry over medium-low heat until it is just cooked, about 10 minutes. There should be a little liquid.

2. Cut the tortillas into 1-inch strips and fry them in ½ inch of oil, a few at a time, until they are pale golden and beginning to crisp, about 20 seconds. Remove them as they are done to paper towels to drain. Preheat the oven to 350 degrees.

3. Mix the chorizo with the red chile sauce. Lightly oil a 1½-quart ovenproof casserole. Spread about one-third of the fried tortillas on the bottom of the casserole. Spread about one-third of the chorizo mixture over the tortillas. Sprinkle about one-third of the cheese over the chorizo. Pour about one-third of the chicken stock over this layer.

4. Continue layering the ingredients until the chilaquile dish is complete. Bake for 30 minutes, or until the chilaquiles are heated through and bubbling. Let them stand for about 5 minutes before serving. Garnish them with the pepper slivers and serve hot.

Chilaquiles with Eggs

≣ Serves 2

3 tablespoons corn oil
6 Corn Tortillas (page 92), cut into ½-inch strips
½ small-to-medium-sized onion, halved and sliced
4 extra large eggs
Salt and freshly ground black pepper
⅔ cup Red Chile Sauce (page 85)
¾ cup grated Monterey Jack or Cheddar cheese
Chopped fresh cilantro leaves for garnish
Sour cream for garnish

1. In a large skillet, heat 2 tablespoons of the oil and sauté the tortilla strips for 3 to 4 minutes, turning so they are evenly coated. Set aside on a warm plate. Add the remaining oil to the pan and sauté the onion for 4 minutes.

2. Beat the eggs in a small bowl with a few pinches of salt and grindings of pepper.

3. Return the tortilla strips to the skillet with the onion, place over medium heat, add the sauce, and stir quickly for 1 minute.

4. Add the eggs, stirring and scrambling them with the tortillas and sauce until they are done, 3 to 4 minutes.

5. Turn off the heat, sprinkle the chilaquiles with the grated cheese, and cover for a minute or so. Serve on warm plates, garnished with cilantro. Pass the sour cream at the table.

Chorizo and Potato Burritos with Green Chile Sauce

≡ Serves 8

1 pound red or white waxy potatoes
1 pound Chorizo (page 153)
1 tablespoon corn oil
1 medium-sized onion, diced
Salt and freshly ground black pepper
3 cups Green Chile Sauce (page 83)
8 10-inch Flour Tortillas (page 96)

1. Cut the potatoes into ½-inch dice and cook in lightly salted water until barely done. Drain and set them aside.

2. Cut the chorizo into small pieces and cook over low heat until just done, about 10 minutes. Turn the chorizo to brown it all over. Remove the chorizo from the pan.

3. Add the oil to the pan and soften the onion over low heat for 10 minutes. Add the potatoes and chorizo and heat thoroughly. Season the mixture lightly with salt and pepper and stir in ½ cup of the green chile sauce. Keep warm over very low heat.

4. Heat the remaining sauce and keep warm. Heat a serving dish and keep it warm. Heat the tortillas on an ungreased griddle or in the oven and keep them warm.

5. Roll the burritos one at a time. Center one-eighth of the chorizo mixture, about ½ cup, on the lower third of a tortilla. Fold the bottom

up and the sides in and roll the burrito. Place each burrito in the warm serving dish. Finish rolling the burritos, then spread the remaining sauce over them and serve hot.

Duck Burritos

≣ **Serves 4 to 8**

1 4½- to 5-pound duck (The duck must be thawed if it has been frozen.)
Salt and freshly ground black pepper
8 8-inch Flour Tortillas (page 96)
1 recipe Sesame Chile and Tomato Sauce (page 87)
2 or 3 serrano peppers, stemmed, seeded, and finely diced
½ cup finely grated queso cotijo or ricotta salata
½ cup thinly sliced scallions, with some green

1. Preheat the oven to 400 degrees. Rinse the duck and pat it dry. Trim it of excess fat. Reserve the innards for another use. Season the duck lightly with salt and pepper and prick the fatty deposits well.

2. Roast the duck, breast up, on a rack in a roaster pan in the oven for 30 minutes. Turn the duck and roast another 30 minutes. Turn the duck again and finish the roasting for 30 minutes, or until a meat thermometer inserted in the thick part of the thigh registers 170 degrees. Cool the duck to room temperature.

3. Remove the skin and meat from the bones. Reserve the skin for another use, if desired, and reserve the bones for stock. Shred the meat and put it in a bowl.

4. Warm the tortillas and keep them warm. Heat the sauce over low heat until it is very hot. Pour about 1 cup of sauce over the duck meat and toss them together. Stir the diced serranos into the remaining sauce and keep warm over low heat.

5. Place about one-eighth of the duck in the center of the lower half of a tortilla. Fold the bottom of the tortilla over the meat and fold the sides in. Roll to form the burrito. Place each burrito on a warm platter. Cover them with a slightly damp tea towel and keep them in a warm oven for a short while, until ready to serve.

6. Top the burritos with the remaining sauce and sprinkle them with the cheese and scallions. Serve hot.

Crab Burritos

≡ Serves 3 to 6

1 medium-sized shallot, finely diced
1 tablespoon corn oil
2 or 3 serrano or jalapeño peppers, stemmed, seeded, and finely diced
2 tablespoons chopped fresh coriander leaves
½ cup sour cream
1 pound cooked Dungeness or lump crab meat, picked over
Salt and freshly ground black pepper
6 8-inch Flour Tortillas (page 96)
1 recipe Simple Guacamole (page 66), thinned with about ⅓ cup half-and-half

1. Soften the shallot in the oil over low heat for 5 minutes. Transfer to a mixing bowl and mix in the serranos, coriander, sour cream, and crab meat. Season with salt and pepper.

2. Heat the mixture in a shallow heavy-bottomed pan over very low heat. Meanwhile, heat the tortillas and keep them warm.

3. Place about one-sixth of the crab mixture in the center of the lower half of one of the tortillas. Fold in the sides and roll to form a burrito. Place each burrito on a warm platter. Cover them with a slightly damp tea towel and keep them in a warm oven, for a short while, until ready to serve. Serve hot, garnished with some of the guacamole, and pass the rest in a sauce bowl.

Breakfast Burritos

Makes 6 8-inch burritos

2 tablespoons corn oil
½ cup chopped onion
½ pound potatoes, cooked until just tender and cut
    into ½-inch dice
½ cup roasted, peeled, and chopped green chile
4 extra large eggs, beaten
Salt and freshly ground black pepper to taste
½ cup grated sharp Cheddar cheese
6 8-inch Flour Tortillas (page 96), warmed
1 cup Jalapeño Salsa (page 57), or Roasted Tomato
    Sauce (page 86) with a finely minced serrano added
    to it

1. Heat the corn oil in a large heavy skillet. Add the onion and sauté for 2 minutes over medium heat. Add the potatoes and cook for 2 minutes. Add the chile and cook 2 to 3 minutes more. Stir the vegetables occasionally.

2. Add the eggs and stir them, scraping the sides and bottom of the pan, to cook the eggs evenly until they are set. This will take 3 to 5 minutes. Generously salt and pepper the eggs and remove the pan from the heat. Sprinkle the grated cheese over the eggs and cover the pan with a lid.

3. Divide the egg and vegetable mixture among the tortillas. Roll them into burritos and place them on a warm platter. Cover them with a slightly damp tea towel and keep them in a warm oven for a short while, until ready to serve.

4. The Jalapeño Salsa should be served at cool room temperature. The Roasted Tomato Sauce with serrano should be served hot. Place the burritos on warm plates and pass the sauce of your choice.

Burritos with Beans, Avocados, and Tomatoes

≣ Makes 12 8-inch burritos; serves 6 as a main course

1 recipe Chile Beans (page 193)
12 8-inch Flour Tortillas (page 96)
2 firm ripe avocados, peeled, pitted, and cut into ½-inch dice
1 large ripe tomato, cored and cut into ½-inch dice
About 2½ cups Green Chile Sauce with Sage (page 83)
2 cups grated Cheddar, Lappi, or Monterey Jack cheese

1. Heat the beans completely. Warm the tortillas and keep them wrapped in a warm place. Preheat the oven to 300 degrees. Toss the avocados and tomatoes together.

2. Place ⅓ to ½ cup of beans on a burrito and spread a small handful of the mixed avocados and tomatoes on top of the beans. Fold the sides of the tortilla over the beans and roll the burrito. Place the burrito on a baking sheet and cover with a slightly damp towel. Continue filling and rolling all of the burritos in the same manner. Keep them warm in the oven for a short while until ready to serve.

3. Heat the sauce. Place the burritos on warm serving plates, spoon the sauce over them, and garnish with the cheese. Serve immediately.

Green Corn Tamales

≣ Green corn tamales are a special summer treat. No recipe that we have tried at home of our own devising or other cooks', tastes quite like the tamales which make some restaurants in the Southwest renowned. A certain corn with high starch and sugar content is used just for those green corn tamales. It needs no addition of flour, meal, or grits. Our tamales are still a treat for us when we can't get to La Indita in Tucson, Arizona, where Maria makes some of the best green corn tamales we have eaten.

Makes about 28 2½-to-3-inch tamales

1 dozen large ears of corn
4 cups fresh corn kernels
¼ cup unsalted butter, softened
¼ cup vegetable shortening
¾ cup Monterey Jack cheese
¾ cup mild Cheddar cheese
1 cup Masa Harina
1 teaspoon salt
4 large Anaheim or Sandia chiles, roasted, seeded, peeled,
    and chopped

1. Remove the outer tough and dirty two or three husks from each ear of corn and discard them. Run a sharp knife around the stem end of each ear of corn. Carefully remove the next two or three large husks from the ear. Trim off an inch or two of the pointed ends of the husks. Cut the kernels from four to six ears, enough to have 4 cups. Leave the extra corn covered with small tender inner husks. The corn will keep for a day if these husks are left.

2. Bring a large pot of water to a boil and drop the fresh husks into the water. Remove from the heat and let stand for 30 minutes. Drain and cool the husks just before stuffing them. It will not hurt the husks to stay in the water longer, but they should not dry out or they will split.

3. Mix the butter and vegetable shortening together in a food processor until light and fluffy. Scrape down the sides of the bowl two or three times. Add 3 cups of the corn, the cheese, Masa Harina, and salt and blend until smooth. Stir in the reserved cup of corn kernels and the chiles.

4. To fill the husks, lay a husk out so that the natural curl will cover the filling. Place about 2½ tablespoons of the filling in the center of husk lengthwise. Fold the sides in over the filling and then fold the ends up. Place the tamales in the steamer, folded sides down.

5. Place the steamer in a pot with enough water to come just below the bottom of the steamer. Cover and place over high heat. When the water comes to a boil, lower the heat to a simmer, and steam the tamales for 1½ hours. Check to be sure the steamer does not run out of water. Remove the tamales from the steamer with tongs to a serving platter and serve hot.

Sweet Tamales

≡ Makes about 30 small tamales

About 30 dried or fresh corn husks
2 cups Masa Harina
1 teaspoon baking powder
¼ teaspoon salt
1 teaspoon ground cinnamon
½ cup packed dark or light brown sugar
1 teaspoon lemon zest
¼ cup currants
12 tablespoons unsalted butter, cut into 12 pieces
½ cup water
½ pound Rambo, McIntosh, or other tart apples, peeled,
    cored, and chopped into small dice
¾ cup pecan halves, roughly chopped

1. Bring a large pot of water to a boil and drop the husks into the water. Remove from the heat and let stand for an hour. If using fresh husks, let them soak for 30 minutes. Drain and cool the husks just before stuffing them. It will not hurt the husks to stay in the water longer, but they should not dry out or they will split.

2. Put the Masa Harina, baking powder, salt, cinnamon, brown sugar, lemon zest, and currants in a food processor. Blend the ingredients. Or mix the ingredients together in a mixing bowl. Process or cut the butter into the mixture until it is in pea-sized pieces.

3. Add the water and just blend the mixture together. Add the apples and the pecans and distribute them evenly throughout the mixture.

4. Place 2 tablespoons of the mixture in the center of each husk lengthwise, fold the sides in, and fold the ends up. Place the tamales in a steamer insert with the folded sides down and set aside. Add enough water to a steamer pan to come just below the steamer insert. Bring the water to a boil and add the insert. Lower the heat to a simmer, cover, and cook for 1 hour. Check the water level occasionally so that the pan does not run dry. Serve hot or warm. The tamales can be gently reheated, wrapped in aluminum foil, in a low oven or on a comal for a few minutes.

Chiles Rellenos with Tamale Filling

≡ **Makes 8 rellenos**

½ cup pepitas, ground
3 tablespoons Masa Harina
2 cups grated Monterey Jack, Muenster, or Lappi cheese
6 scallions with about 2 inches of green, thinly sliced
3 serrano peppers, stemmed, seeded, and thinly sliced
1 tablespoon currants
10 tablespoons water
1 teaspoon plus 2 pinches of salt
8 Anaheim or other large green chiles, roasted, peeled,
   and seeded
2 extra large eggs
¼ cup cornmeal
⅓ cup unbleached white flour
Vegetable or corn oil
Red or green table salsa for garnish

1. Combine the pepitas, Masa Harina, cheese, scallions, peppers, currants, 6 tablespoons of the water, and 1 teaspoon of the salt in a bowl and mix well.

2. Pat the filling into long cylindrical shapes and carefully stuff them into the chiles; shape the chiles around the filling.

3. Prepare the batter by beating the eggs in a bowl with the remaining 4 tablespoons of water. Add the cornmeal, flour, and 2 pinches of salt and mix well. Thin the batter, if necessary, to a coating consistency, using another tablespoon or two of water.

4. In a deep skillet, heat ¾ inch of oil to 375 degrees, or until it is very hot but not smoking. Dip the chiles into the batter and add three of them to the skillet.

5. Fry the rellenos for about 1 minute on each side, or until they are golden brown. Drain on paper towels. Serve immediately or keep them in a fairly hot oven for a short time until ready to serve. Serve hot with red or green salsa.

CHAPTER NINE

Meat, Poultry & Fish Dishes

Grazing land was practically all the Southwest provided to the first Anglo settlers, but it was there in abundance. For a long while, cattle was king, though the Navajos and then the Basque settlers kept herding sheep. Pigs didn't need much land, or a specialized diet, and for that were easy to keep, especially if a taste for pork went back in the family. Goats were considered a delicacy in northern New Mexico, probably a legacy from the Spanish settlements. Game, such as deer, rabbit, beaver, and in southern Arizona and Texas the *javelina*, a wild pig, was plentiful in the early days. Edible birds were not common, but the quail was prized.

This abundance of meat gave the region reason to develop two particularly-cherished culinary traditions: the barbecue and dried or jerked meat. The barbecue has influenced the rest of the country beyond just meat and game; the grill has become an American institution, for fish, poultry, and vegetables, too. We've read some interesting theories, none completely convincing, about the etymology of *barbecue*. At this point, it means something different in every state, with most of the western, southwestern, and southern states claiming a barbecue of their own. As the Indians everywhere cooked over open fires or in pits, it would be hard to place the origin of the American barbecue, but the Southwest can claim, we think, not only tradition, but popularization. Drying meat was another technique adopted from the Indians. Climate encouraged its practice; custom and flavor made it a true regional delicacy.

The refinements of twentieth century refrigeration technology brought poultry, and more recently fish, into the homes of Southwesterners. Chicken was always around, of course, but more in the role of a once-a-week dish. When the poultry was from the backyard, chickens and turkeys were raised, ducks and geese rarely because of the dryness and heat of the climate. Fish, commonly trout and bass, came from inland streams and lakes. The coasts of Texas and southern California offered an abundance of seafood for local consumption. Today, because of quick saline chilling and rapid transportation, Dungeness and blue crab, Gulf and Baja shrimp, Pacific rockfish, ling cod, grouper, and many other Gulf and Pacific fish and shellfish, are enjoyed in Phoenix and Santa Fe as well as San Diego and Corpus Christi.

Fish and poultry dishes reflect the Mexican influence, often including fresh chiles, tomatillos, and avocados. Chicken and turkey appear in enchiladas, chile rellenos, tacos, and tostadas. Home-cooked fish is frequently grilled or fried and served with a fresh red or green table salsa. The modern preference for lighter foods has brought shrimp and crab into burritos and enchiladas.

The integration of these foods (and others, such as duck, commercially raised rabbit, and quail) is an ongoing and exciting reformation of the region's cooking. Time-honored barbecues and meat stews will remain because they are so good, but no longer is it a choice between beef or pork for the main course.

Meat

Oven-Dried Beef

≡ Air-dried beef is a real Southwestern specialty. No other part of the United States has low enough humidity and strong enough sunlight to produce the beef. Southwestern Indians and Mexicans from the Sonoran desert regions both had methods to air-dry meat and game. The use of beef shows the Mexican influence; it is called *cecina* in Mexican Spanish. This is pounded into shreds to become *machaca*, which is used for filling tacos, tamales, tostadas, and enchiladas, and with scrambled eggs. Oven-dried beef is quite good in its own right, though not the same as air-dried. It can be substituted for air-dried beef and is much tastier than the commercial beef jerky. Small amounts, about an ounce per person, are all you need of the beef in most dishes.

Makes about 1¼ pounds

1 3-pound rump roast or bottom round
2 large limes
1 teaspoon salt
1 teaspoon cracked black peppercorns

1. Trim the meat of excess fat and outer connective tissue. The meat should be as close to a cube shape as possible.

2. Freeze the meat for 3 hours; then slice it ¼ inch thick with the grain in accordion folds so that the meat stays in one piece. Begin by making one cut almost through the meat. Turn the meat over on the board and cut another slice ¼ inch from the first slice, again cutting almost through the meat. Continue the slicing. You should be able to unfold the meat in one long hinged piece.

3. Hang the meat for 8 to 12 hours over two plastic clothes hangers held apart so that the meat does not touch itself. Place the meat in a cool, dry place.

4. Remove the meat from the hangers and rub it all over with the juice from the limes and the salt and pepper. Line your oven with aluminum foil. Place the meat on a rack in the oven and turn the temperature to 150 degrees. Cut the meat, if necessary, so that it fits on the rack.

5. Turn the oven heat off after 1 hour. Turn the meat and leave it in the oven for another 3 hours. The meat should be dry and leathery. Leave it longer, if necessary, checking every 30 minutes. Cool the beef completely. Store it tightly wrapped in the refrigerator for up to a month.

Chili con Carne

≡ Abjuring the extravagant claims chili con carne fans are prone to make, we will say that we prefer a rounded flavor, the texture of hand-cut meat, and the unctuousness provided by oxtails. If we are serving to hot pepper lovers, we add the chipotles. These impart their characteristic smokiness and a ringing counterpoint to the palate which wins over even some avowed "I don't like it too spicy" people. Chili con carne should be made at least one day in advance.

Serves 12 to 15

5 pounds bottom round or boneless chuck
3 pounds boneless pork shoulder roast
1½ pounds oxtails
About 6 tablespoons lard or corn oil
2 medium-sized onions, diced
5 garlic cloves, chopped
¼ cup all-purpose flour
1 quart beef broth
1 35-ounce can whole tomatoes including juice, finely chopped
¼ cup Chili Powder (page 50)
2 tablespoons chopped fresh oregano leaves, or 1½
    teaspoons dried oregano leaves, crumbled
1 teaspoon salt
3 or 4 chipotle chiles en adobo, diced, optional
Salt and freshly ground black pepper

1. Trim the beef and pork of extra fat and connective tissue. Leave the oxtails as they are. Cut the beef and pork into ½-inch cubes.

2. Heat 2 tablespoons of the lard to almost smoking in a large heavy-bottomed pan. Brown the oxtails and remove them to a large pot. Add about a tablespoon of lard or oil to the pan, let it become hot, and brown a small batch of beef. Remove the meat to the pot with the oxtails. Do not crowd the pan. Continue browning the meat in small batches, adding fat and letting it become hot.

3. When the meat is browned, turn the heat to low and add the onions and garlic to the pan. Cover and soften for 10 minutes.

4. Sprinkle the flour over the onions and garlic and stir well. Cook for another 2 to 3 minutes. Add the onions and garlic to the meat.

5. Pour a little broth into the browning pan and scrape the brown bits loose. Add these pan juices to the meat.

6. Stir the rest of the broth, the tomatoes, chili powder, oregano, 1 teaspoon of salt, and the chipotle chiles, if desired, into the meat and vegetables. Bring the mixture to a simmer and cook for 1 hour, skimming the fat carefully.

7. Taste the chili and season lightly with salt, black pepper, and chili powder. Cover and cook over low heat for 1 hour, skimming the fat, if necessary.

8. Cool the chili to room temperature; then cover and refrigerate overnight or for 2 days. To serve, reheat the chili over low heat to very

hot, adding a little more broth or water to keep a thick, yet liquid, sauce. Make the final seasoning adjustments when you reheat the chili.

Albóndigas

≣ Albóndigas are usually served in broth as a soup course. Occasionally they are sautéed and served with chile sauce as a main course. We give directions for both preparations.

Serves 4 to 6
_____

1½ pounds ground pork
⅓ cup finely chopped onion
2 large garlic cloves, finely minced
1 to 2 chipotles en adobo, finely chopped
½ teaspoon coriander seed, toasted and ground
½ teaspoon whole black peppercorns, toasted and ground
½ teaspoon dried oregano leaves, finely crumbled
1 tablespoon ground mild red chile
½ teaspoon salt
2 tablespoons Masa Harina
1 extra large egg

TO SERVE AS A SOUP COURSE
1½ quarts Chicken Broth (page 110)

TO SERVE AS A MAIN COURSE
2 tablespoons corn oil
1½ cups Green or Red Chile Sauce (pages 83 and 85)
Cooked long-grain white or brown rice

1. Put the pork in a large bowl and break it up. Mix in the onion, garlic, chipotles, coriander, pepper, oregano, ground chile, and salt.
2. Beat the Masa Harina with the egg. Work this into the pork mixture. Form the mixture into 1-inch balls. Poach the albóndigas in simmering chicken broth for 15 minutes, and serve hot for the soup course.
3. Or form 2-inch albóndigas, and fry the balls in the oil over medium-low heat for about 15 minutes, turning them to brown all sides. Serve them hot as a main course with green or red chile sauce and rice.

Carne Asada with Salsa Fria

≡ The steak can also be cooked on a grill; timing might vary. When the meat is cut into strips and grilled or quickly fried, it is called fajitas.

Serves 4

1½ pounds round steak
1 large garlic clove
1 teaspoon corn or vegetable oil
Salt and freshly ground black pepper
Lime wedges for garnish
1 cup Salsa Fria with Sage (page 58)

1. Trim the meat of fat and connective tissue and cut the steak in half as for butterflying it. Pound the meat to about a ⅛-inch thickness. Cut the steak into four pieces. Peel the garlic and cut it in half. Rub the cut clove over the meat.

2. Heat the oil in a large heavy frying pan or griddle over high heat until the pan is very hot. Fry the meat, in batches, if necessary, for about 20 seconds on each side. Season the steak with salt and pepper after it is cooked.

3. Keep the carne asada warm and serve it hot on a platter garnished with lime wedges. Pass the Salsa Fria.

Grilled Pork Tenderloin with Salsa Colorado

≡ **Serves 6**

2 to 2½ pounds pork tenderloin
1 recipe Salsa Colorado (page 58)
Salt
½ cup water
1 tablespoon white wine vinegar

1. Trim the tenderloin of connective tissue and fat. Spoon some sauce in a glass or ceramic dish large enough to hold the meat. Arrange the

tenderloin on top of the sauce. Spoon the rest of the sauce over the meat. Marinate at cool room temperature for 6 to 8 hours, or covered in the refrigerator overnight. Turn the meat three or four times.

2. Prepare a wood or wood-charcoal fire. When the coals are medium hot, remove the tenderloin from the marinade and salt it lightly. Cook the tenderloin 6 inches from the coals for about 30 minutes, turning them several times to brown evenly.

3. While the meat is cooking, thin the marinade with about ½ cup water and 1 tablespoon of white wine vinegar. Put the marinade in an enameled or stainless saucepan over medium-low heat and cook for about 20 minutes.

4. When the meat is done, let it rest for 5 minutes. Slice it ¼ inch thick on the diagonal. Pass the sauce separately at the table.

Chorizo

☰ Chorizo may be used immediately, but the flavor improves if it is tightly covered and held in the refrigerator for 2 days. Chorizo keeps in the refrigerator for a week.

Makes about 3 pounds

3 pounds coarsely ground boneless pork shoulder, with
    about 15 percent fat
4 large garlic cloves, minced
2 tablespoons minced fresh oregano leaves or 1½ tea-
    spoons dried oregano leaves, crumbled
4 teaspoons toasted and ground coriander seed
1½ teaspoons toasted and ground cumin seed
1 teaspoon salt
1 large mulato chile, seeded, toasted, and ground
2 guajillo chiles, seeded, toasted, and ground
3 tablespoons ground hot red chile
3 tablespoons rice wine vinegar, or 1½ tablespoons
    each white wine vinegar and water

1. Put the pork in a large bowl and break it up. Sprinkle the garlic, oregano, coriander, cumin, and salt over the meat. Work the seasonings well into the meat.

2. Sprinkle the ground chiles over the meat and work them into it. Add the vinegar and work it into the sausage. The chorizo may be stuffed into casings, formed into patties, or used as bulk sausage.

Grilled Leg of Lamb
with Sandia Jelly

Serves 4 to 6

3-pound shank-end leg of lamb, boned
1 cup dry white wine
6 to 8 fresh parsley sprigs
6 to 8 fresh coriander sprigs
3 garlic cloves, peeled and thinly sliced
1 teaspoon cumin seed, toasted and crushed
1 teaspoon whole black peppercorns, toasted and crushed
Salt and freshly ground black pepper
½ cup Sandia Jelly (page 55), or other hot red pepper
    jelly

1. Trim the lamb of extra fat and fell and butterfly it. Pour the wine in a dish just large enough to hold the lamb. Bruise the parsley and coriander sprigs and add them to the dish. Add the garlic, cumin, and peppercorns. Add the lamb to the dish and distribute the marinade evenly over and under it. Cover the lamb and marinate it for 8 hours at cool room temperature or 24 hours in the refrigerator. Turn the lamb three or four times.

2. Remove the lamb from the refrigerator 1 or 2 hours before grilling it. Prepare a medium-hot wood-charcoal fire and remove the lamb from the marinade. Season the lamb lightly with salt and grill it for 15 to 20 minutes, turning it to brown evenly. The lamb should be rare to medium-rare.

3. Make the sauce while the lamb is cooking. Pour the marinade into a skillet and add the jelly. Simmer for 10 minutes; then strain the sauce. Season with salt and pepper and keep the sauce warm.

4. Let the lamb rest for a few minutes before carving it into diagonal slices about ⅜ inch thick. Arrange the meat on a warm serving dish and pour the sauce over it. Serve hot.

Lamb Mixed Grill

☰ Southwestern grilled meat is often served well done. We like this lamb a little on the rare side. The tripe tastes best when it is quite done, crispy and a bit black on the edges.

Serves 6

3 pounds breast of lamb
1 pound lamb heart
½ pound lamb tripe
2 quarts water
2 teaspoons salt
¾ cup olive oil
¾ cup Hot Pepper Vinegar (page 52)
1 tablespoon ground medium-hot red chile
2 teaspoons whole black peppercorns, crushed
15 juniper berries, crushed
3 garlic cloves, crushed and roughly chopped
2 large fresh sage sprigs, or 1 teaspoon dried sage leaves, crumbled
5 or 6 large fresh parsley sprigs
Salt

1. Trim the lamb breast of extra fat and fell. Divide the breast every 2 or 3 rib sections. Cut the meat back from the bone about 2 inches so that the marinade will penetrate.

2. Trim the hearts of fat and cut them lengthwise into ⅜-inch slices.

3. Rinse the lamb tripe. Poach it in 2 quarts of water with 2 teaspoons of salt for 30 minutes. Drain and cut into it strips about 1 inch wide.

4. Mix the oil, vinegar, ground chile, peppercorns, juniper berries, and garlic in a dish just large enough to hold the meat in one layer. Bruise the fresh sage and parsley sprigs and add them to the marinade. Add the meat to the marinade and coat it well.

5. Cover and marinate it in the refrigerator for 24 to 48 hours, turning the meat two to four times. Remove the meat from the refrigerator 1 or 2 hours before cooking.

6. Cook the lamb over a large, medium-hot, wood-charcoal fire. The breasts will take 30 to 35 minutes for medium-rare. The tripe will be done in 15 to 20 minutes. The heart will be cooked in 8 to 10 minutes. Turn the meat frequently to brown it evenly, and baste it often with the marinade. Season the meat lightly with salt before serving.

Lamb Picadillo

≡ There are many recipes for picadillo, undoubtedly because it is so versatile. It excels as a filling for tacos, tostadas, gorditas, sopaipillas, it is sometimes served with tortillas, and it is good with rice. We have not seen a picadillo with lamb; it seemed appropriate to us because of the complex spicing which must have come through Mexico from Moorish Spain. In fact, we now think that lamb makes a better picadillo than beef, the usual meat; it is especially good with brown rice. We sometimes use it as a ravioli filling and poach the ravioli gently in some nice chicken broth.

Makes about 1½ quarts, enough for
10 to 12 tacos, 6 to 8 tostadas; serves 6 to 8

½ medium-sized onion, finely diced
2 garlic cloves, finely diced
1 tablespoon olive or corn oil
1½ pounds ground lamb
1 teaspoon toasted and ground coriander seed
1 teaspoon toasted and ground cumin
1 teaspoon dried oregano leaves, crumbled
⅛ teaspoon ground cinnamon
⅛ teaspoon ground cloves
1 tablespoon ground mild red chile
Salt and freshly ground black pepper
About ½ cup chicken broth or water
½ pound ripe tomatoes, peeled, seeded, and diced, or
    7 ounces canned whole tomatoes, seeded and diced
⅓ cup sliced green olives
2 tablespoons currants, soaked and drained

1. Soften the onion and garlic in the oil for about 10 minutes. Raise the heat and add the lamb. Brown it well and drain off the fat.

2. Add the coriander, cumin, oregano, cinnamon, cloves, and ground chile. Season lightly with salt and pepper. Stir the mixture well and add ½ cup broth.

3. Add the tomatoes, olives, and currants. Bring the picadillo to a simmer and cook, uncovered, for 30 minutes. Add a tablespoon or two of broth if the picadillo sticks to the pan. The mixture should be moist but not juicy when it is done. Adjust the seasoning and serve hot.

Chile Verde

≡ Opinions about chile verde in New Mexico are as strongly held as those about chile con carne in Texas. This recipe is adapted from the Taos Inn's prize-winning chile verde. It is more complex than versions which call for just one kind of meat, green chiles, and salt; we think the flavor benefits from using lamb, pork, and beef. All ground meat, or all cubed meat could be used, but the texture would not be as interesting.

Serves 8 to 12

1 pound coarsely ground lamb
1 pound coarsely ground pork
6 tablespoons corn or olive oil
1 pound rare roast beef, trimmed and cut into ½-inch dice
1 large onion, diced
3 garlic cloves, finely chopped
¼ cup all-purpose flour
5 cups Chicken Broth (page 110)
¼ cup chopped fresh parsley leaves
3 tablespoons chopped fresh cilantro leaves
2 teaspoons toasted and ground cumin seed
1 teaspoon dried oregano leaves, crumbled
Salt and freshly ground black pepper
1 cup light Mexican beer
2 to 2¼ pounds hot green chiles, New Mexico 6 or
    Sandia, roasted, peeled, and diced
1 large ripe tomato, peeled, seeded, and diced, optional

1. Brown the ground lamb and pork in 3 tablespoons of the oil in one layer. Remove the browned meat to a platter and toss with the roast beef. Add the remaining oil to the pan and soften the onion and garlic over low heat for 10 minutes. Add the meat to the pan and sprinkle the flour over it. Stir and cook the mixture for 5 minutes over medium heat.
2. Add 4 cups of the broth to the pan along with the parsley, cilantro, cumin, and oregano. Season with salt and pepper. Cook for 1 hour over low heat.
3. Add the remaining broth, beer, and chiles. Cook for 30 minutes. Season with salt and pepper. If you are using the tomato, add it during the last 10 minutes of cooking. Serve hot with corn or flour tortillas.

Veal Tongue with Mole Sauce

Moles are another Mexican import and they do not confine themselves to the Southwest, but reach as far north as the San Francisco Bay. Americans, even those with a Mexican heritage, are less likely to prepare the chocolate moles. The tongue is good with the red mole, and with the addition of chocolate.

Serves 4 to 6

TONGUE

    2 pounds veal tongue
    1 small carrot, peeled
    3 garlic cloves, peeled
    3 whole cloves
    1 small onion, peeled and halved
    1 1-inch piece cinnamon stick
    1 teaspoon whole black peppercorns
    1 large bay leaf, broken
    1 12-ounce bottle dark beer, preferably Mexican
    1 teaspoon salt

MOLE SAUCE

    1 cup Red Chile Sauce (page 85)
    1 cup of the poaching liquid from the tongue
    1 teaspoon toasted and ground coriander seed
    ½ teaspoon toasted and ground cumin seed
    Salt and freshly ground black pepper
    ½ ounce Mexican chocolate, optional

1. Put the tongue in a pot and barely cover it with water. Add the carrot and garlic. Stick the cloves into the onion and add it to the pot. Make a bouquet garni bag for the cinnamon, peppercorns, and bay leaf and add it to the pot.

2. Cover the pot, bring it to a boil, and lower the heat to a simmer. Cook the veal for about an hour, skimming occasionally, and turning the tongue once.

3. Remove the tongue and cool it. When it is just cool enough to handle, skin it and return it to the pot. Add the beer and salt. Bring the liquid to a simmer and cook the tongue for 30 minutes, turning frequently to prevent sticking. Meanwhile prepare the sauce. Reserve 1 cup of the poaching liquid.

4. Put the chile sauce, reserved poaching liquid, coriander, and cumin in a small saucepan and reduce the sauce over high heat by half, about 10 minutes. Remove from the heat and season with salt and pepper; stir in the chocolate, if desired.

5. Slice the tongue on a slight diagonal about ¼ inch thick. Pour some of the hot sauce in a warm serving platter and arrange the tongue on it. Drizzle a little sauce over the tongue and serve the remaining sauce at the table.

Rabbit Adovada

≡ *Adovada* refers to meat braised in a rather thick red chile sauce. Pork chops and round steaks are commonly prepared this way. Rabbit is especially delicious.

Serves 4

6 large dried New Mexico chiles
8 dried red serranos, or other dried hot red peppers
1 cup boiling water
1 large rabbit (about 4 pounds)
3 garlic cloves
1 teaspoon dried oregano leaves, crumbled
½ teaspoon toasted and ground cumin seed
½ teaspoon salt
3 tablespoons rice wine vinegar
About 1 cup Chicken Broth (page 110)

1. Break up the chiles, remove the stems, and shake loose most of the seeds. Soak the chiles in the water for 30 minutes.

2. Rinse the rabbit and pat it dry. Joint it and reserve the innards for another use.

3. Chop the garlic and add it to the chiles along with the oregano, cumin, salt, and vinegar. Blend the mixture in a blender to a medium-smooth purée in which there are still bits of chile.

4. Place the rabbit in a dish just large enough to hold it and pour the chile mixture over it. Coat the rabbit well, cover, and refrigerate for 24 hours, turning the meat two or three times. Preheat the oven to 300 degrees.

5. Put the rabbit and marinade in an ovenproof casserole and cover with a lid or aluminum foil. Bake for 1 hour.

6. Remove the cover and turn the meat. Bake the rabbit for 1 to 1½ hours longer, adding chicken broth as necessary to keep the sauce a thick but not dry consistency. Turn the meat every 30 minutes. The rabbit should be very tender. Serve hot, accompanied by Ranch Bread or warm corn or flour tortillas.

Poultry

Chicken with Avocado and Tomatillo Sauce

The sauce is a version of green mole. Mexican cooking has many green moles, and a few have made their way into the Southwest. The dish has an appealing rustic look and a well-balanced richness.

Serves 4 to 6

1 3½- to 4-pound chicken
Salt and freshly ground black pepper
2 tablespoons corn oil
½ cup finely diced onion
1 garlic clove, finely chopped
1 serrano or jalapeño pepper, stemmed, seeded, and
    finely diced
1 large ripe Hass avocado
½ pound tomatillos, roasted and husked
½ cup pepitas, toasted and finely ground
1 cup Chicken Broth (page 110)
1 tablespoon chopped fresh oregano leaves, or 1 tea-
    spoon dried oregano leaves, crumbled
5 or 6 large celery leaves, finely chopped

1. Joint the chicken. Reserve the innards, backbone, and wing tips for another use. Sprinkle the chicken lightly with salt and pepper.

2. Brown the chicken in the corn oil over medium-high heat. Remove

the chicken from the pan and keep it warm. Drain all but 2 tablespoons of fat from the pan.

3. Soften the onion, garlic, and serrano in the fat, covered, over medium-low heat for about 10 minutes.

4. Meanwhile purée the avocado with the tomatillos. Stir in the pepitas, broth, oregano, and celery. Add the mixture to the pan and stir well. Season the sauce.

5. Add the chicken thighs, drumsticks, and wings to the pan, along with any collected juices. Cook, covered, over medium-low heat for about 10 minutes. Add the breasts and finish the cooking with the pan covered for about 15 minutes, or until the chicken is done. Serve hot.

Grilled Chicken in Yucatán-Style Marinade

≣ **Serves 4 to 6**

1 tablespoon achiote seed
½ cup water
1 4- to 5-pound chicken
1 small pink grapefruit
2 medium-sized oranges
1 large lime
2 garlic cloves
Salt and freshly ground black pepper

1. Simmer the achiote seed in ½ cup water for 10 minutes and let them soak for 3 to 4 hours or overnight. Grind them in a spice grinder or crush them and then grind them with the soaking water in a blender.

2. Joint the chicken. Reserve the back, wing tips, and innards for another use. Squeeze the fruit and strain the juice; there should be about 1½ cups of juice.

3. Peel and smash the garlic. Stir the garlic and achiote with its soaking liquid into the juice and pour it into a shallow dish just large enough to hold the chicken.

4. Cover the dish with plastic wrap and marinate the chicken in the refrigerator for 24 hours. Turn the chicken once during the marinating.

5. Remove the chicken from the refrigerator 2 to 3 hours before

grilling. Prepare a wood or wood-charcoal fire and put the chicken on the grill when the fire is medium-hot. Turn the chicken two or three times until it is done, 15 to 20 minutes. Serve hot.

Chicken Sonoran-Style

≡ Serves 4 to 6

¼ pound bacon
1 4- to 5-pound chicken
Salt and freshly ground black pepper
1 small onion, diced
2 or 3 large garlic cloves, finely diced
2 pounds ripe tomatoes, peeled, seeded, and diced, or
    1 28-ounce can whole plum tomatoes, seeded and
    chopped
½ cup sliced pitted green olives
3 fresh güero or jalapeño peppers, stemmed, seeded,
    and finely diced
¼ cup chopped fresh coriander leaves

1. Cut the bacon into ½-inch pieces. Fry the bacon over low heat until the fat is rendered and the bacon is crisp. Joint the chicken, reserving the innards for another use.

2. Remove the bacon to a paper towel to drain. Pour off all but about 2 tablespoons of the fat. Sprinkle the chicken pieces lightly with salt and pepper. Brown the chicken over medium-high heat for about 10 minutes. Remove the chicken from the pan and keep it warm. Pour off all but about 2 tablespoons of the fat.

3. Soften the onion and garlic in the fat over low heat for about 10 minutes. Add the tomatoes and the olives to the pan. Cook for 10 minutes over medium heat. Add the chicken thighs, drumsticks, and wings to the pan, along with any collected juices. Cook, covered, over medium-low heat for about 10 minutes, turning the chicken once. Add the breasts to the pan and cook for about 10 minutes.

4. Add the peppers, the bacon, and half of the coriander. Cook for 5 minutes. Remove to a warm serving platter and garnish with the remaining coriander. Serve hot.

Chicken in Red Chile Sauce with Goat Cheese

≡ Serves 4 to 6

2 pasilla chiles
3 dried chipotle chiles
1 cup very hot Chicken Broth (page 110), or very hot water
1 3½- to 4-pound chicken, roasted or poached
Salt
1 large onion, finely diced
3 garlic cloves, finely chopped
1 medium-sized red bell pepper, finely diced
1 or 2 jalapeño peppers, stemmed, seeded, and finely diced
4 to 5 ounces mild California or French goat cheese
8 to 12 warm Corn or Flour Tortillas (pages 92 and
    96), for serving

1. Stem and seed the pasilla and chipotle chiles and tear or cut them into pieces. Soak the chiles in the hot broth for 30 minutes.

2. Remove the chicken meat and skin from the bones. Shred the meat and season it with salt.

3. Pour the soaked chiles and their liquor into a blender and add the onion, garlic, and red pepper. Blend to a purée in which there are still small bits of chile and vegetables. Simmer the sauce for 15 minutes and season it with salt. Stir in the jalapeños. Preheat the oven to 375 degrees.

4. Spread about 1 cup of sauce in an ovenproof casserole. Layer the chicken over the sauce. Pour the remaining sauce over the chicken. Crumble the goat cheese over the sauce.

5. Bake for 20 to 25 minutes, or until the sauce is bubbling. Serve hot with warm tortillas.

Spiced Sautéed Chicken Breasts

≡ This dish is simple, quick to prepare, and tasty. It is especially good with *rajas*, mixed green and red, mild and hot chile strips sautéed in a little olive oil and sprinkled with hot pepper vinegar.

Serves 4

4 chicken breast halves, skinned and boned
Salt and freshly ground black pepper
2 extra large eggs
2 garlic cloves, finely minced
1½ teaspoons toasted and ground cumin
1½ teaspons dried oregano leaves, crumbled
1½ teaspoons toasted and ground coriander seed
¼ teaspoon ground cloves
¼ teaspoon ground cayenne
½ cup all-purpose flour
1½ cups fine dry bread crumbs
4 tablespoons olive oil

1. Trim the chicken of connective tissue. Pound it between wax paper to an even thickness, about ⅜ inch. Season the chicken lightly with salt and pepper.

2. Beat the eggs in a flat bowl large enough to hold a chicken breast. Beat the garlic, cumin, oregano, coriander, cloves, and cayenne into the eggs.

3. Dredge the chicken breasts in the flour, patting any excess flour loose.

4. Coat the chicken breasts, one at a time, in the egg mixture. Pat the bread crumbs onto the breasts, being careful to cover them completely. Place the chicken breasts on wax paper and chill them for 30 minutes.

5. Heat the oil until very hot but not smoking over medium-high heat. Sauté the chicken until it is golden brown, 3 to 4 minutes. Turn the chicken and sauté until it is golden brown on the other side. Serve hot.

Chicken Breasts in Sour Cream and Green Chile Sauce

Serves 4

4 chicken breasts, skinned and boned
2 tablespoons corn oil
Salt and freshly ground black pepper

1 small onion, diced
2 large garlic cloves, minced
1 cup chicken or duck stock
½ cup diced roasted and peeled green chiles
3 tablespoons chopped fresh coriander leaves
3 tablespoons chopped fresh parsley leaves
2 teaspoons coriander seed, toasted and ground
½ cup sour cream

1. Trim the chicken of connective tissue. Pound it between wax paper to an even thickness, about ⅜ inch. Sauté the breasts in 1 tablespoon of the oil over medium-high heat until they are just golden and firm, about 1 minute on each side. Season lightly with salt and remove them to a platter and keep them warm.

2. Add the other tablespoon of oil to the pan and soften the onion and garlic over medium heat. After about 10 minutes, add the stock and reduce over high heat for 2 to 3 minutes.

3. Lower the heat to medium and stir in the chiles, herbs, and ground coriander. Cook for 5 minutes and season with salt and pepper. Add the chicken breasts and their juices and cook for 3 to 4 minutes.

4. Remove the chicken to a warm serving platter and stir the sour cream into the sauce. Heat the sauce just through and pour it over the chicken. Serve hot.

Chiles en Nogada

≡ The pomegranates give this dish special flavor and color, but it makes good eating even without them. Poblanos are the best chiles, but other relleno peppers can be used.

Serves 6 to 8

CHILES AND FILLING
6 large poblano chiles, or 8 Anaheim or Sandia chiles,
    roasted and peeled
¼ cup chopped onion
1 garlic clove, finely chopped
2 tablespoons olive oil
2 cups minced cooked turkey

¼ cup green olives, finely chopped
2 teaspoons capers, rinsed and drained
½ cup chicken broth
¼ teaspoon ground cinnamon
⅛ teaspoon ground cloves
¼ cup pomegranate seeds, or about 1 teaspoon lemon
    juice
1 teaspoon sugar
Salt and freshly ground black pepper

SAUCE
½ cup blanched and lightly toasted almonds
½ cup chicken broth
½ cup heavy (whipping) cream
Salt and freshly ground white pepper
Chopped fresh parsley leaves for garnish
Pomegranate seeds for garnish, optional

1. Seed the chiles carefully, leaving the stems intact, if possible. Slit the chiles so that they can be stuffed.

2. Soften the onion and garlic in the oil over low heat for about 10 minutes. Add the turkey, olives, and capers. Add the broth, cinnamon, cloves, pomegranate seeds, and sugar. Season lightly with salt and pepper.

3. Cook the mixture over medium-low heat for about 10 minutes, or until the juices are almost evaporated, but the meat is still moist. Taste for seasoning and add more salt, pepper, spices, or lemon juice.

4. Stuff the chiles with the filling and arrange them on an ovenproof serving platter. Cover them with aluminum foil and keep them warm in a 250-degree oven while you make the sauce.

5. Put the almonds and broth in a blender and purée them. Pour the mixture into a saucepan and add the cream. Season the mixture well with salt and white pepper and cook over low heat for 10 minutes. Pour the sauce over the chiles and garnish the dish with the parsley and the pomegranate seeds, if available. Serve hot.

Duck Stuffed with Chorizo
with Red Wine and
Red Chile Sauce

≡ Red wine and chiles work very well together in this impressive dinner party main course. We use the same wine in the sauce, usually a middle-priced California Cabernet Sauvignon, that we serve with the duck. To make the duck stock for this recipe, crack the bones and place them, along with the wing tips, in a roasting pan. Roast them at 400 degrees for 1 hour. Transfer the bones to a stock pot and deglaze the roasting pan with 1 cup of water. Add the pan juices to the stock pot, along with the giblet and neck. Add 1 quart of water, 5 fresh parsley sprigs, and 2 peeled garlic cloves to the stock pot. Simmer and skim the stock for 1 hour. Strain the stock and reduce it to 1 cup.

Serves 6

1 5-pound duck (The duck must be thawed if it has
  been frozen.)
Salt and pepper
1½ pounds Chorizo (page 153)
1 cup duck stock
1 cup dry red wine
¾ cup Red Chile Sauce (page 85)
1 lime, cut into slices or wedges, for garnish

1. Remove extra fat from the duck and remove the wing tips. Cut the skin along the backbone and bone the duck except for the wings and drumsticks. Reserve the fat and skin for another use. Use the bones and wing tips to make the stock.

2. Preheat the oven to 375 degrees. Sprinkle the duck meat lightly with salt and pepper. Patch the skin if necessary with a needle and kitchen thread or unwaxed dental floss.

3. Spread the chorizo over the meat and gather the skin tightly. Sew or skewer the duck tightly. Pierce the skin well where there are fatty deposits.

4. Place the duck, breast up, on a rack in a deep roasting pan. Roast for 20 minutes, turn the duck and roast for 25 minutes. Turn the duck breast up and roast for about 35 minutes. Prick the skin again after the duck has been turned.

5. Make the sauce while the duck is roasting. Add the duck stock and wine to a saucepan and reduce by about half over medium-high heat. Add the red chile sauce and reduce by about one-third, about 20 minutes. Season with salt.

6. Let the duck rest for 5 minutes or so before removing the thread or skewers and carving and slicing. Arrange on a warm serving platter and drizzle some sauce over the slices. Garnish the platter with lime slices or wedges. Serve hot and pass the sauce separately.

Grilled Quail with Kumquat Jalapeño Marmalade

☰ Serves 6

½ cup Kumquat Jalapeño Marmalade (page 55)
2 cups strong red wine
2 jalapeño peppers, stemmed and sliced
2 garlic cloves, sliced
1 small onion, sliced
6 to 8 fresh oregano sprigs, bruised
2 bay leaves, broken
1 teaspoon whole black peppercorns, cracked
12 quail, split along the backbone
Salt and freshly ground black pepper

1. Melt the marmalade with the wine over very low heat for 3 to 4 minutes. Pour the mixture into a dish just large enough to hold the quail. Stir in the jalapeños, garlic, onion, oregano, bay leaves, and peppercorns. Toss the quail in the marinade.

2. Cover and marinate for 24 hours in the refrigerator. Turn the quail three or four times. Remove the quail from the refrigerator 1 to 2 hours before grilling. Season the quail lightly with salt and pepper.

3. Grill over a medium-hot wood or wood-charcoal fire for 12 to 16 minutes, turning the quail and basting them. The quail will be juicy and rare. Serve hot.

Fish

Cod Veracruz-Style

≣ This is really a Southwestern version of a Veracruz fish preparation. Though far removed from its nameplace, it is good nonetheless. Use any kind of chiles: green or red, hot or mild.

Serves 4 or 5

½ cup chopped onion
½ cup chopped celery
1 bay leaf
2 tablespoons olive oil
⅓ cup sliced pimiento-stuffed olives
½ cup dry white wine
1 medium-sized ripe tomato, peeled, seeded, and diced
½ cup diced roasted and peeled chiles
1 tablespoon chopped fresh oregano leaves, or 1 teaspoon dried oregano leaves
Salt and freshly ground black pepper
2 pounds cod fillets

1. Sauté the chopped onion and celery with the bay leaf in the oil over medium heat for 10 minutes. Add the olives and wine, cover, and simmer for 15 minutes. Add the tomato, chiles, and oregano.

2. Season the fish lightly with salt and pepper. Put it into the pan with the sauce, cover, and cook until just done, 5 to 10 minutes. Serve hot, napped with the sauce.

Marinated Grilled Mackerel

≣ **Serves 4**

2 whole mackerel, about 1½ pounds each, or 4 mackerel, about ¾ pound each
¼ cup fresh lime juice

¼ cup tequila
¼ cup olive oil
1 teaspoon toasted and ground cumin seed
1 teaspoon toasted and ground coriander seed
⅛ teaspoon ground cloves
2 garlic cloves, sliced
6 fresh oregano sprigs
Salt and freshly ground black pepper

1. Have the fishmonger gut the mackerel. At home, rinse and clean them very well. Slash each fish three times on both sides so that the marinade penetrates.

2. Mix together the lime juice, tequila, olive oil, cumin, coriander, cloves, and garlic. Bruise the oregano.

3. Place the fish in a dish just large enough to hold them. Pour the marinade over them and spoon some inside each cavity. Place an oregano sprig in each cavity and place the rest in the dish. Cover and marinate in the refrigerator for 6 to 8 hours. Turn the fish two or three times.

4. Remove the mackerel from the refrigerator 1 hour before cooking. Season the fish lightly with salt and pepper. Grill over a medium-hot wood or wood-charcoal fire until they are just done to the bone. Turn once and baste with the marinade three or four times. Serve hot.

Salmon and Chiles Steamed in Corn Husks with Tomatillo Butter

≡ This elegant dish is perfect served as the fish course of an important dinner. The perfume, when the "tamales" are opened, is as wonderful as that of fish cooked in parchment, with the extra nuance of the corn husks. The preparations are simple but time-consuming and are best done the morning (or early afternoon if you have help) of the dinner.

Serves 4 to 6

CORN HUSKS AND TOMATILLO BUTTER
1 dozen large ears of fresh corn, or 36 to 40 dried corn husks
¼ pound tomatillos, roasted and husked
¼ pound unsalted butter, softened
Salt and freshly ground white pepper

SALMON AND CHILES

1½ pounds salmon fillets, skinned
6 to 8 fresh red and green chiles, such as red hot
cherry, hot Hungarian wax, red or green cayenne,
jalapeño, or serrano, stemmed, seeded, and cut
lengthwise into slivers
3 garlic cloves, thinly sliced
1 tablespoon olive oil
Salt and freshly ground white pepper

1. Remove the outer tough and dirty two or three husks from each ear of corn and discard them. Save the long green leafy tops of the husks. Run a sharp knife around the stem end of each ear of corn. Carefully remove the next two or three large husks from the ear. Trim off an inch or two of the pointed ends of the husks. Leave the corn covered with the small tender inner husks. The corn will keep for a day if these husks are left.

2. Bring a large pot of water to a boil and drop the fresh husks and leafy green tops into the water. Remove from the heat and let stand for 30 minutes. If using dried husks, let them soak for an hour or so. Drain and cool the husks just before stuffing them. It will not hurt the husks to stay in the water longer, but they should not dry out or they will split.

3. Make a rough purée of the tomatillos in a mortar and pestle, molcajete, or food processor. Drain the purée in a sieve for 10 minutes. Blend the tomatillos with the butter and season well with salt and white pepper.

4. Remove the bones from the salmon and cut it crosswise at a 45-degree angle about 1½ inches wide. There should be 12 to 14 pieces of salmon of roughly the same size.

5. Sauté the chiles and garlic in the oil over medium heat until they just begin to soften, 3 to 4 minutes. Season the vegetables lightly with salt and pepper and remove them from the heat.

6. Season the fish lightly with salt and pepper and assemble the ingredients to make the corn husk packages. Divide the chiles and garlic so that there are enough portions for each piece of salmon.

7. Stand the husks upright in a colander and drain them for a few minutes. Choose the largest·husks in order to enclose the salmon in one husk if possible. Cut the longest pieces of leafy green top into ¼-inch strips.

8. Place a piece of salmon in the center of a husk or two husks fitted together if the husks are short and the fish is long. The natural curl of

the husks should cover the fish. Spread the salmon with about 1 teaspoon of tomatillo butter. Scatter a portion of chiles and garlic over the salmon.

9. Fold the short sides of the husk over the salmon. Fold the ends of the husk over the short sides. Ideally they will overlap and you will be able to tie a strip of leafy green top around the width of the tamale. The leafy green ribbons are for presentation; the tamales will stay folded whether they are tied or not.

10. Finish stuffing and folding the tamales. They can be kept covered and refrigerated for a few hours. Remove them from the refrigerator 30 minutes before cooking them.

11. To cook the tamales, bring about 1½ inches of water to a boil in a pan which will hold a steamer. Place the tamales upright in the steamer and place it in the pan. Cover and steam the tamales for 3 minutes. The fish cooks very quickly and continues to cook a bit in its packages after it is removed from the heat. Arrange the tamales on a warm platter and serve immediately. Pass the remaining tomatillo butter at the table.

Sea Bass with Garlic

Serves 3 to 4

1½ pounds sea bass fillets, skinned
Salt and freshly ground black pepper
½ cup all-purpose flour
1½ tablespoons unsalted butter
1½ tablespoons olive oil
2 tablespoons finely chopped very fresh garlic
Lime wedges for garnish

1. Sprinkle the fish lightly with salt and pepper. Dredge the fish in the flour, patting the excess flour loose.

2. Heat the butter and oil in a large skillet over medium-high heat. When the fat is hot, put the fish in the pan, skin side down, and cook for 3 to 4 minutes, or until that side is pale golden. Turn the fish and cook for another 3 to 4 minutes, until the fish is done.

3. Remove the fish to a serving platter and keep it warm. Stir the garlic into the pan over medium heat and cook, stirring continually, until the garlic is pale golden, about 2 minutes. Spoon the garlic and pan juices over the fish and garnish the platter with lime wedges. Serve hot.

Smothered Sea Bass with Shrimp

≡ Serves 4

½ pound medium-sized (26 to 30 count) shrimp
2 tablespoons olive oil
½ cup finely diced onion
2 garlic cloves, finely diced
2 or 3 fresh red and green hot peppers, such as cayenne,
    serrano, red hot cherry, or jalapeño, stemmed,
    seeded, and finely diced
1 large ripe tomato, peeled, seeded, and finely diced
1 tablespoon chopped fresh oregano leaves, or ½ tea-
    spoon dried oregano leaves, crumbled
½ cup dry white wine
Salt and freshly ground black pepper
1½ to 2 pounds sea bass fillets, skinned (Grouper may
    be substituted.)

1. Sauté the shrimp in their shells in the oil over medium heat until they are just done, about 2 minutes. Cool, shell, and devein the shrimp. Chop some shrimp and reserve some for garnish.

2. Sauté the onion and garlic in the shrimp oil over moderate heat for 5 minutes. Add the peppers, tomato, oregano, and white wine. Cook over medium-high heat until the wine is reduced by half.

3. Season the fish lightly with salt and pepper. Put the fillets in the pan with the sauce. Cover and cook over medium-low heat for 2 to 3 minutes. Turn the fillets and cover them with the chopped and garnish shrimp. Cover the pan and cook until just done, about 3 minutes. Serve hot.

Shrimp and Scallops with Red Chile Cream Sauce

≡ Serves 6

1½ pounds medium-sized (26 to 30 count) shrimp
1 pound sea scallops
1 New Mexico or California dried red chile

1½ cups very hot water
1 small fresh red hot pepper, red hot cherry, or Mexico
    Improved
¼ cup diced red bell pepper
½ cup diced onion
1 garlic clove, finely diced
1½ teaspoons toasted and ground coriander seed
Salt
½ cup heavy (whipping) cream
3 tablespoons olive or corn oil
½ lime
Coriander leaves and blossoms for garnish

1. Shell and devein the shrimp. Rinse and remove the muscles from the scallops. Cut the scallops into even-sized pieces.

2. Stem, seed, and break the dried chile into pieces. Pour the hot water over it in a small bowl and soak for 30 minutes. Stem, seed, and dice the fresh hot red pepper.

3. Put the chile and soaking liquid in a saucepan with the hot pepper, sweet pepper, onion, garlic, and coriander. Simmer the mixture for 20 minutes.

4. Purée the sauce in a blender until it is quite smooth. Season with salt. Put the sauce and cream in a saucepan and reduce it by half over medium-high heat. Season the sauce and keep it warm until ready to serve.

5. Pat the shrimp and scallops very dry. Heat the oil over medium-high heat. Add the shrimp and raise the heat to high. Sauté for 1½ to 2 minutes. Keep the shrimp moving in the pan. Add the scallops and sauté another 1 to 2 minutes. Remove the shrimp and scallops and season them lightly with salt and lime juice. Keep them warm and reduce the pan juices to 2 or 3 tablespoons.

6. Meanwhile, heat the chile sauce over high heat. Add the reduced pan juices to the sauce and heat for a minute or so. Pour the sauce onto a warm serving platter and place the shrimp and scallops on it. Spoon a little sauce over the top of the dish and garnish it with the coriander leaves and blossoms. Serve immediately with warm flour tortillas or bread.

CHAPTER TEN

Egg & Pasta Dishes

There are many egg dishes in Southwestern cooking, and we'll talk of them later, but pasta? Here is cross-cultural cooking in what we think is one of its best manifestations. Pasta dough itself can incorporate any number of vegetables or herbs as it does in Italian cooking, but it takes best to those with definite flavors and colors such as chiles. In both red and green chile pasta, the flavors come through very well in the finished dishes, with the green being more subtle. As the Italians, Chinese, and Thai have proved, even plain egg or flour dough is a match for the most fiery sauces as well as the most delicate.

The events of the last two decades in American cooking, the search for lighter foods, fresh foods, quick dishes which are not made from "convenience" foods, and interest in other cooking traditions, have affected the regional cooks here. Naturally, it has occurred to them to use the ingredients available to give pasta a Southwestern flavor. As pasta lovers, we think of it as the classic impromptu food: especially well-suited to pairing with fresh vegetables and leftovers, easy to make and to buy fresh or dried. It now seems as much at home in the Southwest as fresh seafood, another recent arrival.

Aside from the recipes in this chapter, we think fettuccine noodles are good with *rajas* (assorted roasted and peeled chile strips) and a little goat cheese, or with a butter of fresh coriander and oregano leaf with some toasted and ground cumin and coriander seed. Leftover cooked sauces, especially red or green chile sauce are good with pasta, as are picadillo and chorizo.

Though eggs lend themselves to improvisation as much as pasta, a few dishes are in place as regional classics. Whether *huevos rancheros* came from Mexico or not, we suspect they were born when some cook decided to use that bit of chile sauce from the previous night's dinner. Scrambled eggs are the other great favorite, with variations so numerous and simple that we will describe them rather than give recipes. To have the most regional flavor, find the freshest eggs possible and scramble them with a little butter or leaf lard over very low heat until they are soft and light. The eggs are usually seasoned simply with salt and pepper, sometimes with very small amounts of ground cumin or ground red chile. Cooked chorizo, picadillo, or shredded dried beef are often stirred in during the last minute of cooking. Lightly cooked vegetables, commonly chile, corn, or zucchini, are popular additions, along with canned diced green chiles. Fresh chopped hot peppers and scallions are also stirred in, by themselves, or in rather typical hearty Southwestern style, with any combination of the ingredients above. The eggs are then topped with heated chile or tomato sauce, and/or a little grated cheese. Some people like them with a spoonful of fresh table salsa. Of course, very tasty omelets can be made with Southwestern fillings, but scrambled eggs keep their traditional pride of place. For breakfast, lunch, or supper, however the eggs are cooked, they are served with hot corn or flour tortillas.

Chile Deviled Eggs

≡ **Makes 12 deviled egg halves**

    6 hard-cooked extra large eggs, halved lengthwise, and
        the yolks removed
RED FILLING
    3 hard-cooked yolks (from above)
    2½ tablespoons sour cream
    ½ teaspoon ground red chile
    1 small garlic clove, minced
    Salt and freshly ground black pepper to taste
    Ground hot or mild red chile for garnish

GREEN FILLING
    3 hard-cooked yolks (from above)
    2½ tablespoons sour cream

1 small jalapeño pepper, finely minced
1 tablespoon finely chopped fresh cilantro leaves
Salt and freshly ground black pepper to taste
6 small cilantro leaves for garnish

1. To prepare the red filling, sieve the yolks into a small bowl or mash them with a fork. Add the sour cream, ground chile, garlic, and salt and pepper. Blend well. Fill six of the egg white halves with the red filling. Dust the tops lightly with ground red chile.

2. To prepare the green filling sieve the yolks into a small bowl or mash them with a fork. Add the sour cream, jalapeño, chopped cilantro, and salt and pepper. Blend well. Fill the remaining six halves with the green filling. Garnish each with a cilantro leaf.

3. Arrange the eggs on a plate. Serve immediately or cover and chill. Serve at cool room temperature.

Huevos Rancheros

≡ It is important to have everything ready to go and to work quickly in order to have these ready at the same time. Whether the eggs are sauced with red or green chile, this dish is always popular. We warm extra flour tortillas in order to clean our plates.

Serves 4

Corn or vegetable oil
8 extra large eggs
4 8-inch Flour Tortillas (see page 96)
2 cups Red Chile Sauce (page 85) or Green Chile Sauce
    (page 83), warmed
¼ cup thinly sliced scallions
Sour cream for garnish, optional

1. In a skillet large enough to hold an 8-inch tortilla, add enough oil to come about ½ inch deep in the pan and heat the oil until hot but not smoking.

2. Heat a large griddle or pan with a little oil to fry the eggs. Fry 4 eggs at a time, sunny-side up or over easy.

3. While the eggs are frying, quickly dip two of the tortillas in the hot oil for just 10 seconds. Drain them over the pan and place each one on a warm serving plate.

4. Place 2 eggs on each tortilla, cover them with sauce, and garnish with scallions.

5. Serve those two plates immediately or keep them in a 300-degree oven while preparing the other 2 servings. Serve hot, with sour cream, if desired.

Layered Tortillas and Omelets

≡ Roasted Tomato Sauce (page 86) or Red Chile Sauce (page 85) can also be used in this dish; the flavor effects are very different.

Serves 4 to 6
_____

8 extra large eggs
Salt and freshly ground black pepper
2 serrano or güero peppers, stemmed, seeded, and finely
    diced
½ cup finely diced onion
Corn or vegetable oil
4 8- to 10-inch Flour Tortillas (page 96)
2 cups Simple Tomato Sauce (page 87)
½ cup grated queso fresco, or grated Monterey Jack
    cheese

1. Beat the eggs with the salt and pepper. Stir in the peppers and onion. Fry the mixture in four batches in a little oil in an 8- to 10-inch frying pan over medium-low heat to make four large flat omelets. Keep the omelets warm.

2. Meanwhile, warm the tortillas and the tomato sauce separately. Preheat the oven to 350 degrees.

3. Assemble the tortillas and omelets on a large well-buttered oven-proof serving dish. Put a tortilla on the dish and cover it with an omelet. Spoon about ½ cup of the tomato sauce over the omelet. Continue layering, ending with tomato sauce. Sprinkle the cheese over the sauce.

4. Bake for 8 to 10 minutes, or until the tortillas and omelets are heated through. Cut into wedges to serve.

Corn and Chile Soufflé

≡ **Serves 4**

3 tablespoons unsalted butter
½ small red onion, finely diced
3 tablespoons unbleached white flour
1 cup milk
Salt and freshly ground black pepper
3 extra large egg yolks
2 to 3 serrano peppers, or 2 jalapeño peppers, stemmed,
    seeded, and diced
1 small red hot cherry pepper, stemmed, seeded, and
    diced
1½ cups fresh corn kernels (from 2 or 3 ears of corn)
1½ teaspoons chopped fresh basil leaves, or ½ tea-
    spoon dried basil leaves, crumbled
1 cup grated mild Cheddar cheese
About 1 tablespoon unsalted butter
About 2 tablespoons fine dry bread crumbs
5 extra large egg whites

1. Melt the 3 tablespoons of butter in a saucepan. Soften the diced onion in the butter over low heat. Stir the flour through the onions and cook over medium-low heat for 2 to 3 minutes. Add the milk all at once, stirring vigorously. Cook the béchamel over low heat for 7 to 8 minutes. Season lightly with salt and pepper. Remove the béchamel from the heat, cover, and cool to room temperature.

2. Stir the egg yolks into the cooled béchamel. Stir in the diced peppers, corn kernels, basil, and grated cheese. Adjust the seasoning.

3. Butter an 11- or 12-inch oval gratin dish. Coat the butter with fine dry bread crumbs. Preheat the oven to 400 degrees.

4. Beat the egg whites until they are stiff but not dry. Stir a little of the beaten whites into the béchamel mixture. Fold the rest of the whites into the béchamel in three parts.

5. Carefully pour the soufflé mixture into the prepared dish and bake on the bottom oven shelf for about 20 minutes, or until the soufflé is a rich golden brown on top and still a little soft in the center. Serve immediately.

Cilantro Pasta

≡ This is a delicately flavored, elegant first course pasta dish. We like it best in Chicken Broth (page 110), with Roasted Tomato Sauce (page 86), or with Tomatillo Butter (page 54).

Serves 6

3 extra large eggs
1 tablespoon olive oil
½ teaspoon salt
3 cups unbleached white flour
Water
1 cup whole fresh cilantro leaves

1. Work the eggs, olive oil, and salt into the flour. Add a teaspoon or so of water, if necessary. The dough should be stiff. Or combine the flour, eggs, olive oil, and salt in a food processor and make a fine meal. In either case, knead the dough well for 5 minutes.

2. Divide the dough into three portions and cover it with plastic wrap. Let it rest for at least 30 minutes.

3. Roll one portion of dough through the first two or three settings of the pasta machine, until it is about ⅛ inch thick.

4. Cover one half of the width of the rolled pasta with whole coriander leaves laid closely together. Carefully fold the other half of the pasta over the leaves and press gently yet firmly to sandwich the leaves between the pasta.

5. Set the pasta machine back one notch from the last setting used and roll this pasta through the machine until it is ¹⁄₁₆ inch thick, usually the next to the last setting.

6. Lay the pasta on a lightly floured surface and cut it with a pasta cutter into 1½-inch squares. Repeat the rolling and cutting process with the other two portions of dough.

7. At this point the pasta can be spread on baking sheets and left to dry a bit or covered with plastic wrap and refrigerated until ready to use; it is best used fresh. Cooking time will vary depending on how fresh the pasta is, but it should be served *al dente*. Cook it in gently boiling well-salted water, and have the broth or tomato sauce hot.

Green Chile Pasta

≣ The chile concentrate which flavors the pasta takes awhile to prepare so we sometimes double this part of the recipe and freeze a batch to have on hand. It keeps in the refrigerator for a day or two.

Pasta for 6

1 teaspoon olive oil
6 ounces green chiles, roasted, peeled, seeded, and
    chopped (about ½ cup)
3 ounces jalapeño peppers, seeded and finely minced
    (about ½ cup)
3 cups unbleached white flour
½ teaspoon salt
2 extra large eggs
¼ cup cooked chopped spinach, squeezed dry and
    packed (5 ounces of trimmed fresh leaves, wilted,
    or 5 ounces frozen spinach, thawed)
1 recipe Tomatillo Butter (page 54)
Freshly grated Parmesan cheese for garnish

1. Heat the olive oil in a skillet. Add the chopped chiles and jalapeños and sweat them over low heat, covered, stirring occasionally for 20 minutes.

2. Purée the peppers in a blender until smooth. Return the purée to the skillet and cook over low heat, stirring often, for 10 to 15 minutes, or until very thick. Remove from the heat and cool. There should be about ¼ cup of concentrate.

3. Combine the flour, salt, eggs, spinach, and chile concentrate in a food processor and process until the dough just starts to come together. Or mix the ingredients together in a bowl.

4. Turn the dough onto a board, gather the crumbs, and knead for 2 to 3 minutes. Wrap the dough in plastic and let it rest for at least 30 minutes.

5. Divide the dough into three parts and keep them covered until needed. Roll the dough, dusting it lightly with flour, if needed, through each setting of the pasta machine.

6. Roll the remaining dough through the pasta machine. Lay the sheets of pasta out to dry a bit after cutting them into 8- or 9-inch lengths and trimming off the uneven end pieces. Let the pasta rest, turning once, for about 20 minutes.

7. Roll the pasta through the fettuccine cutter and cook immediately or refrigerate until ready to cook. Cook the pasta in boiling salted water until it is *al dente*. Drain well and transfer the pasta to warm serving bowls. Divide the tomatillo butter equally among the portions of pasta and serve immediately. Pass the Parmesan cheese at the table.

Red Chile Pasta

Serves 4

2 extra large eggs
2 teaspoons olive oil
½ teaspoon salt
1¾ cups unbleached white flour
¼ cup ground mild red chile
¼ cup ground hot red chile
Water
1 recipe Crème Fraîche and Jalapeño Sauce (page 82)
3 tablespoons chopped fresh cilantro leaves for garnish

1. Work the eggs, olive oil, and salt into the flour and ground chile. Add a teaspoon or so of water, if necessary. The dough should be stiff. Or combine the flour, red chile, eggs, olive oil, and salt in a food processor and make a fine meal. In either case, knead the dough well for 5 minutes.

2. Divide the dough in half and cover it with plastic wrap. Let it rest for at least 30 minutes.

3. Roll one portion of the dough through each setting of the pasta machine, up to the last one, dusting it if necessary with a little flour. Cut the pasta into fettuccine or 1½-inch squares or diamonds and toss it lightly with flour. Roll and cut the other portion of dough.

4. At this point, the pasta can be spread on baking sheets and left to dry a bit or covered with plastic wrap and refrigerated until ready to use; it is best used fresh.

5. Make the sauce and keep it warm. Cook the pasta until it is *al dente* in abundant well-salted boiling water. Cooking time will vary depending on how fresh the pasta is.

6. Drain the pasta, toss it with the sauce, and serve in warm pasta plates, garnishing with the chopped cilantro.

Goat Cheese Ravioli with Pecan and Coriander Sauce

≣ Serves 4 to 6

PASTA

2 extra large eggs
1 teaspoon olive oil
½ teaspoon salt
2 cups unbleached white flour
Water

FILLING

½ cup thinly sliced scallions, with some green
5 ounces mild goat cheese
5 ounces ricotta
Salt and freshly ground black pepper

SAUCE

2 cups half-and-half
3 ounces pecans, finely ground
½ cup chopped fresh coriander leaves
2 garlic cloves, finely chopped
½ to 1 teaspoon ground cayenne
Salt and freshly ground white pepper
Small coriander leaves for garnish

1. Work the eggs, olive oil, and salt into the flour. Add a teaspoon or so of water, if necessary. The dough should be stiff. Or combine the flour, eggs, olive oil, and salt in a food processor and make a fine meal. In either case, knead the dough well for 5 minutes.

2. Divide the dough in half and cover it with plastic wrap. Let it rest for at least 30 minutes. Meanwhile, make the filling.

3. Mix the scallions, goat cheese, and ricotta together in a small bowl for the ravioli filling. Season well with salt and pepper.

4. Roll out one portion of pasta through each setting of the pasta machine. Cut the pasta into 12-inch lengths, trimming uneven ends, if necessary.

5. Make three rows of filling, each with six 1-teaspoonfuls of filling. Moisten lightly with water around the filling. Cover with another 12-inch length, pressing to eliminate air pockets. Cut into ravioli with a crimper-cutter or a knife.

6. Continue until all the pasta and filling are used. Place the ravioli as they are done on a floured baking sheet.

7. Purée all the sauce ingredients, except the salt and white pepper in a blender until the sauce is very smooth.

8. Bring abundant well-salted water to a gentle boil. Cook the ravioli until they are *al dente*.

9. Meanwhile, pour the sauce in a large pan and heat over low heat. Season with salt and pepper.

10. When the ravioli are done, drain them and toss them in the sauce. Serve hot, garnished with the coriander leaves.

Corn and Green Chile Lasagne with Roasted Tomato Sauce

≡ **Serves 8 to 10**

PASTA

    3 extra large eggs
    2 teaspoons olive oil
    1 teaspoon salt
    3 cups unbleached white flour
    Water

FILLINGS AND ASSEMBLY

    1 small onion, finely diced
    3 garlic cloves, finely minced
    4 tablespoons unsalted butter
    2 cups fresh or frozen corn kernels
    Salt and freshly ground black pepper
    Pinch of ground cayenne
    2 tablespoons all-purpose flour
    1½ cups milk
    2 cups roasted, peeled, and diced mild, or mild and
        hot, green chiles
    1¼ pounds sharp natural Cheddar cheese, grated
    1 recipe Roasted Tomato Sauce (page 86)
    Abundant cold water with 1 or 2 tablespoons vegetable oil
    Abundant well-salted boiling water
    About 2 tablespoons unsalted butter

1. Work the eggs, olive oil, and salt into the flour. Add a teaspoon or so of water, if necessary. The dough should be stiff. Or combine the flour, eggs, olive oil, and salt in a food processor and make a fine meal. In either case, knead the dough well for 5 minutes.

2. Divide the dough into three parts and cover it with plastic wrap. Let it rest for at least 30 minutes.

3. To prepare the corn filling, cook the onion and garlic in 2 table-spoons of the butter over medium heat for about 3 minutes. Add the corn and cook another 7 to 8 minutes. Season generously with salt and pepper and a pinch of cayenne.

4. To prepare the béchamel, melt 2 tablespoons of the butter over low heat in a heavy-bottomed saucepan and add 2 tablespoons flour. Stir to form a smooth paste and cook 6 to 7 minutes, taking care not to brown the roux.

5. Add the milk all at once and stir vigorously. Cook the béchamel over low heat for 8 to 10 minutes, stirring occasionally to prevent lumps from forming.

6. Stir the béchamel into the corn mixture and adjust the seasoning. Cover to prevent a skin from forming and set aside. Have the chiles, cheese, and tomato sauce ready for assembling the lasagne. Butter a 9-by 12-inch lasagne pan with ample butter.

7. Roll the pasta through each setting of the pasta machine, up to the last one. Cut each strip of pasta into 4- or 5-inch lengths.

8. Fill a pot or bowl with 3 or 4 quarts of cold water and pour in 1 or 2 tablespoons of cooking oil. Have this next to the pasta cooking pot.

9. Cook the pasta, four pieces at a time in the boiling water for 10 to 12 seconds. Remove the pasta as it is parcooked to the cold water. When the pasta is all parcooked, lay it on tea towels or paper towels to drain.

10. Line the lasagne pan all around with pasta, allowing about 1½ inches to drape over the sides of the pan. Line the bottom of the pan with pasta.

11. Spread half of the corn mixture over the bottom of the pan and cover with pasta. Spread half of the chiles over this pasta and sprinkle half of the cheese over the chiles. Cover with pasta and spread half of the tomato sauce over. Cover with pasta and repeat the filling procedure.

12. After the last layer of tomato sauce has been covered with pasta, fold the outside edges of pasta over the top. Dot with butter. The lasagne may be covered and refrigerated overnight at this point. Remove it from the refrigerator 1 hour before baking.

13. Bake the lasagne in a preheated 375-degree oven for 25 minutes.

The top will be light golden brown and crunchy. Let the lasagne stand for about 15 minutes before cutting and serving.

Lasagne with Chorizo

≣ Homemade lasagne is well worth the effort in our opinion. It always satisfies and often impresses. The component ingredients can be prepared at convenient early times, and the whole lasagne can be made ahead and refrigerated overnight.

Serves 8 to 10

1½ pounds Chorizo (page 153)
3 tablespoons unsalted butter
3 tablespoons all-purpose flour
2 cups milk
Salt and ground cayenne pepper
2 recipes Red Chile Pasta (page 182); you will need 3
    portions of dough for this recipe. Reserve the other
    portion for another use.
Abundant cold water with 1 or 2 tablespoons vegetable oil
Abundant well-salted boiling water
Olive oil
1 recipe Simple Tomato Sauce (page 87)
½ pound Monterey Jack cheese, grated
½ pound queso fresco, grated

1. Crumble the chorizo and fry it over medium-low heat for about 15 minutes. Drain the fat from it and set it aside.

2. To make the béchamel, melt the butter over low heat in a heavy-bottomed saucepan and add the flour. Stir to form a smooth paste and cook for 6 to 7 minutes, taking care not to brown the roux.

3. Add the milk all at once and stir vigorously. Cook the béchamel over low heat for 8 to 10 minutes, stirring occasionally to prevent lumps from forming. Season the béchamel well with salt and cayenne pepper. Cover to prevent a skin from forming and set aside.

4. Roll three portions of the pasta through each setting of the pasta machine, up to the last one. Cut each strip of pasta into 4- or 5-inch lengths.

5. Fill a pot or bowl with 3 or 4 quarts of cold water and pour in 1 or 2 tablespoons of vegetable oil. Have this next to the pasta cooking pot.

6. Cook the pasta, four pieces at a time in the boiling water for 10 to 12 seconds. Remove the pasta as it is parcooked to the cold water. When the pasta is all parcooked, lay it on tea towels or paper towels to drain.

7. Oil a lasagne pan and line it all around with pasta, allowing about 1½ inches to drape over the sides of the pan. Reserve the best-looking pieces of pasta for the top of the lasagne. Line the bottom of the pan with pasta.

8. Spread about one-third of the tomato sauce over the pasta. Spread about one-third of the chorizo over the sauce. Cover with pasta. Spread about one-third of the béchamel over the pasta. Sprinkle about one-third of the cheeses over the béchamel and cover with pasta. Repeat the layering until the fillings and pasta are used.

9. Drizzle a little olive oil over the top of the lasagne. The lasagne may be covered tightly and refrigerated at this point. Remove the lasagne from the refrigerator 1 hour before baking.

10. Bake the lasagne in a preheated 375-degree oven for 25 minutes. The top will be golden brown and crunchy. Let the lasagne stand 10 to 15 minutes before cutting and serving.

CHAPTER ELEVEN

Dried Bean, Corn & Rice Dishes

No Southwestern larder is complete without this trinity of staples. They are all ancient foods, haricot beans and corn from the New World, and rice from the old. As Waverley Root mentions in *Food,* haricot derives from the Aztec *ayacotl.* This class of bean includes all snap beans as well as dried beans of every color. Their reception in the rest of the world was as avid as that of chiles. Corn, or maize, (from another Aztec word *maíz*) did not sweep the other continents in the same brushfire way, probably because there were already many established grains. In its homelands, Mexico through the American Southwest, it remains the bedrock of the cuisine, with more cultural and religious significance than any other single food. Rice came with the Spaniards to Mexico. Its acceptance there is surprising considering the limited areas where it could be grown and the entrenchment of corn. Still, it claimed an important role and traveled to the Southwest with the Mexicans and Spaniards.

Corn was preserved in many forms, dried on the cob, dried and ground, cooked with slaked lime to remove the kernel husks, then dried whole for hominy (also known as *nixtamal*), or ground into *masa* for tortilla-making. Whole dried corn kernels are *chicos,* a New Mexican specialty. *Posole,* or *pozole,* properly refers to the stew made with hominy, though in the vernacular the terms are often used to refer to hominy itself. In this chapter we use the whole grains, hominy or chicos, mainly as side dishes but they also appear in soups and stews. The various kinds of dried cornmeal are treated in the bread chapter.

The pinto bean has gained ascendancy in the Southwest, though red and black beans form the basis of dishes brought with settlers from Sonora and the Yucatán. Chick-peas and lentils are not uncommon; there is interest in recent years in exploring beyond the traditions of the pinto. In this area, as with vegetables, meat, fish, and poultry, the cuisine is being reshaped with the modern ingredients of availability, variety, and lightness.

Lard was formerly an important seasoning agent and calorie provider in bean and corn dishes. Some cooks still use lard because it has been used for as long as anyone can remember. The generally available commercial lard is not worth using we think. It adds preservatives and cholesterol to dishes without adding the smooth balanced richness that fresh lard furnishes. If you can find leaf lard from a butcher who renders it freshly, try it instead of oil with the hearty dishes here. Fresh leaf lard is as delicate and rich as really fresh butter or milk are.

Rice is usually prepared in mild ways, to provide contrast to spicy foods. When the menu has enough quiet dishes, rice is quite good with a little red or green chile spark. Brown rice, though not traditional, has a nutty definite flavor that goes well with chiles, onions, and garlic.

Black Beans

Black beans taste better to us if they are first soaked overnight and then cooked slowly. However, they may be quick-soaked by pouring ample boiling water over them, covering the pot and letting them stand for an hour or so. Black beans can be cooked in a pressure cooker for 12 to 15 minutes, after the steam gauge is up. The amount of cooking time for any method depends on the freshness of the beans and whether they will be cooked further.

The amount of water to add will vary according to the size of the pot, and if the cooking liquid is necessary in the recipe. Half an inch above the beans is sufficient for most pressure-cooked beans, and one inch above the beans for simmered beans. It is better to have a little too much liquid, than to have beans stuck to the bottom of the pot. Salt should always be added to beans after they are cooked because it toughens them.

Makes about 2 quarts

1 pound black beans, sorted and rinsed
3 large garlic cloves, peeled
2 large epazote leaves, or ½ teaspoon dried epazote
   leaves, or 1 large bay leaf
Salt

1. Soak the beans overnight in 2 to 3 quarts of water. Drain them, put them in a pot, and cover with 1 inch of fresh water. Add the garlic and epazote. Cover and simmer until the beans are done, 1 to 2 hours.

2. Salt the beans and let them stand covered for 10 minutes. Use the beans as desired. To use the beans for enchiladas, or as an appetizer, drain the beans and reserve the cooking liquid. Mash the beans well, adding liquid as necessary to make a fairly loose paste.

Black Beans with Garnishes

≡ Serves 8 to 10

1 pound black beans
5 tablespoons plus ¼ cup corn or olive oil
1 large onion
1 large celery stalk
4 jalapeño peppers, stemmed and seeded
4 garlic cloves
2 teaspoons achiote seed
½ teaspoon toasted and ground cumin seed
1 teaspoon salt
2 teaspoons finely grated orange zest
3 dashes of bitters, or to taste

GARNISHES
½ cup finely chopped scallions
2 hard-cooked extra large eggs, finely chopped
½ cup sour cream

1. Sort and rinse the beans. Soak them overnight in 2 to 3 quarts cold water. Drain the beans and cover them with 1 inch of cold water. Stir in 2 tablespoons of the oil and cook the beans until they are just tender, 1 to 1 ½ hours.

2. Rough chop the onion, celery, peppers, and garlic. Make a purée of the vegetables with 3 tablespoons of the remaining oil in a blender or food processor.

3. Heat the achiote seeds with ¼ cup of oil over medium-low heat for 10 minutes in a skillet. Strain the seeds from the oil and sauté the vegetable purée in the oil over low heat for 10 minutes, stirring occasionally.

4. Add the vegetables and the cumin to the beans and simmer over low heat for 30 minutes. Add 1 teaspoon salt, the grated orange zest, and the bitters. Simmer for another 20 to 30 minutes and adjust the seasoning. Serve the beans hot with the chopped scallions, chopped hard-cooked eggs, and sour cream on the side.

Pinto Beans

≣ Pinto beans, like black beans, need to be soaked overnight in cold water, or quick-soaked in boiling water for an hour in a covered pan. The beans may then be simmered for 45 minutes to 1½ hours, or pressure-cooked for 10 to 12 minutes after the steam gauge is up. Salt is added to the pintos after they are tender. One inch of water above the beans is usually enough for simmered beans, and gives a little liquid for mashing the beans or using as stock. Half an inch of water above the beans is enough for most pressure-cooked beans. The actual amount of water used depends on the size and freshness of the beans.

Makes about 2 quarts, serving 6 to 8

1 pound pinto beans, sorted and rinsed
2 tablespoons corn or olive oil, bacon fat, or lard
1 teaspoon salt
1 small onion, chopped, optional
2 cloves garlic, minced, optional

1. Cover the beans with 2 to 3 quarts of water and soak them overnight or pour boiling water over them and soak for 1 hour.
2. Drain the water from the beans and cover them with fresh water to ½ inch above the beans. Add the oil, stir, and simmer in a pan or cook in a pressure cooker.
3. When the beans are cooked, still firm but tender, add the salt. They can be served plain, or add the onion and garlic and cook, covered, over low heat for 15 minutes, stirring occasionally so that they do not stick.

Charro Beans

Charro is a fascinating word, in Southwestern Spanish meaning elegant, in Mexican Spanish horseman, and in Spanish rustic. From what we know of cowboys' methods of cooking beans, we think the term was taken from Mexican Spanish. This dish, like most bean dishes, is best made one day ahead and gently reheated.

Serves 6 to 8

1 pound pinto beans, sorted and rinsed
¼ pound bacon, diced
1 medium-sized onion, diced
3 garlic cloves, finely diced
Salt and freshly ground black pepper

1. Put the beans in a heavy-bottomed pan and cover with water by about 2 inches. The beans for this dish should not be presoaked.

2. Cook the bacon over low heat until it is crisp and the fat is rendered. Remove the bacon to a plate. Soften the onion and garlic in the bacon fat for 10 minutes or so.

3. Add the bacon, onion, and garlic to the beans. Cover the beans and bring to a simmer over medium heat.

4. Simmer the beans until they are completely tender, 1½ to 3 hours, depending on the freshness of the beans. The beans should not be falling apart and the stock should be fairly clear. Add a little water, if necessary, to have a slightly soupy consistency when you serve the beans. Season well with salt and pepper.

Chile Beans

Serves 6 to 8

1 pound pinto beans, sorted, rinsed, and soaked overnight in 2 or 3 quarts of water
3 tablespoons corn or olive oil or bacon fat
4 large garlic cloves, minced
3 jalapeño peppers, sliced
1 cup chopped onion

1 tablespoon ground hot red chile
1½ teaspoons toasted and ground cumin seed
About 1 teaspoon salt
Chopped fresh coriander leaves for garnish

1. Drain the beans and cover them with fresh water by about 1 inch. Add 1½ tablespoons of the oil. (Read about cooking Pinto Beans, page 192.)

2. Cook the beans, covered, for 45 minutes to 1 hour, stirring occasionally, until they are tender.

3. Heat the remaining oil in a small skillet over medium heat. Sauté the garlic, jalapeños, and onion for about 5 minutes, or until just tender.

4. Add the sautéed vegetables to the beans with the ground chile, cumin, and salt, and stir well. Cook over low heat for about 10 minutes. Adjust the seasoning. The beans may be prepared ahead of time and reheated. Serve as a side dish garnished with cilantro, or use in other dishes.

Hominy with Spinach

Serves 6

1 30-ounce can hominy, drained and rinsed
3 tablespoons corn oil
1 large red onion, diced
4 garlic cloves, finely chopped
2 jalapeño peppers, stemmed, seeded, and finely diced
½ teaspoon dried oregano leaves, crumbled
2 pounds fresh spinach leaves with stems removed,
    washed and drained
Salt

1. Cover the hominy with water and simmer covered over medium heat for 25 minutes. Drain the hominy and return it to the pan.

2. Heat the corn oil in a large frying pan and sauté the onion and garlic over medium heat for 3 minutes. Add the jalapeño peppers and sauté for another 2 to 3 minutes. Add the vegetables to the hominy along with the oregano.

3. Rough chop the spinach leaves and wilt them in the pan used to sauté the vegetables. When the spinach is wilted, add it to the hominy and heat through for 2 to 3 minutes. Season with salt and serve hot.

Hominy and Summer Squash

Serves 6

4 tablespoons olive oil
8 ounces red onion, sliced in ⅜- by 1-inch slices
8 ounces 2- to 3-inch long zucchini squash, cut lengthwise into ⅜-inch-thick slices
8 ounces 2- to 3-inch yellow squash, cut lengthwise into ⅜-inch-thick slices
1 large garlic clove, slivered
1 30-ounce can hominy, drained and rinsed
2 tablespoons chopped fresh parsley leaves
2 tablespoons chopped fresh basil leaves
Salt and freshly ground black pepper to taste
Grated sharp Cheddar cheese for garnish, optional

1. Heat the oil in a large heavy skillet. Add the onion, squash, and garlic and sauté for about 5 minutes over medium heat, stirring occasionally. Add the hominy and cook for 5 minutes, stirring occasionally.
2. Stir in the parsley, basil, and salt and pepper. Cook for 2 to 3 minutes and season. Serve hot with the grated cheese for garnish, if desired.

Chicos and Lamb

Serves 4 to 6

½ pound chicos
2 pounds bone-in lamb neck and shoulder meat, or shanks
1 fresh or dried New Mexico red chile

1 medium-sized onion, diced
2 garlic cloves, chopped
6 sprigs fresh oregano, or 1 teaspoon dried oregano
    leaves
1 tablespoon ground mild red chile
1 teaspoon salt
Freshly ground black pepper

1. Sort and rinse the chicos. Soak them overnight in 3 to 4 quarts of water. Drain them and cover with 3 inches of fresh water, about 3 quarts. Bring the chicos to a simmer and cook for 2 hours.

2. Trim the lamb of extra fat. Add it to the chicos. The lamb should be just covered. Bring it to a simmer and cook for 1 hour, skimming occasionally.

3. Stem and seed the fresh or dried chile. Dice the fresh chile, or cut the dried chile into 3 or 4 pieces. Add the chile to the chicos, along with the onion, garlic, oregano, ground chile, and salt. Cover and simmer for 1 hour.

4. Uncover the pan and reduce the liquid to about 2 cups over medium heat. Season the chicos with salt and black pepper. Serve hot with tortillas.

Rice with Corn and Carrots

Serves 6 to 8

1½ cups long-grain white rice
3 cups water
1 scant teaspoon salt
1 tablespoon corn oil
Generous pinch of saffron threads
3 tablespoons olive oil
¾ cup thinly sliced scallions
1 cup fresh or frozen corn kernels
¾ cup grated carrots
Salt and freshly ground black pepper to taste

1. Stir the rice, water, salt, corn oil, and saffron together in a heavy-bottomed saucepan with a tight-fitting lid. Bring the water to a boil, lower the heat to a simmer, and cover the pan. Cook for about 12 minutes, depending on the type of rice. Do not remove the lid while the rice is cooking and let the rice stand off the heat for about 10 minutes before removing the lid.

2. Heat the olive oil in a large skillet over medium-high heat. Add the scallions and cook for about 1 minute. Add the corn and cook for 2 minutes. Add the carrots and cook for 1 minute. Cover and cook for another minute; then add a little salt.

3. Add the rice to the skillet, toss with a fork to blend the ingredients, cover, and cook over low heat for 3 to 4 minutes.

4. Add freshly ground pepper, toss, and taste for seasoning. Serve hot. The rice can be made ahead and reheated in a low oven.

Green Rice

Serves 4 to 6

1 cup long-grain white rice
1⅔ cups water
½ teaspoon salt
1 medium-sized zucchini, grated and squeezed dry
6 scallions, trimmed with 2 inches of green and sliced
⅓ cup chopped fresh coriander leaves
1 to 3 serrano peppers, stemmed, seeded, and finely
    diced, optional
½ cup grated queso fresco, or ricotta salata, optional

1. Stir the rice, water, and ½ teaspoon salt together in a saucepan. Bring the water to a boil, lower the heat to a simmer, cover, and cook for 10 minutes.

2. Stir in the zucchini, scallions, coriander, and peppers, if desired. Cover and cook for 2 minutes longer. Remove from the heat and steam, covered, for 5 minutes. Test the rice for doneness; steam a few minutes longer, if necessary.

3. Serve hot, or cool to use as a stuffing. Stir in the grated cheese when the rice is cool.

Spicy Brown Rice with Chipotle and Epazote

≡ Serves 4 to 6

3 tablespoons corn oil
1 cup diced mixed red and yellow bell peppers, or 1
    cup diced red bell pepper
⅓ cup sliced scallions
1 large chipotle en adobo, minced
2½ teaspoons minced epazote leaves
3 cups *cooked* brown rice
1 cup peeled and diced ripe tomato
¼ teaspoon toasted and ground cumin seed

1. Heat the oil in a large skillet. Sauté the peppers and scallions over medium heat for 5 minutes. Add the chipotle, epazote, and rice. Mix well and cook for 1 to 2 minutes.

2. Add the tomato and cumin and cook over medium heat, covered, stirring occasionally, for 10 minutes. Taste for seasoning and serve hot.

CHAPTER TWELVE

Vegetables

More than the advent of Anglo settlers during the last half of the nineteenth century, the construction of the enormous federal dam system in the 1930s brought a cornucopia of produce to what before was range land. Without irrigation, people were restricted to small crops of what had been grown in the region for centuries: corn, squash, and chiles, with a leavening of onions and garlic. After the dams, more people flooded into the Southwest, bringing with them favorite vegetables and fruits in the determination to transplant some of their heritage. They learned to plant cabbage in the winter in order to have coleslaw; they grew summer squash in the spring; they seeded spinach and beets for greens to reliably replace the wild native lambs' quarters and purslane. Especially after World War II, people learned to appreciate and cultivate a staple of Mexican cooking, the avocado.

Today, most of the common vegetables are grown for market. Delicacies such as asparagus are grown hard by the Mexican border in the Imperial Valley of California and the diversity of crops from snap beans to tomatillos has greatly influenced the cooking of the region. The availability of fresh produce, the changed manner of life, have altered the style of eating. Some of the oldest dishes come from the time when a fresh vegetable or fruit was a rarer treat than meat. New vegetable dishes have not yet become traditions because experimentation still continues. We think today's transitional period must be similar to the periods when Indians, Mexicans, Spaniards, and Anglos in New Mexico borrowed from each other's cuisine. Vegetables favored in the tropics, chayote and jícama, are popular not only because they have been well-promoted, but because they taste good with the food.

Grilling, a favored Southwestern technique, is a excellent way to cook vegetables; accompanied by chile butter or salsa, the vegetables taste naturally right next to other grilled foods. The boil-em-to-death method for cooking vegetables has been largely banished here as in other parts of the country. Modern cooks think that vegetables need to have a certain liveliness in order to complement the rich and often spicy main courses.

Artichokes with Chorizo and Cheese

☰ Serves 4 to 6

½ pound Chorizo (page 153), crumbled and cooked
½ pound farmer's or pot cheese
¼ pound queso fresco, queso cotijo, or ricotta salata, grated
2 garlic cloves, finely minced
3 tablespoons chopped fresh coriander leaves
4 large or 6 medium-sized artichokes
1 lime
2 teaspoons Chili Powder (page 50)
2 teaspoons coriander seed

1. Mix the chorizo, farmer's cheese, and queso fresco in a bowl with the garlic and chopped coriander.
2. Cut the stems from the artichokes so that the bases are flush. Trim the thorns and remove the choke from the artichokes. Rub the cut surfaces with half a lime as you work.
3. Fill the artichoke centers with most of the filling. Spread the leaves of the artichokes and put half teaspoonfuls between the leaves until the filling is used.
4. Cut the remaining half lime in slices and put them in a pan with the chili powder, coriander, and about 1½ inches of water. Put a steamer in the pan and arrange the artichokes in it. Steam over low heat for 20 to 30 minutes, or until the artichokes are just done. Serve hot.

Asparagus with Roasted
Garlic Cream Sauce

≣ **Serves 4**

1½ pounds asparagus
1 recipe Roasted Garlic Cream Sauce (page 86)

1. Trim and peel the asparagus. Blanch or steam until it is crisp-tender. Drain the asparagus and keep it warm. Heat the roasted garlic cream sauce.

2. Arrange the asparagus spears decoratively on a warm platter and nap with the sauce. Serve hot.

Chayote and Onion Fritters

≣ **Makes about 6 3-inch fritters**

2 chayote squash (about 1 pound total)
½ cup grated onion
1 extra large egg, beaten
¼ teaspoon toasted and ground coriander seed
Salt and freshly ground black pepper
2 tablespoons unsalted butter

1. Wash the chayote and cut it into quarters lengthwise. Cover it with water in a saucepan and simmer for 15 minutes.

2. Drain and refresh the chayote. Peel it and grate it coarsely. Place it in a strainer and squeeze out the excess liquid. There should be about 1 cup of grated pulp.

3. Combine the chayote, onion, and egg in a bowl and stir with a fork until well blended. Add the coriander and season well with salt and pepper.

4. Heat a griddle and melt 1 tablespoon of the butter on it. Using about half of the batter, spoon three equal-sized rounds onto the griddle, about 3 inches in diameter and ½ inch thick. Fry on each side until golden brown. Keep the fritters hot in a warm oven while frying the other batch in the same manner. Serve immediately.

Baked Chayote with Salsa Fria

≡ Serves 4

2 cups Salsa Fria with Sage (page 58)
1¼ pounds chayote squash
Salt and freshly ground black pepper
½ pound queso fresco, grated
1 cup stale corn tortillas, cut into julienne strips

1. Preheat the oven to 350 degrees and butter a 10-inch round baking dish. Simmer the salsa for 10 minutes over medium-high heat.
2. Cut the chayotes in half, remove the seeds, and place them in a shallow saucepan so that all the squash is in one layer on the bottom, and barely cover with water. Cover, bring to a boil, lower the heat, and simmer for 20 minutes.
3. Drain and refresh the chayote under cold water for 1 or 2 minutes. Drain well. When cool enough to handle, peel and slice the squash crosswise in ¼-inch slices. Season lightly with salt and pepper.
4. Place half of the chayote in the bottom of the baking dish, cover with half of the salsa, and then cover with half of the cheese. Repeat the squash and salsa layers; then layer the tortillas and, finally, the remaining cheese.
5. Bake for 20 minutes, or until the cheese is just starting to turn golden brown. Serve hot.

Corn and Green Chile Cakes

≡ Brunch is a good occasion for these cakes. Serve them with butter, hot pepper jelly and sour cream, salsa, even maple syrup. With no embellishments, or with salsa, they accompany simple fried or grilled foods.

Makes about 20 3-inch cakes; serves 6 to 10

⅔ cup stone-ground cornmeal
⅓ cup unbleached white flour
⅓ cup whole wheat pastry flour
1½ teaspoons baking powder
½ teaspoon salt

2 extra large eggs
¾ cup milk
2 tablespoons corn or vegetable oil
1 jalapeño pepper, seeded and chopped
½ cup chopped onion
3 green chiles, roasted, peeled, seeded, and chopped
1 cup fresh or frozen corn kernels
¾ cup grated Cheddar cheese

1. Mix together the cornmeal, flours, baking powder, and salt in a large mixing bowl.
2. Beat the eggs lightly in a small mixing bowl. Add the milk and oil and blend well.
3. Add the liquid ingredients to the dry ingredients along with the chopped vegetables and cheese. Blend well with a wooden spoon, but do not overmix.
4. Heat a lightly oiled griddle over medium heat. Drop about 2 tablespoons of batter for each cake. Cook the cakes for 2 to 3 minutes on each side, or until they are golden brown. Keep them warm in a hot oven while frying the rest in the same manner.

Calabacitas

≡ Serves 4 to 6

2 tablespoons corn or olive oil
1 cup coarsely chopped red onion
2 small zucchini (about 6 ounces total), cut into ¼-inch-thick rounds
2 jalapeño peppers, halved, seeded, and sliced, optional
3 cups fresh or frozen corn kernels
1 large ripe tomato, chopped
⅓ cup packed fresh coriander leaves, chopped
Salt and freshly ground black pepper
1 cup grated sharp Cheddar cheese for garnish, optional

1. Heat the oil in a heavy-bottomed saucepan. Add the onion and sauté for 2 minutes. Add the zucchini and jalapeño and sauté for 4 minutes, stirring occasionally.

2. Add the corn and tomato and stir well. Cover, lower the heat to moderate, and cook for about 5 minutes. Covering the pan should bring out enough juices from the corn and tomato so that the addition of liquid is not necessary; if the pan is dry, add a bit of water.

3. Add the coriander and salt and pepper, stir well and cook, covered, for another 2 to 3 minutes. Serve in a warm bowl or in individual plates with the grated cheese as a garnish, if desired.

Baked Eggplant with Corn and Chiles

≡ Serves 4

2 small eggplants (about ½ pound each)
Wedge of lime
Olive oil
2 tablespoons olive oil
1 large garlic clove
2 large ears of corn (about 1 cup kernels)
1 large ripe tomato, finely chopped
3 Anaheim, Sandia, or New Mexico chiles, roasted,
    seeded, peeled, and chopped
¼ cup sour cream
2 tablespoons chopped fresh parsley leaves
Salt and freshly ground black pepper

1. Preheat the oven to 350 degrees. Halve the eggplants lengthwise, remove the stem end, and hollow the eggplant leaving a ¼-inch shell. Reserve the eggplant pulp. Rub the shells with lime and then with a bit of oil. Place the eggplant shells in a lightly oiled baking dish and bake for 30 to 40 minutes, or until they are just tender, not overcooked.

2. Finely mince the reserved eggplant pulp. Heat the 2 tablespoons of olive oil in a skillet. Sauté the eggplant in the skillet for 2 minutes. Add the garlic and sauté for another minute. Add the corn, tomato, and chiles. Cook, covered, over low heat for 8 to 10 minutes, stirring occasionally.

3. Add the sour cream and parsley. Season with salt and pepper. Stuff the shells with the vegetable mixture. Place them in a baking dish and bake for 15 minutes. Serve hot.

Green Beans with Green Chile

≡ Serves 6

1½ pounds thin green beans
2 tablespoons corn oil
1 medium-sized onion, diced
1 garlic clove, finely minced
1 large ripe tomato, peeled, seeded, and diced
1 cup chopped, roasted and peeled, mild green chile
1 tablespoon chopped fresh oregano leaves, or 1 tea-
    spoon dried oregano leaves, crumbled
Salt

1. Top and tail the green beans. Blanch them until they are crisp-tender. Drain and refresh the beans and cut them into 2-inch lengths.
2. Heat the oil over medium heat in a large frying pan and sauté the onion and garlic in it for 5 minutes. Add the green beans, tomato, and green chile to the pan. Lower the heat to medium-low and cook for 5 minutes.
3. Add the oregano and cook for 5 minutes longer. Season with salt. Serve the beans hot or at room temperature.

Greens with Bacon

≡ A mixture of greens, such as spinach, Good King Henry, lambs' quarters, dandelion greens, and rocket, is best for this dish.

Serves 4

¼ pound bacon, cut into ¼-inch dice
3 quarts washed and stemmed greens
Freshly ground black pepper

1. Cook the bacon in a large pan over low heat until it is crisp and has rendered its fat.
2. Add the greens to the pan with the water which clings to their leaves. Cover and increase the heat to medium. Wilt the greens for 2 to 3 minutes. Uncover, stir and cook for another 2 to 3 minutes. Season with pepper and serve hot.

Potatoes with Tequila Lime Butter

≡ Serves 6

2½ pounds small red potatoes
3 tablespoons unsalted butter
3 tablespoons gold tequila
2 teaspoons fresh lime juice, or to taste
Salt and freshly ground black pepper

1. Scrub the potatoes well. Steam them in a little lightly salted water until they are almost done. When they are cool enough to handle, halve them.
2. Melt the butter over medium-low heat in a large frying pan. Stir in the tequila and lime juice. Add the potatoes and sauté gently, turning them once, for 5 to 6 minutes. Season with salt and pepper and serve hot.

Cheese and Jalapeño Stuffed Potatoes

≡ Serves 6

6 baking potatoes (about ½ pound each)
1½ cups sour cream
1 teaspoon salt
½ teaspoon freshly ground black pepper
3 jalapeño peppers, stemmed, seeded, and diced
1½ teaspoons toasted and ground cumin seed
3 tablespoons chopped fresh coriander leaves
1 cup grated sharp Cheddar cheese

1. Preheat the oven to 375 degrees. Scrub the potatoes. Pierce them with a knife and bake them for about 50 minutes, or until they are quite done.
2. Remove the potatoes from the oven and let them stand at room temperature until they are just cool enough to handle, about 10 minutes. Cut the tops from the potatoes, about one-third. Lower the oven temperature to 350 degrees.
3. Scoop the flesh from the tops and the potatoes, leaving ¼-inch

shells. Mash the potatoes in a bowl and stir in the sour cream. Add the salt and pepper and adjust the seasoning.

4. Stir in the jalapeños, cumin, and coriander. Fill the potato shells with the mixture. Bake for about 20 minutes. Remove the potatoes from the oven and sprinkle the cheese over the tops.

5. Turn the oven to broil and place the potatoes 5 inches from the heat and broil for 1 to 2 minutes, or until the cheese is bubbling and slightly browned. Watch carefully. Serve hot.

Caldillo de Papas

≡ This is a dish particular to Santa Fe. Santiago Soto told us about his grandmother's recipe and we were very pleased when we tried it.

Serves 4 to 6

1 medium-sized onion, thinly sliced
2 garlic cloves, chopped not too finely
2 tablespoons lard or corn oil
½ pound boneless pork, cut into ½-inch dice
½ teaspoon toasted and ground cumin
1 cup water
1 pound red or white waxy potatoes
Salt and freshly ground black pepper
1 tablespoon chopped fresh mint leaves, or 1 teaspoon
    dried mint leaves
1 large ripe tomato, peeled, seeded, and diced

1. Fry half of the onion and all of the garlic to a golden color in the lard over medium heat. Add the pork and raise the heat to high. Sear the pork briefly and stir in the cumin. Add 1 cup of water, cover, and lower the heat. Cook at a bare simmer for 1 hour.

2. Meanwhile, scrub the potatoes, peel them, if necessary, and cut them crosswise into ¼-inch-thick slices.

3. Season the meat well with salt and pepper and stir in the mint. Arrange the potatoes on top of the meat and sprinkle lightly with salt. Scatter the remaining onion slices over the potatoes and the tomatoes over the onions.

4. Cover the pot and bring it to a vigorous simmer. Remove the cover and cook until the potatoes are just tender, about 15 minutes. Serve hot.

Grilled Nopales

≡ We like to cook different things on the grill to maximize its use and our pleasure. Thickly sliced onions and homemade garlic-rubbed bread have been longtime favorites. Cactus leaves are a treat when grilled so that they are just charred black around the edges. They go especially well with the Marinated Grilled Mackerel (page 169) and the Grilled Leg of Lamb (page 154).

Serves 4 to 6

1 pound nopales
Olive oil
1 cup Salsa Fria with sage or Jalapeño Salsa (pages 58
   and 57)
¼ cup piñons, lightly toasted

1. Scrub the nopales with a vegetable scrubber to rid them of the prickles. With a small sharp paring knife, cut out the little nodules from around the base of the thorns. Be sure to get them all, especially around the edges, taking as little skin as possible.
2. Grill the cactus leaves over a moderately hot wood or wood-charcoal fire for about 10 to 12 minutes on each side. It may take a few minutes more or less to cook the nopales, depending upon whether the leaves are thin or thick and how hot the fire is burning. Brush the nopales lightly with a little olive oil while they are cooking.
3. When the nopales are done, arrange them on warm plates, spoon a little salsa on each one, and sprinkle the piñons over the top. Serve immediately.

Garden Zucchini with
Roasted Tomato Sauce

≡ Baby zucchini are becoming available in some produce stores and supermarkets. Be rigorous in your selections of these, as they have often been stored much too long, resulting in loss of flavor and even off-flavors, which are far from the delicacy of garden zucchini. This is one of those wonderfully simple dishes that depends on the freshest ingredients.

Serves 4 to 6

1½ pounds 2- to 3-inch-long zucchini
1 cup Roasted Tomato Sauce (page 86)
3 or 4 zucchini blossoms
Salt and freshly ground black pepper

1. Wash and trim the zucchini. Cut them into small fan shapes by making two or three cuts from the blossom end of each squash, about two-thirds of the length.

2. Pan-steam the squash in a little lightly salted water for 2 to 3 minutes, or until they are crisp-tender. Heat the sauce and cut the blossoms crosswise into fine shreds.

3. Season the zucchini lightly with salt and pepper and serve them on the sauce on a warm platter. Sprinkle the blossoms over the platter as garnish.

CHAPTER THIRTEEN

Salads

Salads, like vegetables as side dishes, are recent arrivals to Southwestern cuisine. There is no history of salads served as separate courses; because of the scarcity of salad vegetables, shredded lettuce, chopped tomatoes, and onions were put on the table as relishes, or even in a little mound on a plate with beans, meat, or enchiladas. The idea of the salad on its own has spread as the raw materials have become available and the cooking has been influenced by immigrants with ideas of their own as to the importance of freshness in a meal.

People from other vegetable-rich parts of the country settled in large numbers after the Second World War and began to make salad-eating a part of the regional tradition. The importance of salads continued to grow as the nutritional benefits became apparent. More than this, we think that right now there is an awareness of and search for proper salads to complement traditional specialties. It is not enough to have the wedge of iceberg drizzled with bottled French dressing (though we recognize that in some minds this *is* the traditional salad) on a separate plate, or even to serve delicate butter lettuce and mache leaves with virgin olive oil and raspberry vinegar (though this might be appropriate with some meals). The richness of chile-thickened stews, lard-cooked beans, meat and tortillas with every meal, does call for the counterpoint of something un-cooked, crunchy, tangy, in short a salad, but a salad of definite flavors whose ingredients lend themselves to the seasonings of the area, garlic, coriander, oregano, cumin. Our opinions here are strongly held, but by no means represent a consensus. Cooks, like sports fans, are passionate about details; even though they don't have recourse to stat books, they can still justify style.

While all this is being sorted out, there remain those salads that have been accepted for some time: potato, slaw, and filled avocado. These usually have some local pepper or chile to set them apart from German potato salad, dilled slaw, or Caribbean avocado salad. In the meantime, we are eating the salads we present here with satisfaction and learning of new ones with great interest.

Avocado and Rice Salad

≡ Serves 6

3 tablespoons fresh lime juice
6 tablespoons olive oil
1 tablespoon Chili Powder (page 50), or to taste
1 garlic clove, finely chopped
Salt
2 medium-sized or large Hass avocados
1 medium-sized red bell pepper, seeded and cut into
    medium dice
1 medium-sized onion, cut into medium dice
2 serrano or jalapeño peppers, stemmed, seeded, and
    finely diced
2 tablespoons chopped fresh coriander or parsley leaves
3 cups *cooked* long-grain white or brown rice
Lettuce leaves for garnish, optional

1. Make the vinaigrette by whisking together the lime juice, olive oil, chili powder, garlic, and salt to taste.

2. Peel and pit the avocados and cut them into medium dice. Toss the diced vegetables and the coriander gently with the rice. Toss the salad with the vinaigrette.

3. Allow the flavors to meld for an hour or so before serving the salad at cool room temperature. Serve with lettuce, if desired.

Dried Beef, Carrot, and Romaine Salad

≣ If you have time, it's good to let the meat marinate in the vinaigrette for an hour or so.

Serves 4 to 6

12 to 16 baby carrots or 4 to 5 medium-sized carrots
⅓ cup plus 2 tablespoons Hot Pepper Vinegar (page 52)
⅓ cup water
1 fresh sage sprig, or 2 or 3 dried sage leaves
6 ounces Oven-Dried Beef (page 148)
⅓ cup olive oil
1 garlic clove, minced
¼ cup chopped fresh parsley leaves
1 tablespoon chopped fresh oregano leaves
Salt and freshly ground black pepper
½ teaspoon toasted and ground cumin seed
1 bunch scallions
1 or 2 heads romaine lettuce

1. Trim and peel the carrots. If using the larger carrots, cut them into pieces about ⅜ inch wide and 2 inches long. Put them in a small pan with the ⅓ cup vinegar, water, and sage. Cover and simmer until they are crisp-tender, 8 to 10 minutes. Remove the carrots to cool and mince the sage leaves. Add the 2 tablespoons hot pepper vinegar to the cooking liquid; there should be about ½ cup.

2. Shred the beef into fine shreds. Mix the cooking liquid and sage with the oil, garlic, parsley, oregano, and cumin. Toss the vinaigrette with the shredded meat. Season to taste with salt and pepper.

3. Clean and trim the scallions, leaving about 2 inches of green. Clean and trim the lettuce to the hearts.

4. Arrange the dried beef and vinaigrette, the carrots, and the scallions on the romaine hearts. Each person should fold a lettuce leaf around a carrot, a scallion, and some dried beef and eat the little packets. Or the salad may be served and cut.

Cabbage and Pineapple Slaw with Fresh Chile Vinaigrette

≡ If you wish to make this salad ahead, it is best to have the ingredients ready separately, and let the slaw stand for just 30 minutes with the vinaigrette. It becomes a different thing, much more like a relish, though quite good, if it is leftover or stands for several hours.

Serves 6

¼ cup very finely diced mixed fresh chiles (There should be some hot and mild varieties, and red, green, and yellow peppers if possible. Cayenne, red hot cherry, Mexico Improved, Hungarian Wax, Santa Fe Grande, Anaheim, jalapeño, and serrano are good choices.)
½ cup olive oil
3 tablespoons fresh lime juice
Salt and freshly ground black pepper
4 cups finely shredded cabbage
2 cups diced fresh pineapple
½ medium-sized red onion, thinly sliced

1. Mix the diced chiles in a bowl with the olive oil and lime juice. Season well with salt and pepper.
2. Toss the cabbage, pineapple, and onion with the vinaigrette. Let the salad stand for 30 minutes, covered, in the refrigerator.

Chick-pea, Lime, and Avocado Salad

≡ **Serves 4**

1 large California avocado, peeled, pitted, and quartered lengthwise
1 medium-sized lime
2 cups cooked chick-peas
½ cup thinly sliced red onion
2 tablespoons olive oil

1 to 2 teaspoons Hot Pepper Vinegar (page 52)
¼ cup chopped fresh parsley leaves
1 tablespoon minced fresh peppermint or other mint
    leaves
Salt and freshly ground black pepper
Lettuce for garnish
Fresh parsley or mint sprigs for garnish

1. Slice the avocado crosswise into ¼-inch slices. Peel the lime and cut it into quarters lengthwise; then slice it into ⅛-inch wedges.

2. Toss the avocado, lime, chick-peas, and onion gently together in a bowl. Add the oil, vinegar, parsley, mint, and salt and pepper and toss gently. Taste for seasoning.

3. Let the salad stand at cool room temperature for about 30 minutes before serving. Serve on a bed of lettuce, garnished with parsley or mint sprigs.

Corn Off the Cob Salad

≡ Serves 4 to 6

⅓ cup olive oil
3 tablespoons hot pepper vinegar, or to taste
1 tablespoon coarsely chopped fresh marjoram or
    oregano leaves
1 tablespoon ground mild red chile
Salt
4 large very fresh ears white or yellow corn
1 small red bell pepper
1 small green bell pepper
1 bunch scallions

1. Make a vinaigrette with the oil, vinegar, marjoram, and red chile. Season with salt.

2. Husk and remove the silk from the corn. Cook the corn in lightly salted simmering water until the corn milk has just set, from 30 seconds to 2 minutes, depending on the freshness of the corn. Refresh the corn under cold water.

3. Seed the peppers and cut them into small dice. Trim the scallions, leaving 2 inches of green, and slice them thinly. Cut the corn from the cob and break the cut corn into kernels. There should be about 4 cups of corn.

4. Put the vegetables in a bowl and toss them with the vinaigrette. Season with salt. Let the salad stand at cool room temperature for an hour or so before serving.

Green Salad with Blood Orange Vinaigrette

≡ Serves 6

⅓ cup blood orange juice
⅓ cup olive oil
Salt and freshly ground black pepper
3 quarts trimmed and washed mild salad greens, such
    as oak leaf lettuce, Bibb lettuce, butter lettuce,
    Simpson lettuce, and romaine lettuce
6 scallions, trimmed with 2 inches of green and thinly
    sliced

1. Put the orange juice in a small bowl and gradually whisk in the olive oil. Season with salt and pepper.

2. Just before serving, toss the greens and scallions with the vinaigrette.

Jícama and Pepper Salad

≡ Serves 4 to 6

¾ pound jícama, peeled, trimmed, and cut into ¼- by
    3-inch pieces
2 cups red and yellow bell peppers, sliced ¼ inch thick
¼ cup olive oil

3 tablespoons fresh lime juice
1 tablespoon chopped fresh oregano leaves
⅓ cup loosely packed chopped fresh chives
Salt and freshly ground black pepper

1. Combine the jícama and peppers in a bowl. Mix the oil and lime juice together and pour it over the vegetables. Add the herbs and salt and pepper and toss well.
2. Let the salad stand for 30 minutes at cool room temperature before serving. Taste for seasoning. If you hold the salad any longer, cover and refrigerate it.

Jícama Guacamole

☰ This is an especially versatile dish; it can be served as a salad, used as a garnish for tostadas, or served as a dip with tortilla chips.

Serves 6

2 firm ripe avocados
1½ cups grated and squeezed jícama
1 large ripe tomato, diced
2 serranos or 1 jalapeño pepper, stemmed, seeded, and
    minced
1 garlic clove, finely minced
2 tablespoons olive oil
2½ tablespoons fresh lime juice, or to taste
Salt and freshly ground black pepper

1. Peel the avocados and remove the pits. Dice the avocados and put them in a small bowl. Add the jícama, tomato, peppers, and garlic and toss lightly.
2. Sprinkle the olive oil and lime juice over the vegetables. Season well with salt and pepper and toss the salad gently.

Pasta and Roasted Pepper
Salad with Piñons

≡ This is a good picnic salad; it keeps well, there is plenty of it, and it is compatible with many foods.

Serves 8 to 10

1 pound dried pasta, such as macaroni, fusilli, or ca-
    vatappi
5 tablespoons olive oil
1 tablespoon plus 1 teaspoon ground mild red chile
4 tablespoons fresh lime juice
1½ teaspoons toasted and ground coriander seed
3 cloves garlic, finely minced
6 tablespoons chopped fresh cilantro leaves
6 tablespoons chopped fresh parsley leaves
2 large red bell peppers, roasted, seeded, peeled, and
    chopped
4 Anaheim, Numex Big Jim, or New Mexico chiles,
    roasted, seeded, peeled, and chopped
½ cup toasted piñons
Salt and freshly ground black pepper
Lettuce and tomatoes, optional

1. Cook the pasta until *al dente*; then drain and toss it with 1 table-spoon of the oil.

2. In a small bowl mix the remaining oil, ground chile, lime, corian-der, garlic, cilantro, and parsley. Toss with the pasta.

3. Add the peppers, chiles, piñons, and salt and pepper. Toss well and taste for seasoning. Let the salad stand for at least 30 minutes before serving; or refrigerate for a few hours and allow to come to cool room temperature before serving.

4. Serve the salad alone or on a bed of greens, garnished with ripe tomatoes, if desired.

Potato, Snap Bean, and Red Pepper Salad with Jalapeño Mayonnaise

≡ Serves 6

1 pound new red potatoes, scrubbed, halved, and sliced
¼ inch thick
10 ounces yellow wax or green beans, topped and
tailed, and snapped into 1-inch pieces
1 large red bell pepper, roasted, peeled, and seeded
Salt and freshly ground black pepper
¼ cup packed fresh coriander leaves, roughly chopped
½ cup thinly sliced onion rings
¾ cup Jalapeño Mayonnaise (page 52)
Fresh lime juice to taste
Lettuce leaves, such as oak leaf, red leaf, or butter lettuce
¼ cup toasted pepitas

1. Steam the potatoes for about 10 minutes or until just barely tender.
Drain and cool. Blanch the beans until they are tender; young beans take
about 4 minutes, older beans 8 to 10 minutes. Drain and cool. Cut the
roasted pepper into strips of about ¼ by 2 inches

2. Combine the potatoes, beans, and pepper strips in a large bowl.
Season lightly with salt and pepper.

3. Add the coriander, onion, and mayonnaise and toss gently to coat
the vegetables. Taste for salt, pepper, mayonnaise, and lime juice.

4. Line a platter with lettuce leaves and mound the salad on the platter.
The salad may be covered and refrigerated for 3 to 4 hours. Let the salad
stand at room temperature for 30 minutes and garnish with pepitas just
before serving.

Rocket and Spinach Salad with Bacon

≡ Serves 4

¼ pound bacon, cut into ¼-inch dice
About 3 tablespoons olive oil
About 1½ tablespoons white wine vinegar
1 to 2 jalapeño peppers, stemmed, seeded, and finely
    diced
1 garlic clove, finely minced
½ quart stemmed and washed rocket leaves
1½ quarts stemmed and washed spinach leaves
Salt and freshly ground black pepper
2 tablespoons toasted piñons

1. Cook the bacon over low heat until it is crisp and the fat is rendered. Remove the bacon from the pan with a slotted spoon and drain
it on paper towels.

2. Pour the fat into a measuring cup and add enough olive oil to
equal ¼ cup. Stir the vinegar vigorously into the oil and stir in the jalapeño
peppers and garlic.

3. Just before serving, toss the rocket and spinach leaves with the
bacon and the vinaigrette, and season the salad with salt and pepper.
Garnish with the piñons.

Shrimp and Avocado Salad
with Jalapeño Mayonnaise

≡ Serves 4

1 teaspoon ground mild red chile
½ teaspoon sea salt
1 lime slice
1 pound medium-sized (26 to 30 count) or large (16
    to 20 count) shrimp
2 large ripe California avocados
1 tablespoon fresh lime juice
½ cup Jalapeño Mayonnaise (page 52)

Salt and freshly ground white pepper
1 small head mild lettuce, such as butter, oak leaf, or
    salad bowl, trimmed and washed

1. Put the ground red chile, sea salt, and lime in a pan just large enough to hold the shrimp. Add about 1 inch of water. Bring to a simmer and add the shrimp. Poach the shrimp until they are just done, 2 to 3 minutes.

2. Shell and devein the shrimp. Reserve 4 shrimp for garnish and cut the rest into bite-sized pieces.

3. Peel and pit the avocados. Cut the flesh into bite-sized pieces. Toss the avocados gently with the lime juice. Toss the shrimp and avocados gently with the jalapeño mayonnaise. Season the salad with salt and pepper and lime juice. Arrange on lettuce leaves and serve.

Spinach, Beet, and Onion Salad with Coriander Cumin Vinaigrette

≡ Serves 6

½ pound trimmed small red or golden beets
1 tablespoon fresh lime juice, or to taste
⅓ cup olive oil
1 teaspoon coriander seed, toasted and ground
½ teaspoon cumin seed, toasted and ground
Salt and freshly ground black pepper
1 pound fresh spinach leaves, stemmed and washed
1 small mild salad onion, thinly sliced

1. Cook the beets in lightly salted, gently boiling water for 15 to 20 minutes, or until they are just done. Drain the beets and refresh them under cold water. Peel and trim the beets and slice them ¼ inch thick.

2. Put the lime juice in a small bowl and whisk the olive oil into it. Whisk in the coriander and cumin and season the vinaigrette with salt and pepper.

3. Toss the spinach and onion with about two-thirds of the vinaigrette. Arrange the salad on a platter or in a bowl with the beet slices over it. Drizzle the rest of the vinaigrette over the salad and serve.

Summer Squash Salad

≡ Serves 4 to 6

1 pound tender 4- to 6-inch-long yellow and green squash
About 1 teaspoon salt
1 cup thin red onion slices
½ cup grated carrots
4 tablespoons Hot Pepper Vinegar (page 52), or to taste
2 tablespoons rice wine vinegar
¼ cup olive oil
½ teaspoon toasted and ground cumin seed
1 garlic clove, finely minced
2 tablespoons chopped fresh coriander leaves
3 tablespoons finely shredded fresh basil leaves
Salt and freshly ground black pepper
Lettuce leaves for garnish

1. Trim and wash the squash. Grate the squash, place it in a colander, and salt it lightly. Let it stand for 15 minutes, rinse, and then squeeze it very dry. Transfer the squash to a mixing bowl and add the onion and carrots.

2. Whisk the vinegars, oil, cumin, and garlic together in a bowl. Pour the vinaigrette over the vegetables and add the herbs. Season with salt and pepper and toss well.

3. Let the salad stand for at least 30 minutes before serving. Taste for seasoning and serve on lettuce leaves

Tomatoes with Cilantro and Oregano

≡ This salad depends on the freshest summer ripe tomatoes and good quality virgin olive oil. If your cilantro is in bloom use the blossoms or a few of the green seeds to garnish the plates.

Serves 4 to 6

⅓ cup extra virgin olive oil
3 tablespoons chopped fresh cilantro leaves
1 tablespoon chopped fresh oregano leaves

4 large tomatoes, cored, halved lengthwise,
    and cut into ⅜-inch-thick
    slices
Salt and freshly ground black pepper
1 large garlic clove, thinly slivered
4 to 6 handfuls garden greens, such as
    ruby or green leaf lettuce, mache, rocket,
    or lamb's quarters
Cilantro blossoms for garnish, optional

1. Pour a few tablespoons of the olive oil into a large flat dish. Sprinkle 1 tablespoon of the cilantro and 1 teaspoon of the oregano over the bottom of the dish. Lay half of the tomatoes in the dish. Grind black pepper generously over the tomatoes and season them lightly with salt.

2. Sprinkle another tablespoon of cilantro, another teaspoon of oregano, and half of the garlic over the tomatoes. Drizzle half of the remaining olive oil over them.

3. Repeat the next layer, using the rest of the tomatoes, more salt and pepper, herbs, garlic, and oil. Let the salad marinate at room temperature for 1 hour.

4. Place a handful of greens on each salad plate and arrange the tomatoes on the greens. Drizzle a little of the marinade over each salad and garnish with cilantro blossoms if you have them.

Watercress Salad with
Cactus Fruit Vinaigrette

≡ The bright green and red contrast in this salad mades it festive. The cactus fruit is slightly sweet, so the dressing also goes well with sliced mangos, papayas, and peaches.

Serves 6

8 ounces fresh prickly pear cactus fruit
2 tablespoons olive oil
2 teaspoons red wine vinegar, or to taste
Salt and freshly ground black pepper
2 or 3 bunches watercress, trimmed and washed

1. Peel the cactus fruit and put it in a food processor or blender, seeds and all, and process until smooth. Pour through a strainer to remove the hard seeds.

2. Mix together the cactus fruit purée, oil, vinegar, and salt and pepper with a fork in a small bowl. Taste the vinaigrette for seasoning.

3. Arrange the watercress on salad plates and spoon the dressing over the cress and serve immediately.

CHAPTER FOURTEEN

Desserts

A taste for the tinglingly sweet and the solidly comforting marks traditional Southwestern desserts. They call for black coffee and appetites honed on the range. Puddings of all kinds, bread, pumpkin, rice, cornmeal, and *panocha* were made by the Indians, Mexicans, Spanish, and Anglos. In times when fresh milk and eggs were scarce, they were made with water, evaporated or condensed milk, and often sweetened with honey and dried fruit. Brown sugar became popular, along with the dried fruit still added for tradition's and embellishment's sake. Cheese, sometimes wine, or both together were added to bread puddings.

Some heirloom pie crust and cake recipes traveled with settlers from the Midwest and East. They were given local flavor by enclosing dried fruit and nut fillings (the many versions of *empanadas* and *empanaditas*), and by adding more spices to the batters. The use of lard in pastry was much favored by early Southwestern cooks; lard was more available than butter and had the virtue of being easier to work with in the hot climate.

Fried foods, especially breads, are favored in this cooking. The best-loved of these are *sopaipillas* and *buñuelos*. Some cooks make a yeast dough for buñuelos; others use baking powder for a dough very similar to that of sopaipillas. Sometimes the doughs are folded around fruit or cheese, then fried. We think the best way to eat either is piping hot with a little honey and perhaps butter and cinnamon. The recipe for sopaipillas (also served as a main course) is in the bread chapter.

The Spanish influence was most direct in the dessert realm: rice puddings, flans, the soft custards called *natillas*. These have kept their popularity while the Southwestern sweet tooth has turned to the tropical fruits from Mexico and the fine variety of fresh fruits and nuts grown in the region. The citrus of Arizona, California, and Texas is famous, pecan orchards flourish in New Mexico, and pistachios in California. Melons and berries concentrate their flavors in the dry southerly areas, and the peaches of southern Colorado and northern New Mexico are prized by the residents.

We have translated the old or standard recipes freely to reflect our preference for light and refreshing desserts. Sometimes the ingredients themselves have suggested more refined confections than their original forms. Pumpkin, for example, removed from its dense puddingy setting, becomes a pretty, fresh-tasting ice cream. Ice creams and ices are so good in a Southwestern menu that we have included five recipes for them. Our versions of the filling double-crusted dried fruit and nut-filled empanadas are made with butter crusts and left open to become an apricot tart with a little custard or a pecan tart with some cream and *cajeta*.

Cajeta is sweetened caramelized goats' and cows' milk, a Mexican import usually found close to the border in Arizona and California. In Mexico the term also refers to little caramel and milk candies, or to thickened milk or fruit desserts. It is commonly spread on bread, and used as an ice-cream topping. Although it is not much used in the Southwest, we think the distinctive flavor is a treat that goes well in this cuisine. We have provided a homemade version for those who cannot find the import.

Hazelnut Cake
with Cajeta and Coconut

≡ Serves 8 to 12

1 ½ cups shelled hazelnuts, toasted, peeled, and ground
½ cup unbleached white flour, sifted
¼ teaspoon salt
½ teaspoon ground cinnamon
½ teaspoon freshly grated nutmeg
5 extra large eggs, separated
1 cup granulated sugar
⅓ cup Cajeta (page 245)

4 tablespoons unsalted butter, softened
3 cups confectioners' sugar, sifted
1 tablespoon half-and-half
1 teaspoon pure vanilla extract
1 generous cup coarsely grated fresh coconut

1. Preheat the oven to 350 degrees. Butter and flour the bottoms of three 8-inch round cake pans.
2. Toss the ground hazelnuts with the flour, salt, cinnamon, and nutmeg in a mixing bowl.
3. Beat the egg yolks with the sugar until light and fluffy. Fold the egg and sugar mixture into the nut mixture and blend well. The mixture will be stiff. Beat the egg whites until stiff but not dry and gently fold about one-third of the whites into the nut mixture. Fold the remaining whites into the nut mixture until just blended.
4. Divide the batter among the prepared pans. Bake for 20 to 25 minutes, or until golden brown on top and a tester comes out clean. Cool the cakes on racks and remove them from the pans when cool.
5. To prepare the buttercream, cream the cajeta and butter until light and fluffy. Add the sugar, a little at a time, whipping it in each time, and scraping the sides of the bowl. Add the cream halfway through adding the sugar. Beat in the remaining sugar and the vanilla. The buttercream should be smooth, but will be slightly sticky, due to the nature of the cajeta. Place a damp paper towel over the bowl until ready to use.
6. To assemble the cake, place a cake layer on a serving platter. Using one-third of the buttercream, cover the layer evenly. Sprinkle a generous ¼ cup of the coconut on the buttercream.
7. Repeat with the next two layers, heaping the remaining coconut on the top layer. If the weather is warm or humid, the cake should be stored in the refrigerator. Bring it to cool room temperature before serving.

Blood Orange Skillet Cake

≡ Blood oranges have become available in the Southwest during the past few years. They give this upside-down-style cake a lovely flavor; however, regular oranges or tangerines can be substituted. We make the cake in an iron skillet.

Serves 10

4 tablespoons unsalted butter
½ cup packed dark brown sugar
1¼ pounds blood oranges, peeled, seeded, and cut into
   ⅜-inch-thick slices
3 extra large eggs, separated
2 extra large eggs
1 cup sugar
1¼ cups unbleached white flour, sifted
4 tablespoons unsalted butter, melted and cooled
1 teaspoon pure vanilla extract
1 heaping teaspoon grated zest from blood oranges
2 to 3 tablespoons dark rum, optional
Freshly whipped cream for garnish, optional

1. Melt 4 tablespoons of butter in a 10-inch skillet with an ovenproof handle over medium-low heat. Add the brown sugar and stir well until it is dissolved. Remove from the heat. Arrange the orange slices in the bottom of the pan. Preheat the oven to 350 degrees.

2. Beat the 3 egg yolks with the 2 whole eggs and the sugar until the mixture is light and fluffy. Fold the flour in three parts, alternately with the melted and cooled butter in two parts, into the mixture. Fold in the vanilla and zest.

3. Beat the 3 egg whites until stiff but not dry and fold them gently into the batter. Pour the batter carefully over the orange slices.

4. Bake for about 30 minutes, or until a tester comes out clean. Remove from the oven and let stand for a few minutes. Turn the cake out onto a serving platter while it is still hot, allowing the skillet to rest over the platter for about 5 minutes so that the brown sugar and butter drizzle over the cake. Remove the skillet and serve the cake warm or let it cool. Drizzle 2 or 3 tablespoons of dark rum over the cake, if desired. Serve with whipped cream.

Pecan Peach Cake

≣ Serves 10 to 12

2 large peaches, peeled and cut into slices
3 tablespoons dark or light brown sugar
1 tablespoon fresh lemon juice
3 extra large eggs
⅔ cup granulated sugar
2 cups finely ground pecans (about 7 ounces shelled
    pecans)
⅓ cup unbleached white flour
Finely minced zest of 1 small orange
¼ teaspoon salt
3 extra large egg whites
2 tablespoons unsalted butter, cut into small bits
Fresh whipped cream for garnish, optional

1. Toss the peaches gently with the brown sugar and lemon juice in a small bowl. Preheat the oven to 350 degrees. Generously butter and lightly flour a 9½-inch springform pan.

2. Beat the eggs and sugar together until pale yellow and fluffy. Toss the pecans together with the flour, zest, and salt.

3. Beat the egg whites until stiff but not dry. Fold the pecan mixture into the egg and sugar mixture. Gently fold the egg whites into this batter. Pour the batter into the prepared pan.

4. Arrange the peach slices on top of the batter; do not use their juice. Dot the top of the cake with the butter.

5. Bake the cake for 35 to 40 minutes, or until a tester comes out clean. Cool on a wire rack. This cake is best served on the same day it is made. Serve warm or at room temperature with whipped cream, if desired.

Apricot Piñon Tart

≣ Serves 8

PASTRY

½ cup unsalted butter, well chilled
1 cup unbleached white flour
½ tablespoon sugar
Pinch of salt
1½ to 2 tablespoons ice water

FILLING

½ cup milk
3 ounces dried apricots
¼ cup dark rum or brandy
½ cup sour cream
¼ cup light honey
1 extra large egg
3 or 4 drops pure vanilla extract
2 ounces lightly toasted piñons

1. Cut the butter into small bits. Mix the flour, sugar, and salt. Cut the butter into the flour with a pastry blender to make a medium meal, or do this carefully in a food processor.

2. Add just enough water to bind the dough. Gather the pastry and form a flattened round about ½ inch thick. Cover the dough with plastic wrap and chill for at least an hour. The dough performs better if it is refrigerated for 2 to 3 hours and brought out to soften slightly before pressing.

3. Press the dough into a 9-inch tart pan with a removable bottom. Be sure that the dough extends at least ¼ inch above the rim of the tart pan. Prick the dough in the bottom of the pan.

4. Cover the pastry shell with plastic wrap and chill for at least 1 hour. The dough performs better if it is refrigerated overnight and baked directly. It may also be frozen to good result. Preheat the oven to 375 degrees 20 minutes before baking the pastry.

5. Remove the plastic wrap and bake the pastry shell in the lower half of the oven for about 25 minutes; or until it is pale golden brown all over. Check the pastry after 10 minutes. If the dough is puffed, prick it with a fork. If the sides are shrinking, press them into the rim of the pan with the back of a fork. Let the pastry cool on a wire rack.

6. To prepare the filling, scald the milk and remove it from the heat. Soak 2 ounces of the apricots in it until it has cooled to room temperature. Cut 1 ounce of apricots into ¼-inch strips. Soak them in the rum and reserve for garnish. Reduce oven to 350 degrees.

7. Purée the apricots and milk with the sour cream in a food processor. Add the honey, egg, and vanilla. Pour the mixture into the partially baked pastry shell.

8. Sprinkle the toasted piñons over the apricot purée. Arrange the apricot pieces over the piñons. Bake the tart for 30 minutes, or until a cake tester comes out clean. Cool on a wire rack. Serve at cool room temperature.

Pecan Tart with Cajeta

≡ **Serves 8**

PASTRY

    ½ cup unsalted butter, well chilled
    1 cup unbleached white flour
    1 tablespoon sugar
    Pinch of salt
    1½ to 2 tablespoons water

PECAN FILLING

    1 cup pecan halves
    ½ cup heavy (whipping) cream
    ½ cup Cajeta (page 245)

1. Cut the butter into bits. Mix the flour, sugar, and salt. Cut the butter into the flour with a pastry blender, or in a food processor, to make a medium meal. Add just enough water to bind the dough, and gather the pastry to form a flattened round, about ½ inch thick. Cover the dough with plastic wrap and chill for at least 30 minutes.

2. Press the dough into a 9-inch tart pan with a removable bottom. Prick the bottom of the dough. Cover and chill for at least another 30 minutes. Preheat the oven to 375 degrees.

3. Bake the shell for about 25 minutes, or until it is golden brown. Check the pastry after 10 minutes. If the dough is puffed, prick it with a

fork. If the sides are shrinking, press them into the rim of the pan with the back of a fork. Cool on a wire rack.

4. While the tart shell is baking, combine the pecans, cream, and cajeta in a heavy-bottomed saucepan and heat over medium heat. When contents of pan start to bubble, lower the heat and cook slowly, stirring, for 15 minutes. Remove from the heat and cool. Turn the oven temperature to 350 degrees.

5. When the tart shell has cooled to warm, pour the contents of the saucepan into the shell and spread the nuts and filling evenly.

6. Place the tart pan on a baking sheet lined with aluminum foil and bake in a 350-degree oven for 20 minutes, turning the tart halfway through the baking time for even browning. Remove the tart pan from the baking sheet and cool on a wire rack. Serve at room temperature.

Lime Meringue Pie with Coconut Crust

≡ Serves 8

CRUST

    1 cup lightly packed freshly grated coconut
    ¾ cup fine dry bread crumbs
    2 tablespoons sugar
    3 tablespoons unsalted butter, melted

FILLING

    ¾ cup sugar
    5 tablespoons cornstarch
    1 tablespoon unbleached white flour
    1 cup heavy (whipping) cream
    1 cup half-and-half
    3 extra large egg yolks
    ½ cup fresh lime juice
    Finely grated zest of 1 lime

MERINGUE

    4 extra large egg whites
    3 tablespoons sugar
    Pinch of cream of tartar
    1 to 2 tablespoons grated coconut for garnish, optional

1. Preheat the oven to 350 degrees. Mix the coconut, bread crumbs, 2 tablespoons sugar, and butter in a bowl or in a food processor until blended. Pat the mixture into a 9-inch pie plate, evenly covering the bottom and sides. Bake for 15 minutes, or until the crust is pale golden brown. Cool on a baking rack.

2. To prepare the filling, mix the sugar, cornstarch, and flour in a heavy saucepan. Add the creams, whisking them in until well blended. Place the pan over medium-low heat and cook for 8 to 10 minutes, stirring regularly, until the mixture is slightly thickened.

3. Beat the egg yolks well in a bowl. Add a little of the cream mixture to the eggs, blending well. Add a bit more cream and blend well. Carefully add the egg and cream mixture to the saucepan. Cook over low heat for about 2 minutes; do not allow the mixture to boil. Remove from the heat, stir in the lime juice and zest, cover with wax paper, and let cool to room temperature.

4. Preheat the oven to 400 degrees. Pour the filling into the crust. To prepare the meringue, beat the whites in a bowl until foamy. Add the sugar and cream of tartar and beat the whites until stiff but not dry. Mound the whites onto the filling and spread them evenly, taking care to make sure the whites touch the entire perimeter of the crust.

5. Sprinkle the meringue with the extra coconut, if desired. Bake the pie for 5 minutes, or until the meringue is lightly browned. Let cool on a wire rack and then refrigerate for 2 to 3 hours before serving.

Almond Piloncillo Cookies

≡ If you can't find the piloncillo, substitute the same amount of dark brown sugar for it and add 1 tablespoon of molasses. The flavor will be a little different, but the cookies are still tasty.

Makes 40 to 48 cookies

3 ounces piloncillo, broken into pieces
1 cup whole natural almonds
2 cups unbleached white flour
Pinch of salt
12 tablespoons unsalted butter
½ teaspoon pure vanilla extract
½ teaspoon pure almond extract
Confectioner's sugar

1. Preheat the oven to 350 degrees. Lightly butter two baking sheets. Combine the piloncillo and the almonds in a food processor. Process them into a coarse meal. Add the flour and salt and process until just blended.

2. Cut the butter into 12 pieces and add it to the processor with the extracts. Process until well blended, scraping down the sides once or twice. The dough will be mealy and not quite massed together.

3. Using your fingers, break off bits of dough about the size of a small walnut and pat them gently into crescent shapes. Place them on the baking sheets.

4. Bake the cookies for 20 minutes, or until the bottoms are light golden brown. If using two baking sheets, change shelves halfway through the baking time.

5. Remove the cookies immediately from the baking sheets onto wire racks. While the cookies are still hot, dust the tops with confectioner's sugar through a strainer. Store in tightly-covered tins when cool.

Pine Nut Cookies with Cinnamon Sugar

Makes about 7 dozen cookies

¾ cup plus 3 tablespoons sugar
1 extra large egg
12 tablespoons unsalted butter cut into 12 pieces
½ teaspoon salt
1 teaspoon pure vanilla extract
1⅓ cups unbleached white flour
⅓ cup cornmeal
½ cup pine nuts
1½ tablespoons ground cinnamon

1. Combine ¾ cup of the sugar and the egg in a food processor and mix for 1 minute. Add the butter, salt, and vanilla and mix about 1 minute, stopping once to scrape down the sides. Add the flour, cornmeal, and pine nuts and mix until just blended. Do not overmix. The dough will be soft.

2. Divide the dough into three equal portions and arrange each on a sheet of plastic wrap. Roll the dough into cylinders 1 to 1¼ inches in

diameter using the plastic wrap as an aid. Place the cylinders in the freezer for 30 minutes.

3. Preheat the oven to 350 degrees. Mix the remaining 3 tablespoons of sugar with the cinnamon in a small dish. Remove the dough from the freezer one cylinder at a time. Cut the dough with a sharp knife into ¼-inch-thick slices. Press one side of each slice in the cinnamon sugar. Place on baking sheets, sugared side up, at least 1 inch apart.

4. Bake until the edges are lightly browned, 8 to 10 minutes. If baking two sheets at once, change the position of the sheets halfway through baking time.

5. Remove the cookies from sheets immediately and cool on wire racks. If the cookies are left on the sheets to cool, they will break when removed. Store in a tightly-covered tin.

Spiced Chocolate Soufflé

≡ This can be prepared the night before or the morning of the day you plan to serve it. If you make the soufflé ahead, store it in the refrigerator and let it stand at room temperature about 30 minutes before you serve it. Cool, it is especially good with whipped cream that has a touch of Kahlua added.

Serves 6 to 8

½ cup half-and-half
5 ounces semisweet chocolate, preferably Lindt, Tob-
    lerone, or Callebaut, broken into pieces
6 tablespoons sugar
2 pinches of salt
½ teaspoon ground cinnamon
1 tablespoon instant espresso coffee powder
4 extra large eggs, separated
4 extra large egg whites
½ cup sliced almonds
2 tablespoons water

1. Preheat the oven to 375 degrees. Generously butter and sugar a 1½-quart soufflé dish.

2. Combine the half-and-half, chocolate, 4 tablespoons of the sugar, salt, cinnamon, and espresso in a heavy-bottomed saucepan. Place over medium-low heat. Whisk the chocolate as it melts to make a smooth mixture. Remove from heat when the chocolate is completely melted.

3. Beat the 4 yolks, one at a time, into the chocolate mixture. In a separate bowl, beat the 8 egg whites to soft peaks. Add 1 tablespoon of sugar to the whites and beat them until stiff but not dry.

4. Whisk about a cup of the egg whites into the chocolate mixture. Then pour the chocolate mixture into the whites and fold until just blended. Pour the mixture into the prepared soufflé dish and bake in the lower half of the oven for 20 to 25 minutes, or until the soufflé is set.

5. Combine the almonds, water, and remaining 1 tablespoon of sugar in a small skillet. Place it over medium heat and cook, stirring with a wooden scraper, until the water has evaporated and the almonds are sugar-coated, about 8 minutes. Turn them onto a plate or wax paper to cool.

6. Serve the soufflé hot from the dish sprinkled with the sugared almonds. Or cool the soufflé and refrigerate it; then unmold it onto a serving plate. Pat the almonds onto the top and sides of the soufflé just before serving and slice it at the table.

Pomegranate Flan

≡ This flan has an unusual and attractive mauve color. The unsweetened natural pomegranate juice is available at health food stores. A pineapple flan may be made by substituting canned unsweetened pineapple juice for the pomegranate juice and cutting the sugar back by 2 or 3 tablespoons.

Serves 8 to 10

CARAMEL

 1⅓ cups water
 ⅔ cup sugar

CUSTARD

 3 extra large eggs
 3 extra large egg yolks
 ½ cup sugar
 2 cups half-and-half
 1¼ cups unsweetened pomegranate juice
 Fresh pomegranate seeds for garnish, optional

1. Have a 10-inch pie plate or 4-cup custard mold ready on a piece of foil.

2. Heat the water and sugar together in a small heavy saucepan. Bring the mixture to a boil, stirring to dissolve the sugar. Lower the heat to medium-high. Swirl the pan gently until the syrup turns a rich golden brown, about 12 minutes.

3. Pour the caramel into the mold. Swirl it around to coat the mold evenly. When the syrup sets, turn the mold upside down on the foil.

4. Preheat the oven to 325 degrees. Have ready an ovenproof pan large enough to hold the mold and boiling water bath.

5. Beat the eggs and egg yolks with the sugar until they are well blended. Pour the half-and-half into the egg mixture, beating continually. Pour the pomegranate juice into the mixture and beat until well combined.

6. Pour the custard through a sieve into the mold. Place the mold in the ovenproof pan and pour boiling water halfway up the sides of the mold.

7. Bake for 1 hour and 20 minutes, or until a knife inserted in the center of the flan comes out clean. The flan will be soft and creamy. Remove the mold from the pan and cool to room temperature. Cover and refrigerate for at least 3 hours. The flan may be unmolded onto a flat serving platter, if desired, and garnished with fresh pomegranate seeds.

Cajeta Custard

≡ Serves 8

1 cup Cajeta (page 245)
1 cup heavy (whipping) cream
1 cup milk
3 extra large eggs, lightly beaten

1. Dissolve the cajeta in the cream and milk over low heat. Beat a little of the cajeta mixture into the beaten eggs. Whisk the eggs into the cajeta and cream. Preheat the oven to 325 degrees.

2. Pour the custard into eight buttered 6-ounce custard cups, or into a buttered 1½-quart baking dish. Put the dishes in a large baking dish and pour boiling water halfway up the sides of the custard dishes.

3. Bake for 30 to 35 minutes for the cups and 45 to 50 minutes for

the large dish, or until the custard is just set. Remove from the water and cool to room temperature. Refrigerate for 2 to 3 hours before serving.

Vanilla Custard

≣ We often serve this simple yet satisfying pudding with fruit. In the late spring we like raspberries, in the summer peaches and blueberries, and in the autumn stewed apples with cinnamon.

Serves 6

⅔ cup sugar
5 tablespoons cornstarch
2 cups milk
1 cup half-and-half
1 extra large egg
Pinch of salt
1 teaspoon pure vanilla extract

1. Mix the sugar and cornstarch together in the top of a double boiler. Stir in the milk and cream. Place the top over the bottom of the double boiler with boiling water over medium heat. The water should not touch the top pan. Stir the mixture gently with a wooden spoon for 8 to 10 minutes. Cover and cook for 6 to 8 minutes.

2. Beat the egg well with a pinch of salt. Add a little of the milk mixture to the egg; then add the egg gradually to the custard. Stir gently for 2 minutes.

3. Remove the top of the double boiler from the heat and cover. Cool the custard to lukewarm and gently stir in the vanilla. Pour into 6 custard cups. Cover and refrigerate them for at least 2 hours.

Banana Papaya Mousse

≣ **Serves 6 to 8**

1 very ripe papaya (about 1 pound)
2 to 4 very ripe bananas (about 12·ounces total)
2½ tablespoons fresh lime juice
1 tablespoon granulated sugar
1 cup heavy (whipping) cream
1½ tablespoons vanilla sugar

1. Peel and seed the papaya and cut it into chunks. Purée it in a food processor. Add the bananas, lime juice, and sugar and purée until smooth. Pour the mixture into a bowl and chill well.
2. Whip the cream with the vanilla sugar until stiff. Fold the whipped cream into the fruit purée and chill for about 2 hours, or until ready to serve. Spoon the mousse into ramekins or dessert cups just before serving.

Mango Ice

≣ **Serves 6 to 8**

2 large ripe mangoes, preferably from Mexico
⅓ cup light honey
1½ cups warm water
1 red hot cherry pepper, stemmed, seeded, and coarsely
    chopped
2 tablespoons dark rum
Thin slices of ripe mango for garnish, optional

1. Peel the mangoes and cut the meat from the seeds. Purée the mango in a food processor or blender. Stir the honey into the warm water. Add the honey water to the mango and blend together.
2. Pour the mixture into a bowl, leaving about ½ cup in the processor or blender. Purée the pepper with the mango mixture. There should be some bits of pepper in the purée. Stir the pepper purée and the rum into the mango mixture.
3. Freeze in an ice-cream machine according to manufacturer's in-

structions or pour into a freezer container and freeze for about 1 hour. Process or blend the ice to a smooth texture and freeze until set.

4. Ten minutes before serving, remove the ice from the freezer; it should be slightly softened. Purée again for a creamy texture, if desired. Spoon the sorbet into serving glasses and garnish with mango slices.

Pineapple Lime Ice

The very intense flavor of this ice wakens and refreshes the palate, making it welcome after rich, spicy meals, and on those days when it is too hot to think.

Makes about 1½ quarts

¾ cup sugar
¾ cup boiling water
1 medium-sized pineapple, peeled, cored, and cut into chunks
⅝ cup fresh lime juice
Fresh mint sprigs for garnish

1. Dissolve the sugar in the boiling water and set aside to cool. Purée the pineapple in a food processor, or in batches in a blender. Add the lime juice and sugar syrup to the purée and blend well.
2. Pour the mixture into the container of an ice-cream machine and freeze according to manufacturer's instructions.
3. Serve immediately or allow the ice to ripen in the freezer. Remove it from the freezer and allow it to soften a bit. Serve in glasses or dishes garnished with a sprig of mint.

Strawberry Margarita Ice

Makes about 1½ quarts

1 quart vine-ripened strawberries, rinsed and hulled
¼ cup sugar
Pinch of salt

1 cup water
2½ tablespoons Triple Sec
2½ tablespoons tequila
3 tablespoons fresh lime juice

1. Purée the berries in a food processor. Add the sugar and salt and process for 10 seconds. Add the water, liquors, and lime juice and process for 10 seconds more.

2. Freeze the purée in an ice-cream machine according to manufacturer's instructions. This ice can be served immediately or can be placed in the freezer until ready to serve. If placed in the freezer, it should be thawed slightly before serving. It is best served slightly soft. If it is very hard, it may be puréed for a few seconds in a food processor.

Pecan Ice Cream

≡ We have made this ice cream with both raw and toasted pecans; both are good, but decidedly different in flavor. With raw pecans the taste is cleaner and milder, more delicate and refined; with toasted pecans the oil comes forth to give a stronger nut flavor, and a more buttery texture.

Makes about 1½ quarts

2 cups shelled pecan halves, raw or lighty toasted
3 cups half-and-half
1 cup heavy (whipping) cream
¾ cup sugar
3 extra large egg yolks
Pinch of salt

1. Grind the pecans in a blender or food processor into a medium-fine meal. Heat the half-and-half, cream, and sugar together in a large heavy-bottomed pot until the sugar is dissolved. Add the nuts and cook for 5 to 6 minutes over medium heat. Remove from heat and steep for 30 minutes.

2. Drain the pecan milk through a colander or strainer lined with rinsed cheesecloth into a bowl for about 30 minutes. Stir occasionally to help the draining and squeeze the cheesecloth well to extract all of the nut milk.

3. Heat the pecan cream over low heat for 2 to 3 minutes. Beat the egg yolks lightly. Add a little of the mixture to the beaten egg yolks, blending well, and then add the yolks to the cream. Cook, stirring frequently, until the custard thickens and just coats a wooden spoon, about 10 minutes. Stir in the salt. Chill well.

4. Freeze in an ice-cream freezer according to manufacturer's instructions. Remove the ice cream 10 or 15 minutes to soften it slightly before serving.

Pumpkin Ice Cream

Makes about 2½ quarts

1 cup heavy (whipping) cream
3 cups half-and-half
½ cup sugar
4 extra large egg yolks
2 pounds fresh pumpkin
¾ cup sugar
½ teaspoon freshly grated nutmeg

1. Heat the cream and half-and-half with ½ cup sugar in a heavy-bottomed saucepan, until very hot but not simmering.

2. Whisk the egg yolks lightly. Slowly whisk a few tablespoons of the hot cream into the egg yolks. Gradually add a little more cream, whisking continually, until all the cream has been whisked into the yolks.

3. Return the cream and eggs to the saucepan and cook over medium-low heat, stirring, until the custard thickens and coats a spoon, about 10 minutes.

4. Remove from the heat and pour the custard into a stainless steel bowl. Set this bowl into a larger bowl filled with ice in order to cool the custard quickly.

5. While the custard is cooling, preheat the oven to 350 degrees. Remove the seeds from the pumpkin and cut it into large chunks. Place the pumpkin, skin side up, on a baking sheet sprinkled with water. Bake the pumpkin for 30 to 40 minutes, or until it is tender.

6. Remove the pumpkin from the oven. When it is cool enough to

handle, remove the skin. Purée the pumpkin with the remaining sugar to a smooth purée in a food processor.

7. Mix the custard and pumpkin purée together and add the nutmeg. Pour the pumpkin custard into the container of an ice-cream maker and freeze it according to manufacturer's directions.

Coconut Dipped in Chocolate with Cinnamon

Makes 24 to 36 pieces, depending on the size of the coconut

1 coconut
6 ounces semisweet chocolate, preferably Lindt or Toblerone
¼ teaspoon ground cinnamon

1. Make three holes with an ice pick in the eyes of the coconut and drain the milk. Crack the shell and remove the meat from the shell, keeping the coconut meat in as large pieces as possible.

2. With a vegetable peeler or sharp paring knife remove the brown skin from the coconut meat. Rinse the coconut if necessary, drain well, and pat dry. Meanwhile, melt the chocolate with the cinnamon in the top of a double boiler over simmering water.

3. Cut the coconut into ⅜-inch slices, keeping them as long as possible. Pieces smaller than 1½ or 2 inches long should be reserved for another use.

4. Lay wax paper on baking sheets. Dip the coconut slices into the melted chocolate, covering about two-thirds of their length. Place them on the wax paper to cool and harden.

5. If the weather is hot, chill the slices. They may be stored in the refrigerator overnight, layered between wax paper in a tightly-covered plastic container or tin.

Tropical Fruit Salad

☰ Removing the coconut meat from its shell and inner covering is not an easy task, but the flavor of freshly grated coconut is well worth the effort. The directions for cracking a fresh coconut are included here; work carefully, take your time, and nibble on the little bits as you go.

Serves 8 to 10

1 coconut
1 firm ripe mango, peeled, and cut into bite-sized pieces
1 firm ripe papaya, peeled, seeded, and cut into bite-sized pieces
1 ripe pineapple, peeled, cored, and cut into bite-sized pieces
2 tablespoons fresh lime juice
2 tablespoons Triple Sec
1 handful fresh mint leaves, bruised

1. Preheat the oven to 350 degrees. Carefully punch three holes in the eyes of the coconut (an ice pick works well) and drain the liquid. Place the coconut on a shelf in the oven for 12 to 15 minutes.
2. Remove the coconut from the oven and tap it gently but firmly with a hammer to break the shell away from the meat. Repeat on smaller pieces until all the meat is separated from the shell.
3. Peel the brown skin away from the coconut meat with a vegetable peeler or a paring knife. Rinse and drain the coconut. Grate the coconut and measure 2½ cups. Reserve the rest for another use.
4. Toss the coconut with the mango, papaya, and pineapple in a large bowl. Stir the lime juice, Triple Sec, and mint together in a small bowl and pour the mixture over the fruit. Toss the mixture well.
5. Cover the fruit and chill it for at least 1 hour before serving. Serve at cool room temperature.

Cajeta

≡ Cajeta is traditionally made from half goat and half cow's milk; it can be made from all cow's milk, but it lacks the truly characteristic flavor. Be careful not to brown the sugar too much. Long, slow cooking is required to make this syrup correctly, and constant stirring for the last 10 minutes is important.

Makes about 2 cups

1½ cups sugar
2 cups goat's milk
2 cups cow's milk
¾ teaspoon cornstarch
⅛ teaspoon baking soda

1. Put ¾ cup of the sugar in a small skillet and melt it over medium heat for about 7 to 8 minutes, stirring as it melts. The caramel should be a medium golden brown and free of lumps. Remove the caramel from the heat.

2. Combine the goat and cow's milk and pour 3 cups of the combined milk into a large heavy-bottomed pot. Reserve the other cup of milk. Add the remaining ¾ cup of sugar to the pot and place over medium-high heat. Stir occasionally, bringing it just to the boiling point.

3. Add the cornstarch and baking soda to the reserved cup of milk and stir well.

4. When the milk and sugar just comes to the boil, stir the hot caramelized sugar in all at once. It will foam up alarmingly, but stir it down. Add the milk with the cornstarch and soda and stir well.

5. Cook over medium-low heat, stirring occasionally with a flat-edged wooden spoon, for 50 to 60 minutes. During the last 10 minutes of cooking, the cajeta will begin to thicken. Stir it regularly so that it doesn't stick. The cajeta is ready when it is quite thick and coats the back of a wooden spoon. Cool and store in a jar.

Menus

Spring

Asparagus with Roasted Garlic Cream Sauce
Southwestern Fish Stew
Rocket and Spinach Salad with Bacon
Spiced Chocolate Soufflé

Crab Burritos
Artichokes with Chorizo and Cheese
Spinach, Beet, and Onion Salad
Blood Orange Skillet Cake

Salmon and Chiles Steamed in Corn Husks
 with Tomatillo Butter
Grilled Chicken in Yucatán-Style Marinade
Potatoes with Tequila Lime Butter
Cajeta Custard

Summer

Snapper en Escabeche with Tomatoes
Ranch Bread
Grilled Leg of Lamb with Sandia Jelly
Green Beans with Green Chile
Pineapple Lime Ice

Roasted Pepper Gazpacho with Croutons
Marinated Grilled Mackerel
Calabacitas
Lime Meringue Pie with Coconut Crust

Grilled Nopales with Salsa Fria and Piñons
Corn and Green Chile Lasagna
Jícama and Pepper Salad
Strawberry Margarita Ice

Tomatoes with Cilantro and Oregano
Lamb Mixed Grill or
Grilled Pork Tenderloin with Salsa Colorado
Green Corn Tamales
Pecan Peach Cake

Fall

Shrimp Albóndigas or Oysters with Salsas
Yeasted Corn Bread
Duck Stuffed with Chorizo with Red Wine
    and Red Chile Sauce
Watercress Salad with Cactus Fruit Vinaigrette
Pine Nut Cookies with Cinnamon Sugar
Pears or Grapes

Cilantro Pasta with Tomatillo Butter
Grilled Quail with Kumquat
  Jalapeño Marmalade
Greens with Bacon
Pomegranate Flan

Nachos with Goat Cheese and Pepitas
Veal Tongue with Mole Sauce
Hominy with Spinach
Hazelnut Cake with Cajeta and Coconut

Winter

Tostadas with Cabbage Escabeche and Goat Cheese
Rabbit Adovada
Rice with Corn and Carrots
Pumpkin Ice Cream
Almond Piloncillo Cookies

Black Bean Soup with Jalapeño Sherry
Green Chile Enchiladas with Blue Corn Tortillas
Cabbage and Pineapple Slaw
Pecan Tart with Cajeta

Salsa and Home-Fried Tortilla Chips
Chicken in Red Chile Sauce with Goat Cheese
Sweet Tamales
Green Salad with Blood Orange Vinaigrette
Coconut Dipped in Chocolate with Cinnamon
Tangerines

Suppers

Quesadillas with Roasted Pepper Strips
Vegetables en Escabeche
Frijoles Borrachos

Hopi-Style Lamb and Hominy Stew
Blue Corn Tortillas
Jícama Guacamole

Tortilla Soup
Chiles Rellenos with Tamale Filling
Salsa

Brunches

Layered Tortillas and Omelets
Jalapeño Salsa
Corn Off the Cob Salad
Panocha Coffee Cake with Pecan Topping
Iced Vanilla Coffee

Buttermilk Biscuits with Chiles
Blue Corn Pancakes
Red Pepper or Guava Jelly
Tropical Fruit Salad
Mexican-Style Hot Chocolate

Breakfast Burritos or Chorizo and Potato
  Burritos
Cabbage en Escabeche
Tequila Diablo
Apricot Piñon Tart

Sources

Food Sources

Query for catalogs or price lists. The following outlets sell fresh or dried chiles, and many sell other products as well.

Bueno Foods
2001 Fourth Street SW
Albuquerque, NM 87102

Casa Lucas Market
2934 24th Street
San Francisco, CA 94110

Coyote Cafe General Store
132 W. Water Street
Santa Fe, NM 87501

Frieda's Finest
P.O. Box 58488
Los Angeles, CA 90058

La Palma
2884 24th Street
San Francisco, CA 94110

Los Chileros
P.O. Box 6215
Santa Fe, NM 87502

Midwest Imports
1121 S. Clinton
Chicago, IL 60607

Casados Farms
Box 1269
San Juan Pueblo, NM 87566

Casa Moneo
210 W. 14th Street
New York, NY 10011

Dean & Deluca
560 Broadway
New York, NY 10012

Josie's
1130 Agua Fria
Santa Fe, NM 87501

La Preferida
91 S. Water Market
Chicago, IL 60608

Mercado Latino
148-C Common Drive
El Paso, TX 79901

Mi Rancho
464 Seventh Street
Oakland, CA 94110

Old Southwest Trading Company
P.O. Box 7545
Albuquerque, NM 87194

Seed and Plant Sources

Query for catalogs or price lists.

W. Atlee Burpee
300 Park Avenue
Warminster, PA 18974

Joseph Harris Company
Moretown Farm
Rochester, NY 14624

Horticultural Enterprises
P.O. Box 810082
Dallas, TX 75381

Lockhart Seeds, Inc.
P.O. Box 13613
N. Wilson Way
Stockton, CA 95205

Plants of the Southwest
1812 Second Street
Santa Fe, NM 87501

Redwood City Seed Company
P.O. Box 361
Redwood City, CA 94064

Exotica Seed Company
8033 Sunset Blvd.
Suite 125
West Hollywood, CA 90046

Hastings Seedsmen
P.O. Box 4274
434 Marietta Street NW
Atlanta, GA 30302

Johnny Pepper Seed
4320 Campus Drive, #150
Newport Beach, CA 92660

Pepper Gal
10536 119th Avenue North
Largo, FL 33543

Porter and Son
1510 E. Washington Street
Stephenville, TX 74061

Talavaya Seeds
P.O. Box 707
Santa Cruz Station
Santa Cruz, NM 87567

Works Cited

Andrews, Jean. *Peppers: The Domesticated Capsicums*. Austin: University of Texas Press, 1985.

Dent, Huntley. *The Feast of Santa Fe*. New York: Simon and Schuster, 1985.

Greer, Anne Lindsay. *Creative Mexican Cooking: Recipes from Great Texas Chefs*. Austin: Texas Monthly Press, 1985.

Hughes, Phyllis, ed. *Pueblo Indian Cookbook*. Santa Fe: Museum of New Mexico Press, 1972.

Johnson, Ronald. *Southwestern Cooking New and Old*. Albuquerque: University of New Mexico Press, 1985.

Kennedy, Diana. *The Cuisines of Mexico*. New York: Harper and Row, 1972.

———. *Recipes from the Regional Cooks of Mexico*. New York: Harper and Row, 1978.

Kraig, Bruce. *Mexican-American Plain Cooking*. Chicago: Nelson-Hall, 1982.

Miller, Mark. *The Great Chile Book*. Berkeley, CA: Ten Speed Press, 1991.

Naj, Amal. *Peppers: A History of Hot Pursuits*. New York: Alfred A. Knopf, 1992.

Ortho Books. *Adventures in Mexican Cooking*. San Francisco: Ortho Books, 1978.

Ortiz, Elisabeth Lambert. *The Complete Book of Mexican Cooking*. New York: M. Evans and Company, Inc., 1967.

Root, Waverly. *Food*. New York: Simon and Schuster, 1980.

Sanchez, Irene Barraza, and Yund, Gloria Sanchez. *Comida Sabrosa*. Albuquerque: University of New Mexico Press, 1982.

Index